Tri-County Technical College
Southern Wesleyan University

(C) 864-367-2250   (O) 864-654-7804
Email: frbobmen@yahoo.com

Be

BEING
IN THE
WORLD

Dialogue and Cosmopolis

FRED DALLMAYR

UNIVERSITY PRESS OF KENTUCKY

Copyright © 2013 by The University Press of Kentucky

Scholarly publisher for the Commonwealth,
serving Bellarmine University, Berea College, Centre College of Kentucky,
Eastern Kentucky University, The Filson Historical Society, Georgetown
College, Kentucky Historical Society, Kentucky State University, Morehead
State University, Murray State University, Northern Kentucky University,
Transylvania University, University of Kentucky, University of Louisville,
and Western Kentucky University.
All rights reserved.

Editorial and Sales Offices: The University Press of Kentucky
663 South Limestone Street, Lexington, Kentucky 40508-4008
www.kentuckypress.com

17 16 15 14 13   5 4 3 2 1

Cataloging-in-Publication data is available from the Library of Congress.

ISBN 978-0-8131-4191-6 (hardcover : alk. paper)
ISBN 978-0-8131-4192-3 (epub)
ISBN 978-0-8131-4193-0 (pdf)

This book is printed on acid-free paper meeting the requirements of the
American National Standard for Permanence in Paper for Printed Library
Materials.

Manufactured in the United States of America.

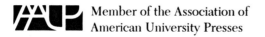 Member of the Association of
American University Presses

For Josefine and Keegan

May their being in this world
be filled with happiness and blessing

Peace is not an absence of war; it is a virtue, a state of mind, a disposition for benevolence, confidence, justice.
—Spinoza

Among nations, a *common feeling* must gradually awaken, so that each can feel itself to be in the place of the other.
—Johann Gottfried Herder

Beauty is in the ideal of perfect harmony which dwells in universal being.
—Rabindranath Tagore

Our task must be to free ourselves—by widening our circle of comparison to embrace all living creatures and the whole of nature and its beauty.
—Albert Einstein

Contents

Preface

A picture, the saying goes, is worth more than a thousand words or verbal explanations. In the following, I want to present a picture and then ask: What is wrong with the picture? Imagine a country in which most of the people are said to be religious or God-fearing. Many or most of the people carry God's name on their lips incessantly or at least on all important occasions. You might say that this is a happy or devout condition. But now add this to the picture: Many or most people in the same country have a gun or several guns and are ready to use these guns to maim or kill fellow citizens at the slightest provocation. Moreover, even when not using guns, they hurl against each other vile and hateful language that even gangsters or streetfighters would be hesitant to employ. What is wrong with this picture?

To make things still worse, imagine that the country in which these people live stockpiles large amounts of weapons of mass destruction with which to slaughter other populations. Most lethal among them is the arsenal of nuclear weapons with which entire continents and even the whole world can be annihilated many times over. Perhaps the coherence of the picture might be salvaged if we assumed that the country was populated by "barbarians" or criminals for whom warfare and wanton killing is a "natural" way of life. But this was not our initial assumption. Hence, the question remains: How can a country inhabited by supposedly God-fearing people mesh or be made compatible with the other features I mentioned? The answer is that it cannot.

It cannot as long as people still remember scriptures and the lessons contained therein. One such lesson is contained in the Sermon on the Mount. There we are told, in plain language (Matthew 5:21–24): "You have heard that it was said to the men of old, 'You shall not kill; and whoever kills shall be liable to judgment.'" But, the sermon continues: "I say to you that every one who is angry with his brother shall be liable to judgment; whoever insults his brother shall be liable to council and whoever says 'You fool!' shall be liable to damnation." And then comes perhaps the most important instruction: "If you are offering your gift at the altar, and there remember that your brother has something against you, leave your gift there before the altar and go: first be reconciled to your brother, and then come and offer your gift." This means: we cannot worship God or bring gifts to the divine as long as we are at enmity with our brothers and sisters; we cannot be faithful to God if we are not faithful to our fellow beings or at least make every effort to be reconciled to them.

This book—like other things I have put to paper—is written from anguish: anguish about the future possibility of life on Earth; about the prospect of a decent, humane, and just "being-in-the-world." This future is jeopardized today by a combination of threats: the threat of large-scale war fueled by reckless power lust; the danger of economic meltdowns promoted by boundless greed; and the peril of ecological disasters nurtured by the desire for instant gratification and consumption. Among these dangers, the threat of nuclear holocaust is surely the most daunting—and also most shocking in a halfway sane world. Have we not seen the utter and brutal devastation in Hiroshima and Nagasaki? Have we not visited the Peace Park and pledged: Never again? Thus, who can contemplate a nuclear war and still claim to be human? In their total denial of humanity, nuclear weapons are simply unusable by human beings—by beings living not *against* but *in* and *with* the world.

The chapters in this book are all committed to the celebration of life and, more particularly, the quest for a good and just life in our contemporary world. In our globalizing context, this quest cannot be pursued in a unilateral, hegemonic, or imperial manner. Only through sustained dialogue and engaged multilateral interactions can we catch a glimpse of cosmopolis, of the just and harmoniously ordered global city promised in all scriptures and philosophical meditations. This city is a place of longing, a hope sustaining all genuine travelers along "the way." It is also a place of beauty, a radiant cosmos or comic vision. As the psalmist says: "How beautiful is your dwelling place" (84:1). Safety or security in this city is not obtained through walls, high fences, or military armaments, but through mutual respect and good neighborly conduct.

To be sure, such a cosmopolis cannot be fabricated or engineered—because its encompassing wholeness (and haleness) vastly exceeds our grasp. Nor, however, does it befall us like a fortuitous accident, like a meteor from outer space, unrelated to our thinking and doing. The chapters in this book do not and cannot present a blueprint of cosmopolis; they are far removed from any intention to reconstruct the Tower of Babel. Yet, from different angles, in different idioms, with different thematic accents, they all point in a certain direction—incessantly and (if you will) prayerfully. They do not articulate a doctrine or systematic theory that could be routinely memorized or recited. They are simply invitations to remain on the way. This, in my view, is what all our thinking and acting are meant to do: not to display a pretentious knowledge but to bear witness to a certain loyalty, a loyalty to the call of peace and justice.

In following the path of wholeness, we do not sacrifice humanity to an alien order nor submerge human awareness in naturalistic impulses. We do not surrender human thought to unreflective nature nor surrender nature to a domineering human rationality. Finally, we do not sacrifice humanity or nature to a sovereign transcendent deity; nor do we submerge the divine indiscriminately in "worldly" things. What we need to accept is a differentiated relationism without enmity or fusion. The Spanish-Indian thinker Raimon Panikkar had a word for it: "cosmotheandric" vision; and the pages of this book frequently pay tribute to him. On the cover of this book there is a painting by Paul Klee titled *With the Eagle*. In the midst of the rich tapestry of the world, the picture shows the emergence of an eye or vision, an eye that sees while being seen. In his *Letters for the Advancement of Humanity*, the philosopher Johann Gottfried Herder makes this comment: "The whole nature knows itself in 'man' as in a living mirror; she sees through his eye, thinks behind his brow, feels in his breast, and works and makes with his hands."[1]

In addition to Raimon Panikkar, the book pays tribute to a number of inspiring cross-cultural thinkers and friends, such as Bhikhu Parekh and Zhang Longxi. It also commemorates the work of two Muslim thinkers who passed away not long ago: the Moroccan Mohammed al-Jabri and the Egyptian Nasr Abu Zayd. Running through its pages—like a *basso continuo*—is the memory of the legacy of the great Indian proponent of nonviolent struggle for justice and peace:

Mahatma Gandhi. Frequently invoked in the pages of the book are the names of intellectual friends who have helped me at various junctures along the way—thinkers like Charles Taylor, William Connolly, Seyla Benhabib, Richard Falk, and Martha Nussbaum. As always, my deepest debt is to my wife and our children. The book is dedicated to our grandchildren, Josefine and Keegan—with a prayer: that the world into which they are growing may grant them glimpses of the city of peace.

Notre Dame, April 2012

Introduction

By now it is a commonplace—a widely accepted commonplace—to say that we live in an age of globalization, that the world is steadily shrinking, and that people around the globe are increasingly pushed together. The saying has a ring of correctness or plausibility. What is correct is that financial markets are relentlessly expanding, that complex information networks are encircling the world, and that military weaponry is stretching around the globe (and capable of annihilating it many times over). What is not often noted is that the correctness of the saying conceals as much as it reveals. Underneath the readily noted surface phenomena, recessed or subterranean shifts are at work that transform the meaning of surface structures. Contrary to the widely held view that globalization is just a quantitative leap—that it is simply "*more* of the same"—the suspicion grows that the "same" is no longer really the same; that an unfamiliar "otherness" intrudes on all sides, making our time one of untapped horizons or open seas. Once attention is granted to these shifts, difficult questions surge to the fore, questions not amenable to quantitative tabulation—like "what is the meaning of 'world'?" How can it be both a habitat and an open horizon? And who are *we* as human beings inhabiting this familiar/unfamiliar terrain? Despite the disappearance of open frontiers, does world or earth still remain basically terra incognita (perhaps *terra nullius*)?

Questions like these throw into disarray or put pressure on traditional conceptions of self-hood, subjectivity, and individual identity—and also on the relation between self and other(s). Perhaps what is dawning now is a connectedness or overlapping of selves, maybe even an intercorporeality (which is more than "intersubjectivity"). Intimated in the latter notion is a strong pressure placed on traditional bifurcations, such as those between mind and body, cogito and nature. And what about collective identity, the identity of nation-states

1

as well as that of ethnic, religious, or cultural collectivities? Can one really say that the so-called Westphalian system of states—the system that has dominated European politics since the religious wars—is today simply globalized and made the canonical model for all societies around the world? Are there not profound tremors affecting all states today, tremors produced by "deterritorialized" agents operating both below and above the state level—and that states seek to control with ever harsher "national security" measures? One prominent exemplar of (potentially) deterritorialized agency is "cosmopolitanism"—a term that has many meanings and raises the difficult issue of the relation between "cosmos" and "polis," between general order and political practice. Other closely connected instances of such agency are transnational religions, cultures, or civilizations, as well as international movements (in such fields as labor, health, and ecology). No doubt, none of the cited tendencies are unambiguous or simply harbingers of "progress." Intimately linked with such boons of "modernity" like human rights, legal equality, and democracy, the Westphalian tradition can be neither piously embalmed nor rashly abandoned. This means that whatever changes are afoot can only be cautiously and interactively pursued, not monologically legislated.

The present volume explores the transition from Westphalia to cosmopolis from many different angles and in many different registers. The opening chapter delves into some of the recessed philosophical underpinnings of globalization and the ongoing turn toward "world" (or worldhood). The chapter takes its departure from a famous phrase used by the philosopher Martin Heidegger to capture the core of human life or existence: the phrase "being-in-the-world." With this formulation, Heidegger radically distanced himself from a central feature of modern Western thought or philosophy: the yawning gulf separating humans from the world, the cogito from external nature, or subject from object. What was intimated by his hyphenated expression is the insight that human beings are not external to but constituted by "world"—including nature and fellow beings— seen as target(s) of intimate concern or "care" (*Sorge*). The chapter discusses this close relationality of humans and world in its different modalities, ranging from the practical "handling" of utensils to forms of ethical-existential "solicitude" (*Fürsorge*). Attention is also paid to Heidegger's later reformulation of relationality under such headings as *"Ereignis"* and *"Geviert"* (fourfold). In order to avoid the impression of a static structuralism, the chapter lifts up another crucial feature of Heidegger's thought: his emphasis on temporality (highlighted in the phrase "Being and Time"). Seen from this angle, human beings are characterized not by a static essence but by their "ek-static" potentiality or openness to an uncharted future. To render this feature more accessible, a comparison is made with the teachings of American pragmatism and the "ontology of becoming" (or "process philosophy") championed by Alfred North Whitehead and his followers. What emerges from this comparison is the notion of a world in the process of "becoming" or gestation—and implicitly the vision of a becoming cosmopolis or cosmo-genesis.

The second chapter turns to prominent social and political ramifications of cosmo-genesis, ramifications typically captured by the term *cosmopolitanism* (or cosmopolitanization). Although it is fashionable and widely used, the meaning of the term is contested and far from self-evident. To contribute to its clarification, the chapter distinguishes among three main interpretations: empirical, normative, and practical or interactive. In the first reading, cosmopolitanism coincides basically with "globalization," where the latter refers to empirical economic and technical processes such as the global extension of financial markets and communication networks. Where these processes are uncritically celebrated, the term shades over into what sociologist Ulrich Beck has called "banal cosmopolitanism," that is, a globe-trotting mentality reducing global "liquidity" and transaction flows to commercial commodities. A very different meaning is given to the term by normative philosophy as formulated by such thinkers as Kant, John Rawls, Jürgen Habermas, and their followers. In this interpretation, cosmopolitanism refers to a set of moral and/or legal norms governing both domestic and international politics—regardless of whether these norms are derived (with Kant) from transcendental consciousness or (with Rawls) from a transempirical "original position" or finally (with Habermas) from an exchange of rational validity claims. What all these formulations underscore is the status of cosmopolitanism as a normative yardstick to which public behavior "ought" to conform. Noting a lingering dilemma in normativism—the conflict between "is" and "ought," between duty and inclination—the chapter introduces the possibility of a further reading where cosmopolitanism relies on practical engagement, on ever-renewed cross-cultural and intersocietal learning experiences conducive to a broadening of experiential horizons. Seen from this angle (indebted to the teachings of pragmatism, hermeneutics, and virtue ethics), the tension between norm and conduct is not removed but mitigated through education and ethical transformation—just as the conflict between the "global" and the "local" is tendentially bridged or reconciled in the vision of a shared "cosmos."

Chapter 3 continues the discussion of cosmopolitanism by reviewing the preconditions needed for any possible "cosmopolis." Starting from the biblical story of the Tower of Babel and the ensuing dispersal of peoples, cultures, and languages, the chapter draws two lessons: first, that cosmopolitanism in our time cannot assume a homogeneous global community but has to proceed through cross-cultural dialogue (what has been called "dialogue among civilizations"); and second, that cosmopolitan endeavors cannot rely on purely technical (or else financial) prowess but must be in tune with cultural, ethical, and spiritual or "symbolic" dimensions of human life. In more concrete terms, such endeavors can follow (with modifications) Plato's construction of the "city in speech" as presented in *The Republic,* where construction begins with the provision of material or subsistence needs and moves from there to ethical and educational needs and finally to the requisites of truth and justice. A similar process is endorsed by Aristotle when he distinguishes between the provision for survival (*esse*) and the cultivation of the "good life" (*bene esse*). What is not fully thematicized by classical writers is the diversity of cultures and religious beliefs and also the detrimental effects of city life (urbanization, industrialization) on nature or ecology. What was not and could not at all have been foreseen by classical writers is the emergence of the modern market economy and especially of financial capitalism, with their detrimental effects on social cohesion, evident in the radical gulf between rich and poor, corporate elites and widespread indigence. The chapter discusses efforts to correct this gulf (without endorsing a coercive collectivism), efforts that are in line with the renewed contemporary focus on public ethics and civic virtues. By way of conclusion, attention is given to issues involved in global citizenship and also to institutional arrangements appropriate for a cosmopolis "after Babel."

The themes of civic education and a possible global citizenship are continued in chapter 4, titled "Humanizing Humanity: Education for World Citizenship." The chief accent of the chapter is placed on the humanities or "liberal arts" as central pillars of civic pedagogy or education for the common good. (The chapter was initially presented as keynote address at the "First World Humanities Forum," organized by UNESCO in Korea in 2011.) This does not mean that other disciplines or sciences are not also important for social and public life. However, what distinguishes the humanities preeminently is that they cannot be instrumentalized for career objectives; in Martha Nussbaum's apt phrase, they are "not for profit." Differently stated, the human studies serve an "intrinsic" (not extrinsic) purpose: namely, the ongoing "humanization" of practitioners. The same idea is also captured in the expression "liberal arts," which indicates the possible liberation of practitioners from external tutelage or from subservience to coercive (political or economic) constraints. The chapter traces the development of human studies from their classical roots to their recent status in the "republic of knowledge." Next, relying on insights culled from philosopher Hans-Georg Gadamer, several distinctive features of the humanities are highlighted, especially three: their contribution to *Bildung* in the sense of human "formation" or transformation; their reliance on prudent "judgment" (*phronesis*) in contrast to apodictic knowledge; and finally their ability to foster the growth of a "common sense" (*sensus communis*), that is, a shared or public sensibility. Equipped with these features, the humanities can play a crucial role in (what Nussbaum calls) "education for democracy." In our time, this role can be translated or expanded into the task of promoting a genuinely cosmopolitan *Bildung* or the formation of "citizens of the world."

Chapter 5 takes up and elaborates further on our situation "after Babel": the absence of a homogeneous global community, which mandates the resort to an interactive or dialogical cosmopolitanism. Such an interactive approach involves multiple forms of border-crossing—between self and other, familiarity and unfamiliarity—with the aim not of excluding or annihilating, but of "befriending the stranger." This notion of befriending or cross-cultural friendship stands in stark contrast to the dominant global "politics of fear," which, in essence, is anchored in the assumption of radical interhuman enmity. The chapter examines the modern roots of this conception in the political philosophy of Thomas Hobbes, especially his notion of a "natural" state of war, and proceeds to trace the offshoots of this legacy to recent formulations, especially Carl Schmitt's definition of "the political" as the friend-enemy polarity. Another term for the fear engendered by enmity is *phobia*—of which our age has a plethora (including Islamophobia and xenophobia). To counter the prevailing orgy of phobias—epitomized in the global formula of "terror wars"—the chapter turns to a number of leading critical intellectuals, especially the international politics and law expert Richard Falk. As Falk points out in a series of his writings, the ongoing terror wars lift terror or fear to the level of a "megaterrorism" that blurs the lines between military conflict and violence against civilian populations and also between interstate war and political insurgency; as a result, the international laws of warfare are jeopardized or completely eroded. To round out and further corroborate the critique of megaterror, attention is given to religious scriptures and to the testimony of some prominent Christian theologians—a testimony that, in the end, affirms the soundness of a politics not of fear but of the "common good' (as articulated by Aristotle, John Dewey, and others).

The latter testimony also confirms my own conviction that what is most needed in our time is a politics of the common good that requires the cultivation of public ethics and civic responsibility—and this in the domains of both domestic and international politics. Although sometimes feebly acknowledged in the former arena, the requirement is almost universally rejected in the latter—where the "realism" of power politics tends to have unlimited sway. Chapter 6 contains my attempt to delineate the role and relevance of ethics in international politics. The chapter is the outgrowth of a conversation held at the University of St. Andrews with three distinguished colleagues—Richard Shapcott, Anthony Black, and Richard Beardsworth—who questioned me on a number of issues, but especially on international ethics. Of necessity, my response to them follows the specific focus of their queries. Shapcott's interrogation provides a useful opening gambit, because it shows the interconnection of my various commitments—especially the commitments to hermeneutics, dialogue, comparative theorizing, and cosmopolitanism. Although appreciating the lucidity and helpful character of his intervention, I notice a remaining difference, which revolves around my own preference for a "dialogi-cal cosmopolitanism" over "liberal" or purely "procedural" types of universalism. As a learned intellectual historian, Black reminds me of certain historical antecedents of contemporary globalization—examples that I readily acknowledge as precursors. His critical edge, however, has to do with a presumed neglect of international "reality." My quick response (needing elaboration) is that the horrors of that reality—which I acknowledge—are an invitation not to apathy but to ethical-political struggle. Concern with political realism is also central to Beardsworth's comments—which are informed by complex "post-modern" arguments. Beardsworth is troubled by dangers of a certain "moral (or moralizing) politics" to which he counterposes the concep-tion (derived from Machiavelli) of a "responsible politics of power" or (with Deleuze) of politics as "a dynamic force-field of weighted, mobile forces." Although appreciating the emphasis on contextual limits or bounded constraints, what in the end I find lacking here is the human face, the aspect of ethical-political engagement—without which even "limited violence" quickly descends into total violence and destruction.

Beardsworth's comments are significant also for drawing attention to the issue of bodily contexts or public "embodiment." As previously indicated, modern Western thought is troubled by a set of ingrained dualisms or bifurcations, including those between mind and body, cogito and world. Contemporary cosmopolitan initiatives clearly need to transgress this legacy; chapter 7 seeks to take some steps in this direction. As the chapter indicates, ancient thought tended to view the political community as a homogeneous organism nurtured by convention. This conception was ruptured by the onset of modern thought, which came to see "mind" as a creative or constructive force confronting the external world. Under the impact of this change, the political community was perceived no longer as an organism but as an artifact or artificial construct, that is, a "body politic" created through deliberate design or a contractual mechanism. The chapter examines closely this conception of the "body politic" as it was articulated by leading modern thinkers, including Thomas Hobbes, John Locke, and Rousseau. Although differing in important details, the respec-tive versions followed a three-step formula: leading from a presocial condition ("state of nature") via a contract to the "civil" condition of the "state." Under the impact of nineteenth-century positivism and scientism this formula was collapsed into a single strand that equated politics tendentially with physical or biological processes (sometimes termed "dynamic force-fields"). In opposition to both contractual and physicalist treatments, the chapter in the end sketches the alternative conception of the political community seen as an interactive or relational body, that is, as a shared "embodied praxis" or an affective "interbody."

Another major dilemma or bifurcation troubling modern Western thought is that between faith and reason, between religion and secular life. A major assumption dominating modern social science is that of the progressive "secularization" of society, coupled with the retreat if not disappearance of religious belief. This assumption has been challenged or thrown into disarray by the recent upsurge of religion in many parts of the world (what some have called the "revenge of God"). The challenge has been accompanied by complaints about a presumed "crisis of modernity," a basic loss of "meaning," and perhaps an end of traditional culture. In a celebrated text, political philosopher Charles Taylor has depicted our time as a "secular age," where "secular" refers to a widespread inability to embrace and affirm faith. In Taylor's view, the modern age is marked above all by a religious deficit: a slide into agnosticism, into "exclusive humanism," and (most important) into an "immanent frame" excluding "theistic transcendence." What surfaces here in stark form is the bifurcation between faith and mundane existence, between "transcendence" and "immanence"—with the added accent that modernity appears characterized mainly by a loss or denial. What is not considered, or ruled out of court, in this perspective is the possibility that God (or the divine) and human life are embroiled in such a way that historically both sides are undergoing constant transformation.

This possibility is at the core of chapter 8, which introduces as an antipode to the "immanence-transcendence" binary the thought of the philosopher of religion Raimon Panikkar. Inspired in part by the Indian tradition of nondualism (*advaita*), Panikkar holds that the problem or "loss of meaning" in our time is due not simply to "secularism" but to the collusion of radical transcendentalism and agnostic immanentism. To recover a proper balance of life, in this view, requires a basic acknowledgment of our "being in the world": our insertion into a cosmic "rhythm of being" that happens not in a fragmented or dualistic but in a relational or "cosmotheandric" mode (linking nature, humans, and the divine). What is involved in Panikkar's work is a critique of both an immanentism neglectful of deeper spiritual aspirations and an abstract transcendentalism neglectful of social problems and ethical standards of public conduct. The latter neglect is particularly grievous in our contemporary period: a time marked (especially in America) by the massive upsurge of organized religion and the simultaneous decay of minimal levels of social responsibility and civic virtues. This situation is obviously damaging to public life and basic requisites of democracy; but it is equally damaging to religion, which acquires the character of a smokescreen or "opium" (in Marx's well-known phrase) drawing people's attention heavenward while plundering their democratic entitlements. What is required at this point is a resolute rethinking of both politics and religion: in such a manner that politics or public life is rescued from the relentless pursuit of immanent self-gratification, while religion is transformed from a form of dogmatic authoritarianism into (what I have called elsewhere) a "religion of service."[1]

This rethinking also involves a reformulation of the meaning of "secularism" and its relation to religious faith—an issue that is discussed in chapter 9. Taking its departure from the term "post-secularity" (coined by Jürgen Habermas), the chapter explores two main directions in which the expression has been interpreted: one direction where religious faith is in a way "secularized" by being adapted or rendered acceptable to modern secular discourse; and another direction where faith triumphs over secularism by expunging the latter and its modern (Enlightenment) corollaries. What surfaces behind this divergence is a new version of the immanence-transcendence conundrum: a version accentuating a presumed contrast of language games in which one linguistic idiom is said to be more readily accessible or simply takes precedence over the other. On this issue I tend to agree with Charles Taylor (whose "theistic transcendentalism" I have previously questioned) when he challenges the assumption of an "epistemic break" between modern secular reason and "nonrational" religious discourse. Pursuing this challenge further, chapter 9 insists on the primacy of ordinary language and on the need of all texts or discourses (secular and religious) to undergo interpretation and reflective interrogation—a need that concurs with Hans-Georg Gadamer's axiom of the "universality of hermeneutics."[2] Once this axiom is taken seriously, it becomes possible to offer a new definition of "post-secularity" that departs from the two meanings mentioned above: a definition where the prefix *post* refers neither to a secular nor to a religious triumphalism but to an ethical-political task—the task of liberating public life from its attachment to "worldly" self-interest and the unmitigated pursuit of wealth, power, and military adventures.

This is a task that needs to be shouldered by people in all countries and all walks of life; but it is an obligation resting particularly on public or political leaders, whose conduct serves as an example for others to follow. Unfortunately, there is today a great scarcity of such leaders—given the prevailing tendency to cater to the lowest chauvinistic instincts. Yet, the situation is not entirely bleak; it is relieved by some prominent and inspiring counter-examples. Chapter 10 draws attention to one such example, the Mahatma Gandhi, with a focus on his lessons for modern and contemporary democracy. Together with many political thinkers, Gandhi saw the essence of democracy in popular self-rule or self-government; however, under the influence of classical Indian texts as well as basic religious teachings, he identified this essence not with "selfish rule" or the unhampered pursuit of self-interest but with the cultivation of an ethical and just community. Seen from this angle, "self-rule" (*swaraj*) does not mean autocratic rule over others, but the ability to tame and transform selfish impulses in the direction of shared well-being. On a concrete political level, Gandhi's aim was not simply to replace British domination with domestic Indian domination, but rather to rethink and transform the entire conception of self-government through the invocation of such guiding maxims as nonviolence (*ahimsa*) and the pursuit of justice and truth (*satyagraha*). Viewed from this perspective, the dominant Western equation of democracy with liberalism or neoliberalism is shown to be deeply flawed and misleading—as a number of critics have noted. By way of conclusion, chapter 10 explores possible parallels between Gandhi's thought and arguments advanced by recent Western political thinkers—finding the strongest parallel with the teachings of John Dewey, whose entire life-work was devoted to rescuing democracy from the derailment into laissez-faire liberalism or "minimalism."

Gandhi's legacy was not extinguished with his assassination in

1948. In the ensuing years, many social and political struggles sought to pattern themselves on his example. As we know, the American Civil Rights Movement, led by Martin Luther King Jr., drew its inspiration in large measure from the Gandhian practice of *satyagraha;* the same is true of Nelson Mandela's struggle against South African apartheid and also some of the "velvet" resolutions in Eastern Europe against Soviet domination. More recently, Gandhian ideas and practices were invoked in a somewhat unexpected context: the Egyptian uprising during the so-called Arab Spring (2011). As it happens, many of the participants in that uprising had studied Gandhian texts and methods of nonviolent resistance for some time. Chapter 11 seeks to shed some light on the character of the uprising by comparing it with two other instances of radical change in the Muslim world: the Kemalist "revolution" in Turkey after World War I and the Iranian revolution of 1979. In each case, the revolutionaries or change agents sought to rectify a deficit perceived in the preceding regime. While the Kemalists challenged the absence of Western-style secularism and modernism in the Ottoman Empire, the Iranian revolutionaries attacked precisely the opposite: the relentless modernizing and secularizing policies of the Shah's regime. Differentiating themselves from both Kemalists and Iranian fundamentalists, the Egyptian insurgents attacked a different kind of deficit: the lack of democratic self-rule during the long years of autocracy. Thus, they embarked on the difficult path of social and political reform, the path of building a responsible ethical democracy—thereby bypassing the conundrums of secular reason versus faith, of immanence versus transcendence.

Such, at least, was the initial aspiration and promise of the Egyptian uprising. In the meantime, political realities—including geopolitical machinations of "great" powers—have conspired to tarnish the initial animus of the Arab Spring. Today, democracy in the Gandhian sense of self-rule hangs in the balance everywhere in the Muslim world, including Egypt. In their effort to guard nascent democratic institutions, insurgents have to be vigilant about dangers threatening self-rule from many sides. The common denominator of these dangers is autocracy—which, in turn, can appear in many guises: secular, religious, or a combination of the two. Since, in most Muslim countries, religion is strongly rooted, friends of Gandhian-style self-rule cannot ignore perils stemming from these quarters. In fact, they must learn that one of the basic requisites of democracy is freedom of conscience and thought—which generates freedom of conduct and action. Freedom of conscience and thought involves the capacity to interpret and understand in one's own terms all traditional teachings, including religious teachings—a capacity that underscores the "universality of hermeneutics" previously mentioned. Chapter 12 commemorates two leading Muslim philosophers and intellectuals—the Egyptian Nasr Abu Zayd and the Moroccan Mohammed al-Jabri—who both passed away in 2010. Both, in their different ways, sought to vindicate the right of free interpretation (*ijtihad*) of scriptures as a gateway toward a more democratic way of life. When joined by other intellectuals in other parts of the world—I believe—their example can pave the way toward a generously tolerant, dialogical, and immanent-transcendent cosmopolis.

The appendixes contain some papers that flesh out the scope of the present volume. The essay "Beyond Multiculturalism? For Bhikhu Parekh" discusses the present status of multicultural policies, which, in recent times, have been increasingly challenged or attacked by defenders of a nationalistic or populist "identity politics." The paper upholds the continued viability of the perspective (properly reformulated), paying tribute in this context especially to the crucial contributions of political philosopher Bhikhu Parekh. The second essay deals with a similar issue, this time with reference to Confucianism. The question addressed is whether Confucianism is merely a part of Chinese cultural property, a feature of "Han" identity that, in a globalizing context, could be used for expansionist or hegemonic goals; or whether it is a generous, open-ended legacy available for cosmopolitan dialogue. In the third paper, dedicated to a discussion of the East Asian thinker Zhang Longxi, the emphasis is placed on the needed reconciliation of universalism and particularism, of sameness and difference, in any conceivable cosmopolitan venture. The concluding paper is the text of a conversation between myself and representatives of a "Youth Forum" held on the island of Rhodes, Greece, in fall 2010. Given the fact that cosmopolitanism for me is largely an educational endeavor, and that my preferred version stresses concrete, interactive engagement, the conversation with young people exemplifies the character of such engagement.

The conversation with young people also provides a desirable antidote to an excessive dose of geopolitical "realism." It is one of the temptations of old age to become disillusioned and hence to fall prey to cynicism or pessimism. This is a temptation—as most older people realize—that needs to be resisted. Faced with the expectations of a young generation, cynicism or pessimism simply has no appeal. On the contrary, it is one of the chief obligations of older generations to do everything possible to facilitate and promote the well-being of young people and thus to enable them to search for the "good life." This does not mean wishful thinking or the embrace of blind optimism. Actually, with regard to preparing and pursuing the proper way, optimism and pessimism are equally irrelevant. It is part of the moral equipment of a mature person to know that the rightness of ethical standards does not depend on the success or the failure of particular actions. As we know from classical teachings—extensively invoked in chapter 4—right actions carry their worth or dignity in themselves and do not depend on extrinsic considerations of utility. Hence, cosmopolitans striving for a more equitable, dialogical, and peaceful world cannot have their gaze fixed entirely on the formidable obstacles encountered along the way. Instead, in full awareness of these obstacles, they have to nurture a deeper hope or promise. Seen from this angle, cosmopolis might be called a "realistic utopia." It is such a realistic utopianism that was at the heart of the life-work of Albert Camus and especially of *The Myth of Sisyphus* and its account of the protagonist's ever-renewed ethical struggle. The text ends with a stunning phrase: "We must imagine Sisyphus happy."[3]

1. Being in the World

A Moving Feast

> All people are my brothers and sisters, and all things are
> my companions.
>
> —Chang Tsai, *Western Inscription*

Our age of globalization conjures up a host of challenging problems,
mostly of a cultural, economic, and political nature. A steadily expanding literature deals with these problems. What is not often noticed is
that globalization also harbors terminological and semantic quanda-
ries. We know at least since Copernicus and Galileo that our Earth is
a "globe" and not a flattened landscape. Given this knowledge, what
does it mean that our habitat is "globalized" in our time? Surely, its
physical "global" shape is not modified. In aggravated form, similar
semantic problems beset other terms often used as equivalents: like
world or *earth*. Can it be that the world, in our time of globalization, is
becoming more "worldly" or simply a bigger world? Or that the Earth
acquires a more "earthly" character? In addition to having descriptive referents, the two latter terms are additionally weighted down
by metaphysical and theological connotations. Thus, *world* often is
used to designate "this" world in opposition to another "transcendent"
world, while the adjective *worldly* frequently serves as a synonym for
"secular" or "temporal" in opposition to "spiritual" and "transtemporal" (or eternal). In a similar way, *earth* and *earthly* often stand
as monickers for a domain of flux and imperfection, in opposition to
"heaven" or a "heavenly" domain marked by permanence and perfection. Using these synonyms, is it possible to describe globalization as
a process of steady "secularization" and a turn to merely temporal and
earthly concerns?

In the following, I aspire to take some steps in the direction of a clarification of these issues. I use as my point of departure an initiative famously undertaken by the philosopher Martin Heidegger when he defined human beings as "beings-in-the-world" (an integral term strung together with hyphens). With this definition, Heidegger distanced himself from a number of traditional conceptions that portrayed human existence as a haphazard composite of disparate elements: like animal plus reason (*animal rationale*), creature plus soul, or body plus mind. Moreover, in his usage, the phrase "being-in-the-world" was held together not only by hyphens (a relatively artificial device) but by a mutual openness and close engagement of its constitutive ingredients: a relationality that he captured in the term "care" (*Sorge*). Taking seriously this philosophical initiative, one can ask: How is "being-in-the-world" related to some of the problems referred to before—like globalization, secularization, and temporalization? Can one even build a bridge from the phrase to such notions as "cosmos" and "cosmopolitanism"? I shall proceed in three steps. First of all, I shall examine in some detail Heidegger's discussion of "being-in-the-world" and in particular the meaning he ascribes to "world"—and subsidiarily to "earth." To forestall the impression that this discussion results in a static structure or "system" of world relations, I turn in a second step to the crucial temporal dimension of Heidegger's perspective, where all the constitutive terms must be read as verbs with an active or processual character. In a final step, I shall explore the implications of his thought for such processes as globalization, secularization, and "cosmopolitanization" or cosmo-genesis.

Human Existence and the World

As is commonly known, Heidegger's *Being and Time* (1927) offers a sustained "deconstruction" of traditional Western metaphysics and philosophy; far from being fashionably "post-modern," however, his work also involves a constructive or radically reconstructive enterprise. What renders the former necessary is the tendency of "tradition" to obscure salient questions or to render their meaning self-evident; in modern Western thought, this tendency is aggravated by the habit of treating terms as separate "entities" whose complex relationship is precisely at issue. As Heidegger states, tradition (in the sense of traditionalism) shields from view the very conditions whose grasp permits a "productive appropriation" of the past. The modern tradition, which his book above all seeks to deconstruct, is the mind-body problem deriving from Descartes: the radical separation or juxtaposition of two disparate entities, thought and extension, cogito and external matter or nature. "With the '*cogito sum*,'" we read, "Descartes claimed to put philosophy on a new and firm grounding. But what he left completely open or undetermined was the mode of being of the '*res cogitans*' (thinking substance) and more precisely the ontological meaning of the term '*sum*' (I am)." Descartes's formulation in effect covered over or shielded from view the question that needed to be addressed: namely, the possibility of the separate status of the "cogito." The neglect or oblivion inherent in the Cartesian formula was continued in later "critical" philosophy, especially in the work of Kant. Despite his undeniable critical élan, Kant neglected to investigate the ontological underpinnings of the mind-matter dualism and, even more grievously, to provide a sustained analysis of "the subjectivity of the subject" (or cogito).[1]

Turning to the constructive or reconstructive side of its enterprise, *Being and Time* launches a new conception that completely undermines traditional dichotomies and juxtapositions of entities: the notion of "being-in-the-world." As Heidegger emphasizes: "The compound expression 'being-in-the-world' indicates already in its very phrasing that it stands for a *unitary* phenomenon. This primary datum must be seen as a whole"—which does not cancel the diversity of its "constitutive structural elements." To elucidate the "unity in diversity" of the phrase, *Being and Time* examines three basic dimensions of the formula: the aspect of being "in the world," which brings up the issue of world (*Welt*) and worldliness (*Weltlichkeit*); next, the question of the kind of "being" (human existence) that is in the world; and last, the general problem of "in-being" or immanence as such. Of these three aspects, the first and last deserve here primary attention. Regarding "in-being" and especially being "in the world," Heidegger stresses the radical difference of these phrases from a merely spatial location where one thing or entity is placed in another. When talking about being "in" or inside, he states, one usually refers to one thing being placed in another "like water is 'in' the glass or a garment is 'in' the cupboard." This purely empirical-spatial locution can be extended by saying "the bench is in the classroom, the classroom is in the university, the university in the city, and so forth." With this kind of spatial talk the "in-being" of "being-in-the-world" has nothing whatever to do. What is involved is not the placement of human existence or a human body in a larger container; rather, at stake is a more intimate togetherness or symbiosis, a symbiosis disclosing a mutual familiarity or engagement. Being-in-the-world here means that "I reside or dwell together with the world as something more or less familiar." The phrase "I am" means no longer "cogito" but "being or dwelling with"; thus, "being-in" is "the formal designation of human existence which is basically constituted as being-in-the-world."[2]

To repeat: the latter phrase does not denote a mere juxtaposition or coexistence of separate entities; rather, world or openness to world is a constitutive quality of human being—in such a way that one can speak of a genuine encounter or "touching" relation (*Berührung*) between them. Against this background, the relation between human being and world cannot or should not be misconstrued along purely epistemological lines, namely, in terms of the "subject-versus-object" dichotomy (which has bedeviled Western philosophy at least since Descartes). In the same manner, the connection between existence and world must not be confused with the traditional conundrums of the mind-body or spirit-matter "relationship"—a confusion that would render human "in-being" a purely "spiritual" quality while degrading world into a purely corporeal "extended matter." To obviate these misconstruals and confusions, Heidegger introduces at this point an emphatic link that allows for genuine encounter: the notion of "care" (*Sorge*) together with its verbal instantiation "caring" (*Besorgen*). "All the discussed modes of in-being," Heidegger observes, "display the constitutive feature (still to be specified) of *caring*." The terms "care" and "caring," he adds, are multifaceted and have a variety of meanings, ranging from anxious worry or concern to solicitude and affection. All these meanings and shadings need to be acknowledged and taken into account, at least on a phenomenal level. However, in a deeper sense, care and caring in *Being and Time* are used as "existential-ontological" terms to designate "the nature of a possible being-in-the-world." Differently put: the expressions are "structural-ontological concepts," because human being in its core "is (constituted by) care."[3]

Constituted in this manner, human beings have access to, or are familiar with, "world"—although not necessarily in a cognitive or epistemic sense. In Heidegger's words, "world" is always already disclosed (*erschlossen*) to human beings and thus understandable or understood at least in an inchoate way: "The tentative or preliminary disclosure of whatever is encountered amounts to a kind of understanding (*Verstehen*) of world to which human existence is inevitably oriented." Differently phrased, "world" in Heidegger's presentation has the status of a broad framework of significance within which phenomena are encountered as more or less intelligible, more or less meaningful or relevant. "The familiarity of the world," the text states, "does not necessarily involve the theoretical transparency of the complex fabric constituting the world. However, the very possibility of an existential interpretation of this fabric is grounded in the world-familiarity characterizing human life." The extent to which even an inchoate familiarity allows people to manage their lives is illustrated in the domain of practical or pragmatic affairs where the issue is the adequate handling of utensils or instruments. Here, the frame of significance of the world is a frame of practical involvement or management. The "in-being" of human existence in this case occurs in the mode of practical orientation, which allows concrete phenomena to be encountered for the sake of distinct purposes. This mode of providing orientation to phenomena in a distinct frame of significance, Heidegger adds, is what we call "the phenomenon of the world." And the structure of the fabric to which existence orients itself is what is meant by "the worldhood of the world" (*Weltlichkeit der Welt*).[4]

As indicated before, the empathic link between existence and world can take different forms—whose depth structure, however, is anchored in "care" (*Sorge*). In a section of the book devoted specifically to the discussion of the basic character of human existence "as care," Heidegger elucidates a number of modalities reflecting different kinds of encounters "in-the-world." One modality has to do with practical-pragmatic dealings in the world, with the "handling" of everyday utensils or equipment (what he calls *Zuhandenheit*). This modality he terms practical "caring" or "taking care of" (*Besorgen*). A different modality emerges when the encounter involves other creatures, especially other human beings; in this case the preferred term is "caring for" or being "solicitous about" someone (*Fürsorge*). Purely hypothetically, one might also think of a third modality involving carefulness about oneself or self-care (*Selbstsorge*). However, given that human existence is structurally anchored in care, Heidegger treats this modality as a potentially misleading tautology. One closely connected aspect, strongly emphasized in *Being and Time,* is that, for human beings, care or caring means first of all to care about their possibility of being and hence about their possible future(s). From this angle, a whole range of horizons or possible trajectories comes into view—and with this the challenge of human freedom. In Heidegger's words: "In this anticipation of its own potentiality for being we find the ontological condition of the freedom (*Freisein*) of human existence for its authentic possibilities."[5]

A sprawling and challenging work, *Being and Time* soon gave rise to a plethora of interpretations—including a host of misreadings and misunderstandings. What was and is often not recognized is that the work was uncompleted or a work still "in progress." Undeniably, the book contained some narrowly "humanist" or anthropocentric passages—or at least passages that could be interpreted along anthropocentric lines. During the ensuing decades, the latter kind of reading became in fact predominant in the European context, especially under the influence of Jean-Paul Sartre's "existentialism." As it happened, the ascendancy of this reading coincided with Heidegger's move in the very opposite direction, namely, away from anthropocentric self-assertion (a move that is frequently called *Kehre*). Given this divergence of trajectories, it became necessary for Heidegger at some point to disassociate himself from existentialist readings and, at the same time, to provide a clearer account of his perspective in the face of misunderstandings. This double aim was pursued and accomplished in the famous "Letter on Humanism," written in 1946. Responding to a question posed by a French colleague (Jean Beaufret) regarding whether the term *humanism* still made sense or carried some meaning, Heidegger stressed the need to dislodge anthropocentrism or to decenter human existence by highlighting the latter's caring openness to Being and all beings encountered in the world. If this is done, he observed, "then 'humanism' (if we decide to retain the word) means that humanity or human existence is indeed crucial for the disclosure of the truth of being—but in such a way that everything does no longer depend on human beings as such. Hence, we are thinking of a curious kind of 'humanism': it resembles the phrase '*lucus a non lucendo*'" (where a term is defined by its negation).[6]

In the course of clarifying his position on existentialism and humanism, Heidegger's "Letter" also offered some pointers regarding the proper meaning of *world, worldly,* and *being-in-the-world.* In this respect, a host of metaphysical and even theological interpretations had descended on *Being and Time,* trying to present its argument as spiritual or antispiritual, religious or antireligious, Christian or anti-Christian. Countering these construals and misconstruals, the "Letter" placed the emphasis again on relationism: the caring openness of human existence to "Being," seen as the dimension allowing all beings "to be." As Heidegger states: "The phrase 'being-in-the-world' used to pinpoint the humanity of human existence does not assert that 'man' is a merely 'worldly' creature understood in a Christian sense, a creature turned away from God and so cut loose from 'transcendence.'" In line with the immanence-transcendence doublet, the phrase is sometimes read as an endorsement of sensual worldliness in contrast to a "supersensible" or intelligible realm, which, in turn, is linked with God. Again, the "Letter" demurs. "The phrase 'being-in-the-world,'" it continues, "does not in any way designate an 'earthly' (*irdisch*) realm in opposition to a heavenly realm, nor is 'worldly' (*weltlich*) here contrasted to 'spiritual' (*geistlich*)." Above all, the phrase does not imply a decision about "whether in a theological-metaphysical sense 'man' is merely a this-worldly or an other-worldly creature." Moving beyond all these binary formulations, the "Letter" zeroes in on a notion of "world" where the latter does not at all designate a fixed or circumscribed domain (in opposition to others) but rather a radical openness or an open "clearing" in which all beings can be encountered. In the cited phrase, Heidegger states, "world" does not signify a distinct being or a realm of distinct beings but rather "the openness of Being as such." Human beings stand out "ek-statically" into this openness, which solicits their caring or careful attention. Differently put: "World is the clearing (*Lichtung*) of being into which humans reach out from their particular (projected) condition."[7]

Temporality and World

As indicated before, human existence is linked with the world in the mode of care—that is, through careful attentiveness to the meaning and possibilities of its being. From this angle, "world" (in "being-in-the-world") is not only a general framework of significance but a temporal horizon in which past, present, and future possibilities are disclosed. Underscoring this point, *Being and Time* presents temporality (*Zeitlichkeit*) as the depth structure and ontological significance of care. By exploring still-untapped possibilities or trajectories, existence projects itself into the future. This projection, however, does not occur in a vacuum, but against the backdrop of already completed possibilities, that is, the backdrop of past circumstances. What we call "the present" (*Gegenwart*) is nothing but the confluence and negotiation between past and future possibilities. In Heidegger's words: "*Temporality* is the phenomenon which brings together past, present, and future"—a bringing together or negotiation that is possible only through careful resoluteness: "Thus temporality emerges as the meaning of authentic care." As is clear, temporality here does not just mean clock time or an external measurement applied to events, but rather a constitutive and mobile horizon permeating human experience from beginning to end. Differently put: time is not a fixed or static concept but itself temporal, exhibiting the qualities of timeliness or untimeliness. The same is true of the cognate term *world*. Like temporality, world is not a fixed or static entity, but a moving horizon making possible the encounter of existence with "inner-worldly" phenomena. At the same time, serving as constitutive element of "being-in-the-world," world also permeates human experiences from beginning to end. What this brings into view is the "transcendent-immanent" status of world and time (a notion that transgresses the bounds of traditional metaphysics).[8]

Without delving more deeply into the argument in *Being and Time*, it is possible to retain one crucial insight: the central terms in Heidegger's philosophy cannot or should not be read as abstract metaphysical concepts designating substances or fixed essences. This is true already of the key term "Being"—against whose abstract definition Heidegger protests at the very onset of his study (by shifting the accent to the "*question* of being"). But it is equally true of other key terms like "human existence (*Dasein*)," "world," "time," and "language"—all of which should be interpreted not so much as nouns but as verbs, that is, as happenings "in progress" or "in process." In the context of his discussion of the temporality of care, Heidegger uses the stunning expression: "The world temporalizes itself (*zeitigt sich*) in temporality."[9] Phrases like this have tended to antagonize many readers, especially when Heidegger directly transforms a familiar noun into a verbal expression, by saying "the world worlds (*die Welt weltet*)," "language languages (*die Sprache spricht*)" or "the thing things (*das Ding dingt*)." With regard to the term *world*, by the way, its verbalization is not just an idiosyncrasy of some of his later writings, but can be traced to some early texts antedating *Being and Time* by almost a decade. Thus, in a lecture course of 1919 on the "meaning of philosophy" (*Zur Bestimmung der Philosophie*), we find a statement to the effect that only "if the world worlds" can there be anything like a "being-in-the world." This statement, again, is not an abstract metaphysical finding but can be verified by everyone in his or her own life: "Wherever and whenever 'world worlds' for me, I am somehow there."[10]

Despite a certain continuity of perspective and language, one should also note some important modifications or transformations in Heidegger's thought, especially the transformation of "world" and "being-in-the-world" into a more comprehensive fourfold fabric comprised of "earth, heaven, mortals, and immortals (or divinities, *Göttliche*)." As in the case of "being-in-the-world," the elements of the fourfold (*Geviert*) are linked together by an indissoluble bond. As Heidegger states in an essay of 1951, the four belong together in "originary unity"; they are "simply folded into each other (*Einfalt*)." Just as in the earlier phrase the elements were held together by care, we find in the fourfold a similar kind of bonding: Heidegger calls it *Ereignis*, a term that is difficult to translate (and among its renditions "appropriation" or "event" are certainly the least apt). One might see in *Ereignis* a multilateral and perhaps omnilateral kind of caring, or perhaps a kind of co-being in which every element of the fourfold allows all the others properly "to be." Heidegger speaks in this context of "guarding," "keeping hale" (*schonen*), "salvaging" (*retten*), "setting free" (*freilassen*), "bringing to peace" (*zum Frieden bringen*). Seen in this manner, *Ereignis* enables every element and every being to come into "its own" (*eigen*) without stubborn self-enclosure and with generous favor toward all; it promotes amicable concord without uniformity and while respecting (what someone has called) the "dignity of difference." As in the case of other Heideggerian terms, *Ereignis* is not an abstract concept. On the contrary, as he emphasizes, its meaning is instantiated in everyday life, in the sense that a jug, a bridge, and in fact every "thing" (*Ding*) displays the juncture of the fourfold. At the same time, far removed from a static structure, the term points to an ongoing temporal happening; hence one may say that the fourfold constantly "occurs" (*sich ereignet*). Against this background, its concord might be called a moving feast.[11]

Although formulated in complex language, Heidegger's view of moving horizons is not without parallels—of which some are closer than others. At least in some respects, parallels can be found with American pragmatism as the latter was formulated by William James and John Dewey. Like Heidegger, James and Dewey moved away from abstract traditional metaphysics—which they derided as "intellectualism"—and placed the accent more on temporal practice than on inert knowledge. Like the German thinker, the two—in opposing intellectualism—aimed to move away from traditional epistemic dichotomies, like those between cogito and extended matter, between subject and object, between immanence and transcendence. Again like their German counterpart, James and Dewey replaced dichotomies with a closer relational bond called "experience"—a term that (deriving from Hegel) denoted not just a subjective feeling state but a transformative existential openness to society and the world. Again paralleling Heidegger, the two conceived of philosophy not as the construction of a systematic edifice, but as a path or inquiry pursuing ever-new horizons. Admittedly, the cited parallels refer more to the author of *Being and Time* than to the later thinker of *Ereignis* (with its loosely South Asian and Taoist resonances). Also deviating from and even in opposition to Heidegger, pragmatists—most notably Dewey—were more willing to engage themselves responsibly in social and political occurrences of their time. Dewey, in particular, perceived modern democracy as the steady unfolding of human possibilities and hence as an arena of liberating "solicitude"; his notion of democracy as a work "in progress" clearly pointed in the direction of social life as a moving feast.[12]

Another parallel, but of a looser kind, can be found with "process philosophy," as articulated by the English philosopher Alfred North Whitehead and his followers. As it happens, Whitehead wrote and published his seminal work *Process and Reality* roughly at the time of *Being and Time*. Although initially trained as a mathematician and logician, Whitehead moved steadily away from an abstract epistemic formalism in the direction of a closer scrutiny of concrete phenomena and their relationships. Together with Heidegger and the pragmatists, he was opposed to the traditional metaphysical reliance on substances or fixed essences; continuing a path begun by Hegel, he became increasingly concerned with change and transformation rather than permanence, with "movement" and "becoming" rather than static structures. Together with Heidegger and the pragmatists, he was also averse to traditional dichotomies or dualisms (and even to simple "dialectical" formulas); delving more deeply into the actual "processes" constituting "reality," he detected a great deal of contingency, irregularity, and creativity not reducible to neat epistemic designs. In line with the German and American thinkers, Whitehead placed strong emphasis on the temporal character of all processes (although he was willing to acknowledge a certain "atemporal" transcendence). More than in the case of the pragmatists, there are limits in the case of the Whiteheadian parallel. Despite his effort to abandon "intellectualism" in favor of concrete experiences, "process philosophy" always remained close to the findings and methods of modern natural science. An example of this closeness is the focus on ultimate units of analysis (termed "actual entities"), which are uniform and atomistic; another example is the at least partial reliance on causal empirical explanation. A main difference, however, resides in the attitude toward modern technology, which process philosophers almost without qualification tend to support.[13]

Process philosophy has developed in many directions and affected numerous disciplines. Following Whitehead's lead, several philosopher-scientists—including Nicholas Rescher and Ilya Prigogine—have explored the complexity of dynamic processes in a variety of fields, ranging from electromagnetic waves to inanimate matter to living organisms to the "qualia" of human experiences. An important offshoot of Whitehead's initiative—but often striking out in new directions—is the field of "process theology," as initially outlined by Charles Hartshorne and further developed by John Cobb Jr., David R. Griffin, and others. In opposition to the traditional focus on divine omnipotence and transcendence, process theologians emphasize God's intimate involvement or engagement in the world, to the point that, far from being a static idol, God is seen as "becoming" through participation in human joys and sufferings. Temporality also affects the aspects of creation and revelation, in the sense that God appears as a cocreator of the world, disclosing or revealing himself/herself continuously in human lives on both a personal and a societal level.[14]

To a much more limited extent, process thinking has also surfaced in the field of political theory or philosophy, a field traditionally preoccupied with sovereign power, stable legal and institutional structures, and the division between rulers and ruled. A good example is the work of political theorist William Connolly, especially his book *A World of Becoming.* The book draws inspiration from a number of intellectual sources, including pragmatism (William James), process philosophy (Whitehead and Prigogine), and recent French thought (Merleau-Ponty and Gilles Deleuze). Drawing especially on Whitehead's initiative, Connolly explores the notion of "emergent causality" as a possible way of overcoming the dichotomy between human (or anthropocentric) intentionality and external (or "efficient") causality, between human "free will" and "nonhuman force-fields" negating freedom. In the light of Whiteheadian insights, he observes, the contrast needs to be "reconfigured" along the lines of complex processes. The notions of process, temporality, and emergent properties, in Connolly's view, are important not only for contemporary science but also for a proper understanding of social and political life. "The idea of becoming," he states, "can help us to grapple with the place of creative self-organization in both human and nonhuman processes" and thus can assist us "to negotiate more wisely relations between the human estate and the larger world."[15]

A Becoming Cosmopolis?

What do the teachings of Heidegger, pragmatism, and process philosophy tell us about cosmopolitanism and the prospect of cosmopolis? Can they help us to move closer to the realization of this vision? Probably not directly, but they can make us aware of the distance separating us from cosmopolis, of the many obstacles and blockages obstructing the way. Connolly's *A World of Becoming* vividly portrays some of these blockages; prominent among them are the enormous concentration of wealth and of militarized state power—two factors sometimes in competition and often in collusion with each other, which are additionally aggravated by ethnic, religious, and ideological rivalries. Following to some extent the work of Immanuel Wallerstein, Connolly traces the development of capitalism as a "world system" or globalized market, characterized by a steady fluidity of financial transactions, a deepening rift between rich and poor, all sanctioned and safeguarded by the public power of hegemonic elites. The combination of these factors leads him to the image of an "abstract machine," more specifically a "global resonance machine," defined as "a cluster of energized elements of multiple types that enter into loose, re-enforcing conjugations as the whole complex both consolidates and continues to morph." Using Whiteheadian (and Deleuzian) language, the machine can also be termed a "force-field," or else a "resonance machine of global antagonism": "The hubris, resentments, tensions, and injustices accumulated from multiple sources condense into a global machine of revenge and counter-revenge."[16]

The image of a "machine of global antagonism" is surely captivating—and corroborated by daily events. In a world overshadowed by endemic violence, by terror, counter-terror, and perpetual fear, the prospect of a cosmopolis animated by multilateral respect and care seems far removed indeed. The challenge presented by this situation is enormous and nearly overwhelming. One thing that is surely required is that people all over the world would cease to be mere consumers, bystanders, or onlookers and shoulder the task of active participation and citizenship in global affairs. At the same time, active involvement should not amount to mere self-assertion or narrow identity politics, but has to embrace openness and generous hospitality in such a manner as to generate goodwill across borders. Connolly's study reflects on possible "counter-movements" and offers encouraging pointers in that direction. A certain degree of state and interstate pressure to regulate a runaway market, he observes, together with a settlement of Near East conflicts, "would help immeasurably." As he emphasizes, however, what is needed are not only changes in public conditions but also changes in people's dispositions and attitudes: "The hawkish minorities on each side must be matched and surpassed by counter-constituencies anchored in multiple sites" and oriented toward nonviolent, possibly amicable modes of settlement. As it seems to me, this is the most important but also the most difficult challenge for counter-movements, because it involves a change from forceful, possibly domineering self-assertion to responsible civic conduct: "We must work on mood, belief, desire and action together. And as we do so, we amplify positive attachment to existence amidst the political resentments that spur us on."[17]

To move from resentment to nonresentment and life affirmation—this would indeed be a moving feast and "a rainbow after many storms" (as Nietzsche has taught us). The move involves a change from aggressive self-assertion to reconciliation, from unilateralism to omnilateral "*Ereignis*" and "letting-be" (in Heidegger's sense). Stated in Gandhian language, it involves an ascent from violence and revenge to the level of greatest possible nonviolence (*ahimsa*)—where the latter does not just mean avoidance of physical harm but the cultivation of well-being through caring solicitude and "positive attachment to existence." Still in a Gandhian idiom, counter-movements function not so much as destructive forces but as agents of *satyagraha,* a term that signals the active pursuit of existential "truth" and social-political goodness or happiness. To be able to pursue *satyagraha,* participants in the Gandhian freedom struggle had to undergo a process of ethical learning and seasoning, a process aimed at weeding out remnants of destructive hatred and vengefulness. Moreover, this training or discipline was not restricted to a select group but extended (or was meant to extend) to all groups transgressing boundaries of ethnicity, religion, social status, gender, and age. It is not hard to see why Gandhian *satyagraha* came to serve as such a powerful inspiration to freedom movements elsewhere.

To be sure, the difficulties and obstacles are legion. If the task is formidable in domestic societies, the ascent beyond hatred and fear is even more demanding in the global arena. Here territorial animosities coupled with the desire for "spheres of influence" inflame and derail the minds of even prudent political leaders (if such could be found). Add to these factors the global inequalities (previously mentioned) of wealth, power, and technology, and the result is a cauldron of resentment fueling policies of genocide, ethnic cleansing, jihadism, and Armageddon. Small wonder that, faced with these calamities, some people choose to retreat into solitude or familial contentment—forgetting that modern wars do not respect private retreats. For grown people, there is really no alternative to the cosmopolitan agenda, an agenda seeking to minimize mayhem and destruction and to advance global peace.

To enlist in this agenda implies the readiness to stand up for justice, to enlist "skillful means" in the pursuit of justice, and to undergo the disciplined cultivation of civic, now globalized virtues. To become engaged, however, does not mean "activism" of every kind. We need to remember that we are not lords and masters of the universe, but only participants in the unfolding story of a "world of becoming." In Heideggerian terminology, we are "beings-in-the-world" co-constituted by our world; we are modest partners in a "fourfold" that shapes the happenings of our world. To go beyond this role in the direction of mastery is a recipe for failure. Here it is good to recall the timeless-timely words of the *Tao Te Ching*:

> Those who would take over the earth
> And shape it to their will
> Never, I notice, succeed.
> The earth is like a vessel so sacred
> That at the mere approach of the profane
> It is marred
> And when they reach out their fingers it is gone.[18]

2. Cosmopolitanism

In Search of Cosmos

> Who saves one person saves the entire world.
> —Babylonian Talmud

The legacy of Western "modernity" is ambivalent. On the one hand, it has bequeathed to us the inspiring ideas of global brotherhood and universal justice. On the other hand, in the aftermath of the Peace of Westphalia, it has launched the agenda of a compact, exclusivist nationalism or nation-state, an agenda often copied or supplemented by equally self-contained subnationalities. During the nineteenth and twentieth centuries, the nationalist agenda was steadily on the upsurge, engendering first a series of interstate wars and then the violent paroxysm of two World Wars. In the midst of these conflagrations, the broader civilizational vision was not extinguished, with its core often captured by the formula of "cosmopolitanism." In the words of the poet Heinrich Heine, exclusive nationalism or chauvinism was a sign of backwardness, whereas brotherhood harbored a "greater future." Excoriating in harsh terms the "shabby, coarse, unwashed" character of the former, Heine celebrated by contrast "a sentiment which is the most splendid and sacred thing Germany has produced," namely, "humanity, the universal brotherhood of man, the cosmopolitanism to which our great minds—Lessing, Herder, Schiller, Goethe, Jean Paul and all educated people in Germany— have always paid homage."[1]

In recent times, Heine's cosmopolitan vision has come to be challenged again by all kinds of exclusivist backwardness. As a counter-move to social or cultural interaction and interdependence, we witness in many parts of the world the return of virulent forms of "identity politics," where identity is defined in national or ethnic or religious terms (and sometimes in all these terms simultaneously). Exclusivism is manifest in the erection of new walls or fences between peoples and, on a legal level, in the imposition of new restrictions on immigration and citizenship. In this context, there is no doubt a great need to reaffirm and reenact Heine's cosmopolitan agenda—and, fortunately, this need is widely felt and emphasized. As political philosopher Seyla Benhabib has stated, quite correctly: "Cosmopolitanism . . . has become one of the key words of our times"—something that is surely to be welcomed. Unhappily, the popularity of a term does not always help to clarify its meaning—which remains contested.[2]

In the following I shall take some steps in the direction of clarification by differentiating among some possible meanings of the term. In a first step, noting the close connection or affinity between the term and *globalization,* I turn attention to the global extension of markets and communications networks. Taken in this sense, cosmopolitanism refers to ongoing, empirically observable processes of border-crossing and hybridization—processes that are often accompanied by glaring ethical and psychological deficits. In a second step, I move from empirical description to the normative level, that is, to cosmopolitanism as a moral "vision"—whether this vision is formulated as the Kantian demand for global justice in a world confederation or the (linguistically nuanced) stress on the universal redemption of discursive validity claims. Construed in this sense, cosmopolitanism refers (in Benhabib's words) to "the emergence of norms that ought to govern relations among individuals in a global civil society." Noting the dilemma besetting Kantian and post-Kantian formulations—the antinomy between "is" and "ought," between vision and practice—I turn in a final step to cosmopolitanism seen as a practical experience and mode of ethical conduct. Viewed in this light, the term refers to the agenda of a global pedagogy fostering the cultivation of global civic "virtues," such as the virtues of openness, generosity, service, and care. The same pedagogy animates the search for a viable "cosmos" reconciling the split between description and norm and also the gulf between global and local dimensions of public life.[3]

Globalization

Cosmopolitanism and *globalization* are closely connected and on some level overlapping; but they are not synonyms. Although capturing some features of the former, the second term appears limited to various empirical processes—which, to be sure, have gained great prominence in our time. In the view of David Held, one of the chief sponsors of "world order" studies, globalization denotes "a set of processes which are reshaping the organization of human activity, stretching political, economic, social and communicative networks across regions and continents." Among these processes, Held gives pride of place to economic and financial transactions carried out under liberal or neoliberal auspices. "For the past two to three decades," he states, "the agenda of economic liberalization and global market integration—the 'Washington Consensus,' as it is sometime called—has been the mantra of many leading economic powers and financial institutions."[4] Held's view is corroborated by sociologist Ulrich Beck, who is likewise concerned about definitional issues. "In public discourse," Beck writes, "the fashionable term 'globalization' is understood primarily in a one-dimensional sense as *economic* globalization, and is closely connected with what can be called 'globalism,'" a term that captures "the idea of a global market, defends the virtues of neoliberal economic growth and the utility of allowing capital, commodities and labor to move freely across borders." Even opponents of globalization, he adds, tend to agree with the primary identification of the term with economic transactions and their social and cultural ramifications.[5]

In the aftermath of the economic and financial debacle of recent years, the vaunted benefits and accomplishments of neoliberalism and the Washington Consensus have come under critical scrutiny, depriving them of their status as a global mantra. Held is instructive in this respect by exposing the glaring defects or shortcomings of neoliberal globalization. The latter model, he states, bears a "heavy burden of responsibility" for failing to address important areas of market failure: such as the "problem of externalities," illustrated by environmental degradation; the "inadequate development of non-market social factors," including the insufficient provision of such "public goods" as education, health services, and transportation; and the "underemployment or unemployment" of available productive resources in the world. The sketched market failures reached their culmination in the worldwide financial crisis, where "high levels of consumer spending in the West, fueled by easy access to credit," created ultimately a "global liquidity overflow" evident in massive "asset bubbles and excess leverage." In Held's sober assessment, the "key fault lines" of the debacle can be traced to the totalized ideology of privatization and deregulation, which gave rise to "a 'light-touch' regulatory system that encouraged risk-taking and allowed money to be diverted into very specific areas: mortgage securitization and off-balance sheet activity."[6]

The exposed shortcomings of neoliberal globalization do not by themselves challenge or put a dent into the celebration of global liquidity and borderless transaction flows. As Karl Marx noted long ago: under the impact of capital "everything solid melts into air." The fact that present-day globalization is not tightly bound up with market transactions is demonstrated by the rapid expansion of communications facilities and global travel. Ulrich Beck speaks in this context of the "new metaphor of 'liquidity,'" stating that today "neither boundaries nor relations mark the difference between one place and another," in the sense that "boundaries are becoming blurred" while "relations are entering into consistently shifting constellations." Citing a recent sociological study tellingly titled *Global Culture Industry: The Mediation of Things*, Beck reaches the conclusion that "social structures are dissolving into 'streams' of human beings, information, goods and specific signs or cultural symbols." What emerges at this point is "a sociology beyond societies" characterized by a "single-minded empirical and conceptual focus on 'mobility,'" a category that supplants the traditional concepts of "structure" and "community." To corroborate this finding further, Beck also cites a study by Arjun Appadurai that, on the basis of empirical research, argues that "the new units 'flowing' around the world are 'socioscapes' that increasingly set capital, the media, ideologies, technologies, and human beings in 'motion' and establish new relations between them."[7]

As it happens, Beck is not entirely entranced or taken in by the metaphors of liquidity and ceaseless mobility. To register his reservations, he introduces the term *banal cosmopolitanism*, which in many ways resembles what Stanley Fish at one point called "boutique multiculturalism," that is, the delight in exotic foods and customs that characterizes the global consumer society. Under the impact of global consumerism, Beck writes, the familiar and local become the "playground of universal experiences," the "locus of encounters and interminglings or, alternatively, of anonymous coexistence and the overlapping of possible worlds and global dangers." What is "banal" about this kind of cosmopolitanism, above all, is the lack of any commitment or genuine engagement among people, in favor of the indiscriminate search for novelty for the sake of vacuous self-indulgence. In the pursuit of banal aims, Beck adds, cosmopolitanism becomes itself a commodity because "the glitter of cultural difference sells well." The market here is vast: "Images of an in-between world, of the black body, exotic beauty, exotic music, and so on, are globally cannibalized, staged and consumed as mass products for mass markets." Through the erasure of all boundaries and distinctions, products and transaction flows are mingled and "hybridicized"—without leaving an imprint or trace. For example, "someone who listens to 'black music' and wears pictures or quotations of black people on their t-shirts does not have to identify with the culture from which the pictures or quotations are taken"; rather, "black culture, styles and creativity are sold here to a public that knows no borders."[8]

Beck's comments also refer—albeit obliquely—to the human costs of banal cosmopolitanism: flow charts and streams of liquidity are not merely empirical processes but implicate distinct character or personality traits that are fostered in the global arena. In the case of economic globalization (as discussed above), it is relatively easy to delineate the personality profile undergirding the agenda: it is the *homo economicus,* familiar from modern liberal economic theory, the robust entrepreneur or corporate business leader committed to maximizing profits at minimal costs. Globalization has simply projected this profile onto the global screen, where profits and losses are no longer counted in millions but in billions and trillions. No doubt, the vastness of scale puts an enormous strain on the capacity of human management—a fact that accounts for the frequent psychological or psycho-pathological afflictions among global business leaders. The likelihood of such afflictions is greatly intensified in the case of individuals caught up in the flows of total liquidity. No longer tied to, and steadied by, the "Protestant ethic" of economic success, such individuals are bound to drift aimlessly in the ever-shifting "socioscapes" of global life, where closeness and distance vanish together and where no place and every place is "home."

Nobody has portrayed the pathology of "banal" cosmopolitans better than the noted sociologist Zygmunt Bauman. In his book *Globalization: The Human Consequences,* Bauman has pinpointed the social effects of unlimited liquidity and mobility. In his portrayal, the ongoing "time/space compression"—or rather, the erasure of space/time boundaries—encapsulates the gist of the present-day "transformation of the parameters of the human condition." In the course of globalization, he notes, "mobility climbs to the rank of the uppermost among the coveted values," and the freedom to move "fast becomes the main stratifying factor of our late-modern or post-modern times." In our post-modern context, the globalized individual is in a way catapulted into a dimension beyond space and time where the difference between "now" and "then," "here" and "there," "close by" and "far away," drops off. In the words of Paul Virilio, the new transcendent or "cybernating" world is "devoid of spatial dimensions, but inscribed in the singular temporality of an instantaneous diffusion. From here on, people cannot be separated by physical obstacles or by temporal distances." Undaunted by this exhilarating globalism, Bauman injects some sober ethical considerations. The new mobility, he observes, implies in fact a "radical unconditionality," a "disconnection of power from obligations," and ultimately a "freedom from the duty to contribute to daily life and the perpetuation of the social community." This freedom from obligation in turn carries with it a heavy psychological baggage: the exposure to unlimited risk and insecurity: "Being 'far away' [from everything] means being in unprecedented trouble, and so it demands cleverness, cunning, slyness or courage"—a cleverness that overtaxes the psychic arsenal of most human beings.[9]

There is another, even more sobering consequence entailed by nomadic or banal cosmopolitanism, namely, a deep social division. Alongside the emerging "planetary dimensions of business, finance, trade and information flows," Bauman comments, "a localizing and space-fixing process is set in motion"; these two interconnected processes "sharply differentiate the existential conditions of whole populations and of various segments of each one of the populations." Thus, while some of us are becoming "fully and truly global" (in the dimension of liquidity), others are confined to an impoverished and barely habitable "locality" or "localism." However, being local in a global-ized world is "a sign of social deprivation and degradation"—and also a sign of anomie and psychic trauma. In Bauman's words: "The dis-comforts of localized existence are compounded by the fact that, with public spaces removed beyond the reaches of local life, localities are losing their meaning-generating and meaning-negotiating capacity and hence are increasingly dependent on sense-giving and interpret-ing actions which they do not control or influence." This fact may have something to do with the rise of "neo-tribal and fundamental-ist tendencies" today that reflect the experience of people "on the receiving end of globalization," in opposition to the widely acclaimed "hybridization of top culture." Putting the argument of his study in a nutshell, Bauman concludes: "Rather than homogenizing the human condition, the technological annulment of temporal/spatial distances tends to polarize it." While emancipating some people from territorial constraints and rendering social meanings extraterritorial, it has the effect of "denuding" the territory to which other people are confined of its "meaning and identity-endowing capacity."[10]

Cosmopolitan World Order

As indicated before, globalization (as discussed so far) is an outgrowth of Western modernity—more specifically of a certain empiricist strand, which does not exhaust its meaning. There is another, rationalist or normative strand that shifts the accent from description to universal principles and prescriptions. In many ways, this strand was inaugu-rated by Descartes's focus on the inner mind (cogito) and its rules of cognition, in contradistinction from external contexts (*res extensa*). With some modifications, the Cartesian initiative was continued by Immanuel Kant and his emphasis on the invariant-transcendental structures of mind functioning as the premises (or conditions of possi-bility) of both scientific knowledge and practical action. In the broader political arena, Kant also elaborated on the norms or structures suit-able for the interrelation between states and peoples, an elaboration that famously led him to the formulation of the guiding principles of "cosmopolitan law or right" (*Weltbürgerrecht*).

With this formulation, Kant made an important contribution to the development of modern morality and law. As he wrote in his famous treatise "Perpetual Peace," it is necessary to distinguish among three kinds of legal orders: domestic "civil law or right" (*ius civitatis*); "international law/right" between states (*ius gentium*); and "cosmopolitan law/right" (*ius cosmopoliticum*), "insofar as individuals and states, coexisting in an external relationship of mutual influences, may be regarded as members of a universal community of peoples." The latter cosmopolitan community was only possible, for Kant, if all member states were "republican" (not democratic) in character and linked together in a loose confederation. The only and central article of the *"ius cosmopoliticum"* was the principle of "hospitality," which involves "the right of a stranger not be treated with hostility when he arrives on someone else's territory." Although he may be turned away, the stranger "must not be treated with hostility, so long as he behaves in a peaceful manner."[11]

Kant's perspective has been ably carried forward and enriched by a number of later writers and philosophers, always with an emphasis on normative principles and legal rules. During the twentieth century, probably the most famous thinker to continue the Kantian trajectory was the American philosopher John Rawls. In his early work, especially in *A Theory of Justice*, Rawls endeavored to articulate general principles of a just society by invoking, as a transcendental or quasi-transcendental condition of possibility, an "original position" of reasoning where all empirical contingencies are blended out. At that point, the philosopher's attention was mainly focused on domestic society and hence on the domain Kant had called *"ius civile."* In due course, however—and probably as a result of the ongoing process of globalization—Rawls shifted his focus to the global, international, or (more precisely) cosmopolitan arena. The result was his famous study *The Law of Peoples*, whose title refers not properly to traditional international law (*ius gentium*) but rather to "the political principles for regulating the mutual political relations between peoples." Continuing, but modifying the strategy of his earlier book in a global direction, Rawls states: "The content of a reasonable Law of Peoples is ascertained by using the idea of the original position a second time with the parties now understood to be the representatives of peoples." The application of this strategy yields a list of "principles of justice among free and democratic peoples" that includes items like the following: "peoples are free and independent"; they are "equal and parties to the agreements that bind them"; they are "to observe a duty of non-intervention"; they are "to honor human rights," and the like. While following in general the Kantian lead, *The Law of Peoples* departs from this legacy in a number of aspects that I cannot pursue here in detail, but of which two seem particularly relevant: the toning down of Kant's more rigorous transcendentalism; and the emphasis on "free and democratic peoples" (in lieu of "republican" regimes).[12]

In due course, the initiatives of Kant and Rawls came to infiltrate or affect the academic discipline of "international relations" (IR), a field that has tended to be dominated solidly by a "realist" outlook (inspired by Hans Morgenthau and others) averse to ethical considerations. The result—at least among some practitioners of the field—has been a willingness to moderate power-political concerns through attention to normative demands, especially the demand of global justice. Among the group of "normative" practitioners, some pioneering steps were taken by Charles Beitz, Henry Shue, and Thomas Pogge. In a way, it was Beitz who first inaugurated the normative or Rawlsian "turn" with his book *Political Theory and International Relations* (published in 1979). Taking issue with the dominant realist or power-political emphasis, Beitz in his study argued forcefully in favor of introducing the idea of global justice into the international field. As he pointed out, Rawls's theory of "justice as fairness"—with some modifications—was eminently suitable for transforming the traditional conception of "inter-state law" (*jus gentium*) into a properly "cosmopolitan" system of cross-culturally binding ethical rules. This shift to morally binding rules limiting state behavior was soon picked up and applied to concrete issues by other practitioners, for example, by Henry Shue in his study *Nuclear Deterrence and Moral Restraint* (1989), followed later by the coedited work *Preemption: Military Action and Moral Justification* (2007). Perhaps the most prominent proponent of a global or cosmopolitan order inspired by Rawlsian teachings, however, is the philosopher and public ethicist Thomas Pogge, well known for such publications as *Realizing Rawls* (1989) and *World Poverty and Human Rights: Cosmopolitan Responsibilities and Reforms* (2002). In all his writings, Pogge has insisted on the urgency of applying Rawls's idea of the "original position" and his central principles of "equal liberty" and "difference," with appropriate adjustments, to the global arena.[13]

To be sure, among post-Kantian thinkers Rawls is not alone in having fostered a normative approach to international politics. In many ways, his influence has been corroborated, and also subtly transformed, by a European perspective: the critical theory of Jürgen Habermas. While preserving the rationalist tenor of *A Theory of Justice*, Habermas proceeded to reformulate the prelinguistic conception of the "original position" in terms of a "discourse" or communicative interaction in which all people affected by the outcome of deliberations would be entitled to participate. As conceived by critical theory, communicative discourse is meant to apply to a broad field, from epistemology to ethics and politics. In every case, discourse is assumed to lead from the assertion of certain claims through their contestation to the ultimate "validation" or redemption of these claims. Partly under the influence of Rawls, Habermas also envisaged a possible extension of his model to the broader cosmopolitan arena (although his primary concern remained focused on regionalism and European unification). In comparison with the Rawlsian agenda of global justice, the global application of the discourse model exhibits two distinctive features: first, a shift from the "original position" to an exchange of validity claims (congruent with the so-called linguistic turn); and second, a relative deemphasis of the "difference" principle, construed as concern with the fate of disadvantaged people who, for one reason or another, lack the ability or opportunity to raise validity claims.[14]

Among the followers of the discourse model, no one has been more resolute in transplanting this model to the global level than Seyla Benhabib. In a string of writings culminating in her study *Another Cosmopolitanism* (2006), Benhabib has attempted to sketch the path leading from interstate relations to "cosmopolitan law" anchored in discursive principles. In the words of Robert Post, introducing her book: the question taken up by the author is "how we can fashion political and legal institutions to govern ourselves, all together, on this earth"; more specifically, how we can "conceptualize the emergence of cosmopolitan law as a dynamic process through which the [universal] principles of human rights are progressively incorporated into the positive law of democratic states." In her text, Benhabib clearly distinguishes traditional international or interstate law (*ius gentium*) from the ethical and normative character of the emerging cosmopolitan order. As she writes: "Cosmopolitan norms of justice accrue to individuals as moral and legal persons in a worldwide civil society"; their peculiarity consists in the fact that "they endow *individuals* rather than states and their agents with certain rights and claims." Basically, normative cosmopolitanism signals an eventual transition from treaties concluded among states to a cosmopolitan order "understood as international public law that binds and bends the will of sovereign nations." In accentuating the normative quality of public law, Benhabib also is at pains to differentiate it from "globalization" conceived in purely economic terms and from the empirical operation of global "networks" of media and communication systems.[15]

Although committed basically to a normative and quasi-Kantian vision—one should note—Benhabib is troubled by the division between "facts and norms" and also by the tension and possible disjunction between universal principles and domestic practices of self-governance. Following some Kantian intuitions or suggestions, however, she places her trust in the progressive attenuation of the problem, mainly along the lines of what she calls a "dialogical universalism."[16] A similar outlook can be found in the writings of David Held (whose work was previously invoked). As he observes in *Cosmopolitan Democracy* (1995), the end of the Cold War ushered in the possibility of a "new world order" based on the "spirit of cooperation and peace" and hence the prospect of a "cosmopolitan international democracy." Like Benhabib, Held ponders the tension between the emerging global order and the persistence of territorially limited legal orders anchored in the traditional ("Westphalian") model. In a time of regional and global interconnectedness, he notes, major questions arise "about the coherence, viability, and accountability of national decision-making entities." With Benhabib again, he places his hope in the progressive attenuation of the tension—a process effected mainly (though not exclusively) through a restructuring of global institutions both inside and outside the framework of the United Nations. The hope for progressive attenuation is also expressed in Held's emphasis on the need to connect global and local or domestic changes in a mutually complementary or "dialectical" process. Precisely as a result of economic globalization, he observes, "new demands are unleashed for regional and local autonomy as groups find themselves buffeted by global forces and by inappropriate or ineffective [domestic] political regimes."[17]

Cosmopolitanism as Engaged Practice

As advocated by normative writers, the vision of global order and justice is surely captivating and important. Regardless of whether anchored in Kantian transcendental reason or a Habermasian discursive rationality, the vision injects a badly needed moral or prescriptive dimension into an international arena ravished by rampant power politics. Given the predictable effects of the latter—domination, injustice, and violence—nothing appears more required in our world than a cosmopolitan order governed by rational and universal principles. Yet, even while appreciating the normative global design, one cannot quite discard a certain feeling of aloofness, of a troubling remoteness of theoretical construction from lived practice. Especially when—as in the case of David Held—one notices the steady proliferation of global principles and "metaprinciples," one cannot avoid the impression of a certain "apriorism," of an intellectual constructivism intent on starting the global building with the roof. This impression has to do, among other things, with the somewhat uneven or skewed treatment of the tension between norms and facts or else between global rules and local or regional contexts. As this tension is treated by Rawlsian and discursive thinkers, primacy is almost invariably granted to global order or the "application" of global norms, while local or regional conditions appear mainly as obstacles to be alleviated with the passage of time.

This unevenness comes to the fore especially in the relation between rational maxims of justice and the concreteness of cultural contexts. In the normativist construal, cultural contexts often tend to be treated as passive, even reluctant recipients of global rules rather than active contributors or resources. Thus, in his *Cosmopolitan Democracy,* Held makes room for cultural concerns—but on a very subsidiary level. "Distinctive national, ethnic, cultural and social identities," he admits, "are part of the very basis of people's sense of being-in-the-world; they provide deeply rooted comfort and distinctive social locations for communities seeking a place 'at home' on this earth." But, he adds, these identities are "always only *one* possible option among others"; since they are "historically and geographically contingent," they can readily be replaced by another identity (or perhaps by hybridity or no identity). On a cosmopolitan level, their significance in any case remains negligible. The unevenness also surfaces in his later

Cosmopolitanism (2010). "While my account aims at being universal," we read there, "it tries to address cultural and political specificity seriously." As it appears, however, recognition of that specificity does not impinge on the "defining role" of universal principles.[18]

In attenuated fashion, Held's ambivalence can also be found in Benhabib's writings. Like Held, Benhabib treats local and cultural contexts as arbitrary or contingent and in need of "moral justification" through universal norms. As previously indicated, she follows Kant's tradition, by stating: "I view cosmopolitanism as the emergence of norms that *ought* to govern relations among individuals in a global civil society." Yet, as mentioned, she remains concerned about the antinomy between global norms and local customs. Hence, she asks: "How can one mediate moral universalism with ethical particularism?" This question leads her to see cosmopolitanism mainly as "a project of mediations," pointing in the direction of a "dialogical universalism." This outlook also prompts her to embrace the need of a "dialogue with otherness" and ultimately the practical-pragmatic agenda of (what she calls) "democratic iterations." "Culture matters," she states emphatically; "cultural evaluations are deeply bound up with interpretations of our needs, our visions of the good life, and our dreams for the future." And "because these evaluations run so deep, as citizens of liberal democratic politics, we have to learn . . . to live with the otherness of others whose ways of being may be deeply threatening to our own."[19]

This seems to me a correct and commendable observation. However, as one should note, the turn to practical "iterations" has consequences: it involves a shift of intellectual horizons no longer strictly compatible with Kantian, Rawlsian, or discursive parameters. In modern times, the acknowledgment of a certain primacy of practice (vis-à-vis theoretical principles) is associated mainly with the teachings of American pragmatism, hermeneutics, and neo-Aristotelian virtue ethics. One of the most distinctive features of John Dewey's work is precisely his persistent remonstration against the pretense of abstract theory-construction or what he called "intellectualism." From Dewey's angle, the task of philosophical thinking is not to impose readymade maxims from on high (or "top-down"), but rather to be attentive to concrete (often perplexing) encounters and experiences as the nourishing soil of reflection. As he noted in one of his writings: "Thinking is not a case of spontaneous combustion; it does not occur just on the level of 'general principles.'" What this means is that cognitive insight is not the possession of a detached "spectator," but the result of a process of inquiry where "the self *becomes* a knower" or "*becomes* a mind in virtue of a distinctive way of partaking in the course of events." This approach has an important impact on the meaning of education or pedagogy, which, for Dewey, involved not the transfer of finished doctrines from teacher to students, but rather an ongoing process of learning in which all parties are continuously transformed. Perhaps the most crucial implication of this outlook is in the field of politics, where democracy is seen not as a finished system but as an ongoing "iterative" practice: more specifically as "primarily a mode of associated living, of conjoint communicated experience."[20]

Although originating in a different intellectual milieu—that of Continental-European philosophy—hermeneutics likewise is marked by attentiveness to concretely situated experience and practice. This is particularly evident in the work of its chief representative, Hans-Georg Gadamer. Building on Heidegger's notions of "being-in-the-world" and its corollary of "understanding," Gadamer developed his view of hermeneutics as an inquiry proceeding through dialogical engagement between self and other, reader and text, familiarity and unfamiliarity. As he writes in his magisterial *Truth and Method,* hermeneutical engagement requires a diligent openness to the world, which, in the case of interhuman encounters, takes prominently the form of dialogue or of the interplay of "question and response." What such a dialogue yields, or is meant to yield, is a mutual disclosure of "meaning" that goes beyond mere psychic empathy and abstract rational consensus (in the direction of existential "truth"). In all his writings, Gadamer always stressed the close linkage between understanding and human practice, where the latter is not simply deduced from theoretical premises but rather serves as the nurturing soil of understanding and ethical conduct. It is at this point that a fruitful interplay between hermeneutics and Aristotelian and neo-Aristotelian "virtue ethics" comes into view, where ethics means basically the cultivation of personal and social dispositions transgressing the limits of selfishness or self-interest in the direction of mutual recognition and respect.[21]

What the discussed perspectives have in common is the emphasis on the primacy of practice over cognition and, more specifically, the primacy of ethical conduct over the knowledge of normative rules and legal principles. Knowledge of rules and principles can be easily obtained by reading textbooks or memorizing parental instructions. By contrast, ethical conduct in practice requires a steady process of habituation, that is, the cultivation of ethical dispositions conducive to the practice of individual and social virtues. It is the latter cultivation that alone holds out the hope of taming or curtailing the temptations of power lust, greed, and injustice. As experience teaches—on both the personal and the political levels—legal principles and high moral rules can be easily avoided or circumvented in the absence of sound ethical dispositions; clever minds will always find loopholes, detours, and excuses. Moreover, general rules and principles do not interpret themselves and need always to be applied to complex circumstances—a need that provides endless escape routes to people not steeped in habituated ethical conduct. Transferring these considerations to the contemporary global situation, it becomes clear that cosmopolitanism cannot simply rely on the operation of legal principles and rational norms, but has to descend into the formation of conduct and character. As I see it, there is presently no shortage of international norms and conventions—but their impact on the actual conduct of public decision-makers is minimal.

This is not an argument against law and especially not against international legal rules and principles. But law is subsidiary to ethics; it is a fall-back position when ethical dispositions are lacking (and as a fall-back position it remains fragile and vulnerable to evasion). Turning back again to our theme: what is urgently needed in our time is a strengthening of the dispositions conducive to cosmopolitan coexistence and collaboration, chiefly the dispositions of generosity, hospitality, mutuality, and striving for justice. This strengthening involves a large-scale pedagogical effort aiming at the steady transformation of narrow (national, ethnic, or religious) self-interest into a willingness to care for the common interest or "common good" of humankind. As a pedagogy, the effort should start as early as possible, at the elementary and secondary school levels and extending into college and adult education. An excellent mode of cosmopolitan pedagogy is exchange programs involving students, teachers, doctors, and members of other professions. Equally helpful are international nongovernmental organizations or institutions—like the "World Social Forum" and the "World Public Forum–Dialogue of Civilizations"—that bring together people from many countries and from different walks of life. Even some intergovernmental institutions can play an important role; particularly prominent in this respect is the United Nations Educational, Scientific and Cultural Organization (UNESCO) and its affiliates.

Given that, in all these instances, pedagogy involves cross-cultural learning processes, practical cosmopolitanism in large measure relies on communication, mutual interpretation, and dialogue and thus takes a stand against every form of unilateral or hegemonic monologue. It is no accident that, in recent times, cosmopolitanism as practical conduct has been associated with the idea of a "dialogue of (or among) civilizations."[22] The association is also captured in the notion "dialogical cosmopolitanism"—a phrase that is similar to, but not entirely synonymous with, Benhabib's "dialogical universalism." What is distinctive about dialogical or practice-centered cosmopolitanism is the refusal to grant blanket primacy to globalism or "universal" order. In my view, granting such primacy seems to be based on the assumption that "bigger" or larger is always "better." But clearly, by itself, celebrating globalism means only to give preference to quantitative spatial extension—which says nothing about quality. As previously indicated, globalism often means nothing more than a mode of globetrotting or aimless tourism—devoid of any qualitative or ethical engagement. What one has to take seriously here is the necessarily situated character of concrete human action and interaction—the fact that practice or conduct always occurs at a certain place, among a determinate and finite group of people. To this extent, the well-known motto "think globally, but act locally" has its good sense—although the second half of the phrase is often forgotten. This also means that cosmopolitanism as practice cannot shun or sideline local contexts—because we basically learn about ethical conduct in concrete interaction with others. More generally, learning is a "bottom-up" enterprise, and this holds true also and especially for cross-cultural or intercivilizational learning. At its core, cosmopolitanism—to make any headway—requires learning and extending hospitality across borders, which is a difficult task and not sufficiently appreciated in celebrations of hybridity or total mobility.[23]

These comments do not entail the dismissal of universalism or its collapse into the diversity of particular local customs. However, there is a sense in which "global" and "local" are related in ways different from that suggested by the image of a spatial hierarchy. One way to express this difference may be to say that the "cosmos" (of cosmopolitanism) can be found in small and recessed circumstances as much and perhaps more readily than in spatial bigness. This is what may be suggested by the medieval notion of *perichoresis,* denoting the presence or indwelling of truth in everything or every facet of the world. In a slightly different idiom, the philosopher Spinoza captured the idea in the pithy statement that "the more we know individual beings the more we are able to know God." Something along similar lines may also have been meant by Leibniz when he argued that the "monads" (or elements of the universe) do not need windows because that universe is reflected and mirrored in all its diverse parts (in a cosmic kind of "relationism").[24]

The idea of a cosmic indwelling or of a cosmos inhabiting even small places is not a monopoly of Western philosophy but can also be found in East Asian and South Asian traditions. Thus, the great Confucian thinker Mencius left us these memorable lines: "The Way (*tao*) lies in what is near, but people think it in what is far off; one's task lies in what is simple, but people seek it in what is complicated. If everyone would treat their kin as kin and their elders as elders, the world would be at peace." In a more religious or spiritual language, a kindred thought has been expressed by the Indian poet Kabir (of whom one does not know whether he was Hindu or Muslim or perhaps something else) in his famous admonition to believers: "No need to go outside (or abroad); your front yard is the holy Banares."[25]

3. After Babel

Journeying toward Cosmopolis

> Jerusalem aedificata ut civitas.
> —Psalm 122:3

In the earliest times, after the great flood, the Bible tells us (Genesis 11:1–9), "the whole earth had one language and few words." The people took hold of a stretch of land in order to settle there and gain means of subsistence. They soon developed skills as artisans and craftsmen and even ventured into the fields of construction and engineering. After they had acquired sufficient competence and self-confidence, they said to each other: "Come, let us build ourselves a city and a tower with its top in the heavens, so that we make a name for ourselves and not be scattered upon the face of the earth." As the construction of the tower was beginning to take shape, the Bible story continues, God was not pleased with the endeavor and said to himself: "Look, they are one people . . . and this is only the beginning of what they will do and nothing [in their view] will seem impossible for them." Hence, God came down and "confused the language" of the people and "scattered them from there over the face of all the earth." Therefore, the story concludes, the place was called "Babel" because there "the Lord confused the language of all the earth."

The story is memorable at all times, but especially in our age of globalization when there are initial glimmers of "cosmopolis" or an emerging global city or community. The biblical account holds several lessons worth pondering, but especially these two. First, the present global convergence happens "after Babel," that is, after the scattering of languages and peoples. This means that we cannot proceed from a presumed unity or univocity of humankind but have to take seriously the diversity or multiplicity of languages, customs, and cultural traditions. Hence, any move or journey in the direction of cosmopolis today can only occur in the mode of sustained dialogue, the mode of cross-cultural and interreligious interaction. Second, the biblical account should caution us against placing our trust exclusively or even predominantly in our engineering capacity, that is, our capacity for instrumental fabrication or construction. The journey toward cosmopolis, one might say, cannot rely solely or even predominantly on our quality as *homo faber* or designing architect. Going beyond the narrow confines of anthropocentrism, the journey has to make ample room for dialogue and listening, for the humanizing demands of education, ethics, and spiritual insight. Differently put: *homo faber* has to yield pride of place to *homo loquens, home quaerens*, and *homo symbolicus*.[1]

Building a (Global) City

Thus, in embarking on a global endeavor today, we cannot take as our model the work of the early peoples after the great flood. A better model to follow would be the teaching of the philosopher Plato—although even here we have to make several corrections or modifications. As is well known, Plato in his dialogue called "The Republic" sets out to discuss the meaning of "city" or political community (*polis*) and especially to specify what is required for a city, particularly a good or well-ordered city, to exist. For Plato, or rather for Socrates as the protagonist of the dialogue, the origin of the city resides in human need. In his words: "A city, I take it, comes into being because each of us is not self-sufficient but needs many things." Since different people need many different things, the point is to "gather many persons into one place as partners and helpers, and to this common settlement we give the name of 'city' (*polis*)." The most basic and commonly shared need is for survival or subsistence, and to satisfy this need provision must be made for foodstuffs "so that we may live and be." Closely connected with this requirement is the need for clothing, for shelter or housing, and for different utensils. So room must be made in the city for farmers, weavers, builders, shoemakers, and the like; soon other occupations will be added. In this way, Socrates says, "carpenters and smiths and many other such craftsmen become partners in our city and make it big." Traders and merchants will also be added as the city becomes more affluent or opulent. At this point, however, a query or objection is raised whether we are in the presence of a properly human city or whether we have built a "city of pigs" (or fit only for pigs), since the only concern seems to be survival or physical well-being. Responding to this query, Socrates introduces the higher concern for ethical well-being and justice. To meet these demands, the city needs to be well ordered and well governed—a task that is placed into the hands of a caste of "guardians" and ultimately a philosopher-king.[2]

Plato's imaginary *polis* or city constructed "in speech" remains memorable and instructive. Its great value resides in its insistence on a "higher" purpose or *telos:* the goal of justice and ethical well-being as the lodestar of civic life. Despite its inspiring quality, however, we need to modify Plato's city in a number of respects, especially if we shift our focus from the city to cosmopolis. First of all, as mentioned before, the contemporary striving for cosmopolis happens "after Babel," that is, after the dispersal of humanity into a multitude of languages, customs, and cultural traditions. Thus, we cannot accept or take as a model the relatively uniform or homogeneous character of the Greek city. Although Plato recognizes different individual aptitudes and functions, his model does not start from the premise of different languages and cultures. The second aspect in need of modification is the vertical caste structure of the Platonic city, a structure predicated on the sharp distinction between physical survival needs and "higher" ethical aspirations, between material and spiritual dimensions of human life. This aspect was already criticized by Aristotle, who objected to the presumed superiority of an ethical elite (saying, for instance, that the quality of a meal depends not solely on the opinion of the cooks but also, and importantly, on that of the eaters). For Aristotle—and for us following his lead—the concern for survival (*esse*) and for ethical well-being (*bene esse*) are more closely linked or interdependent. What we *do* want to retain from Plato's model is chiefly the accent on justice and shared well-being (what Aristotle called the "good life").[3]

To some extent, we also follow Plato's dialogue in trying to build the global city from the ground up: by proceeding from material survival needs to normative concerns, or from nature to culture. Like any city, cosmopolis cannot exist or flourish without adequate natural and material resources, that is, without sufficient provision for livelihood and material well-being. Here, our time introduces a consideration that was not yet prominent in Greek antiquity: the awareness that civilization or city life cannot be purchased at the price of ecological spoliation or the devastation of natural resources. When nature is eroded or wasted, the preconditions of civil life are jeopardized. Awareness of this correlation was not entirely lacking in ancient times. One of the many lessons of the Babylonian epic "Gilgamesh" is that properly human life depends on the symbiosis of nature and culture, poetically expressed in the friendship between the city ruler Gilgamesh and Enkidu, the man of the wilderness. In modern times, however, this insight has been largely forgotten or shunted aside. Progressively, science and technology have been celebrated as the cure-all for social and material ills; but today it is clear that the "cure-all" cannot cure itself or is itself a source of disease. The process of global warming and a host of natural catastrophes demonstrate the fragility of our natural habitat and the fact that nature's resources are not infinitely renewable.

Material Inequality

In addition to ecological resources, the material conditions of human life are dependent on modes of economic production and exchange. Here, another huge problem arises for cosmopolis, equal to global warming: namely, the haphazard, lopsided, and largely inequitable distribution of wealth and economic resources. Under the impact of modern liberal individualism and market economics, economic activities are undertaken less and less with a view to the common good (in Aristotle's sense) and more and more for the sake of private gain. As this development proceeds, social solidarity increasingly gives way to inequality, particularly to class division or stratification. In recent times, this process has reached its culmination in the system of corporate and financial capitalism—a culmination that revealed its grim side in the financial "meltdown" of 2008–9. As detailed in a report of the Economic Policy Institute in Washington, the income of Americans from wages or salaries declined significantly between 1959 and 2007, while the shares derived from dividends and from interest more than doubled; moreover, income from capital gains rose from 1.6 percent to 8.2 percent in the same period. In the words of Harold Meyerson, analyzing the report: "The big money, in other words, was in big investment, and it went overwhelmingly to the rich. In 1962, the wealthiest 1% of American households had 125 times the wealth of a median household. By 2009, that gap had increased to 225 times the median."[4]

Such a steep discrepancy of wealth clearly is incompatible with any idea of social well-being or the common good. It is also at odds with a measure of social stability, which requires the reining in of extreme wealth and poverty in favor of a common middle ground. In the sage words of Aristotle: as "the best way of life is one which resides in the mean [or middle]," so "the best form of political society is one where power is vested in the middle class. . . . [Hence] it is the greatest of blessings for a state that its members should possess a moderate and adequate property."[5] Obviously, what goes for a single *polis* also goes for the emerging cosmopolis. Unfortunately, under the impact of globalization and neoliberalism, the system of economic stratification evident in the United States is projected or transferred to the global arena. The trend, sad to say, has been going on for some time. According to the Human Development Report issued by the United Nations in 1999, global inequalities in income and living standards had by that time reached "grotesque proportions." For example, the combined wealth of the world's three richest families (about $135 billion) was greater than the annual income of 600 million people in the economically least-developed countries. Whereas in 1970 the gap between the richest one-fifth of the world's population and the rest of the world stood at 30-to-1, by 1990 it had widened to 60-to-1 and at the end of the century to 74-to-1. The same UN report also disclosed that, between 1995 and 1999, the world's richest people doubled their wealth to over $1 trillion, while the number of people living on less than $1 per day remained steady at 1.3 billion. A similar picture was painted by the World Bank in its World Development Report of 2000–2001: at the dawn of the new millennium the average income in the richest twenty countries was thirty-seven times the average in the poorest twenty countries—a gap that had doubled in the last forty years.[6]

Things have not changed much during the last decade. In its

Human Development Report of 2010, titled "The Real Wealth of Nations," the world body noted problems and growing disparities, especially in the area of social and economic equality. Despite some advances in terms of people's health and education in some regions, the report stated, the past years "have also seen increasing inequality—both within and across countries—as well as production and consumption patterns that have increasingly been revealed as unsustainable." The disparities are especially evident in the field of global income distribution. "Despite aggregate progress," we read, "there is no convergence in income because, on average, rich countries have grown faster than poor ones over the past 40 years. The divide between developed and developing countries persists: a small subset of countries has remained at the top of the world income distribution, and only a handful of countries that started out poor [like India and China] have joined that high-income group. . . . Hence, the gaps in human development across the world, while narrowing, remain huge." Despite some improvements on the level of average measurements, the report adds, income inequality during the past few decades "has risen in many more countries than it has fallen." Thus, in most countries of the former Soviet Union, as well as many countries in East Asia and the Pacific Rim, income inequality today is higher than it was a few decades ago. The report also points to the connection between economic disparities and the financial crisis or meltdown in 2008, a crisis "which caused 34 million people to lose their jobs and 64 million more people to fall below the $1.25 a day income poverty threshold."[7]

Anyone seriously yearning for cosmopolis cannot possibly be complacent about this maldistribution of economic means. Close attention to inequality is dictated, first of all, by the looming danger of civil strife, possibly a global civil war. In the crisp language of Aristotle's *Politics:* "The masses become revolutionary when the distribution of property is unequal." But the deeper reason is that stark maldistribution thwarts the striving for human and social well-being in a community. In the felicitous words of the UN report: "The central contention of the human development approach is that well-being [Aristotle's *eudaimonia*] is about much more than money: it is about the possibilities that people have to fulfill the life plan they have reason to choose and pursue. Thus, our call for a new economics . . . in which the objective is to further human well-being."[8] To remedy the plight of maldistribution and to advance the prospect of equity on a global level, some thoughtful people have proposed a number of remedies. Thus, already in the 1970s, the Nobel laureate economist James Tobin proposed a tax on all currency transactions, which then would go into a global distribution fund. Subsequently, the "Tobin tax" idea was reformulated in several ways, especially to include all global financial transactions, but always with a similar purpose. Giving to the idea a religious or theological underpinning, Rabbi Jonathan Sacks in 2002 invoked the biblical notion of *tzedakah*, meaning a just distribution of resources in light of a substantive conception of the common good. As he stated pointedly, *tzedakah* aims to remedy a social condition where "a few prosper but the many starve," where "not all have access to good education, health care, and other essential amenities."[9]

Cultivating the Common Good

Removing gross material disparities is an important requisite in the building of cosmopolis. But by itself it is insufficient and ineffective unless it is coupled with the cultivation of a social ethos, a sense of duty, social responsibility, and shared well-being. Here again, Jonathan Sacks is right on target when he writes: "It is difficult to talk about the common good when we lose the ability to speak about duty, obligation and restraint, and find ourselves only with desires clamoring for satisfaction." The blame, in his view, must be attributed to "the dominance of the market" focused exclusively on private gain and, more broadly, to the modern (Western) infatuation with individual self-centeredness, which has "eroded our moral vocabulary" and "social landscape." Sacks, in this context, refers appropriately to philosopher Alasdair MacIntyre's famous book *After Virtue* and its complaint about the growing incomprehensibility of the older vocabulary. As a result of this semantic slide, "virtues once thought admirable, like modesty, humility, discretion, restraint," have become "dusty exhibits in a museum of cultural curiosities." In eloquent language, Sacks seeks to recover the socializing and humanizing quality of virtues, their ability to sustain networks of relationships as an antidote to divisiveness: "The rewards of the moral [or ethical] order are great. It creates an island of interpersonal meaning in a sea of impersonal forces." Differently put: ethics is "an attempt to *fight despair in the name of hope,* and recover human dignity"; it is "civilization's greatest attempt to humanize fate."[10]

What is needed to recover social ethics from oblivion is the good example of elders and public leaders and the transmission of ethical and religious teachings through education. Here we touch on a crucial fiber in any possible future cosmopolis—but a fiber that is still under-valued and underdeveloped. Sacks refers to an important resolution of the United Nations General Assembly (2002): that, through the intermediary of the World Bank, funds should be provided to ensure universal education throughout the world by 2015. But he also points to the steep hurdle: namely, that education is still "far too unevenly distributed" and that "of the world's children, 113 million do not go to school." Still, the immensity of the task does not dampen his spirit and his conviction that education holds out the best chance of "moving us forward in the long, hard journey to universal human dignity." In this spirited conviction, Sacks is ably seconded by American philosopher Martha Nussbaum, especially in her books *Cultivating Humanity* (1997) and *Not for Profit* (2010). As she writes in the later study, edu-cation plays a crucial role in transmitting and sustaining ethical modes of conduct and invigorating the practice of civic virtues. In perform-ing this role, education relies on schools but also on many other fac-tors: "Much of the work of overcoming narcissism [or selfishness] and developing concern [for others] has to be done in families; and relationships in the peer culture also play a powerful role. Schools, however, can either reinforce or undermine the achievements of the family; they can also shape the peer culture" for good or ill. For Nuss-baum, education is "a huge agenda" that must be implemented with constant awareness of local situations and possibilities. Above all, "it must be addressed not only through educational content but through exemplary pedagogy" (what she calls "Socratic pedagogy").[11]

When properly pursued, the task of ethical education is supported and underscored by religious teachings and good religious practices (although that synergy can be subverted by either secular or religious extremism). It is in this domain that Rabbi Sacks's text issues its most stirring plea: not to impose a uniform doctrine on people everywhere, but to recognize or discern in the variety of religious faiths glimmers of a dimension that is "not for profit" and that we call "divine." As he writes, our global era summons the world's faiths to a supreme challenge: "Can we find, in the human other, a trace of the Divine Other? Can we recognize God's image in one who is not in my image?" More concretely put: "Can I, a Jew, hear the echoes of God's voice in that of a Hindu or Sikh or Christian or Muslim or in the words of an Eskimo from Greenland speaking about a melting glacier?" (Quite appropriately, the cover of Sacks's book carries a picture by Pieter Brueghel the Elder titled *The Tower of Babel*.) For Sacks, religions at their best are not accomplices of worldly powers, but rather expressions of "deep dismay" at some of the features of our world: "its inequities, its consumerism and exploitation, its failure to address widespread poverty and disease." Different religions express this dismay in different languages and with attention to different local or regional conditions. At this point, Sacks introduces one of his most startling thoughts: namely, that the proposition at the heart of monotheism is "not what it has traditionally been taken to be: *one* God, therefore one faith, one truth, one way." Rather, the contrary needs to be affirmed (in our time "after Babel"): that *"unity creates diversity,"* that "the glory of the created world is its astonishing multiplicity." This, he adds, is "what I mean by *the dignity of difference.*"[12]

Global Citizenship

Recognition of difference, to be sure, does not entirely cancel mutual bonds or a sense of interconnection. This is particularly true when (following Plato's dialogue) we move from the level of material needs and social arrangements to the normative level, and first of all that of citizenship. As in any city, members of cosmopolis must be able to claim the status of citizen irrespective of their economic, ethnic, or religious background; differently put: they must enjoy a qualitative (or normative) equality, especially in and before the law. Aristotle is emphatic on this point: citizenship is not a matter of kinship, lineage, or any personal association, because it is established in public law. In his words: "A citizen is best defined by one criterion: an individual who shares in the public administration of justice and in [the possibility of] holding public office."[13] This does not mean that relevant distinctions are entirely discarded. There are in all republics certain age qualifications for the exercise of political rights and the holding of public office; usually, a distinction is also made between natural-born and naturalized citizens. Above and beyond these factors, recognition of the "multicultural" character of most present-day countries or states may entail acceptance of certain differences inside the citizenship category itself. This point has been particularly advanced by political theorist Iris Marion Young in her critique of "the ideal of universal citizenship." Although morally appealing, this ideal—in Young's view—has often forced marginalized or minority groups to assimilate to a dominant cultural and civic model neglectful of their situated needs. To correct this bent to conformism, she argues, "we need a group differentiated citizenship and a heterogeneous public where relevant differences are publicly recognized as irreducible"—though without abandoning concern for the "common good" and the need "to decide together the society's policies."[14]

Pursuing this line of thought further, we need to remember our condition "after Babel," that is, the dispersal of humankind into different cultures and languages. In this situation, cosmopolis cannot possibly be a uniform legal and political structure hegemonically controlling the world; it can only mean a shared aspiration nurtured and negotiated among local or national differences. In the prudent words of Charles Taylor: "We have no choice but to be cosmopolitans *and* patriots, which means to fight for the kind of patriotism that is open to universal solidarities against other, more closed [or chauvinistic] kinds."[15] What this comment brings into view is the need for a layered or "multiple" citizenship where people might be citizens in both a particular city (or cities) *and* cosmopolis. This idea is favored especially by proponents of "cosmopolitan democracy," that is, a cosmopolis making room for national or local forms of democratic self-government. In the words of one of the defenders of this view, the idea of a multiple (including cosmopolitan) citizenship is designed to impose ethical restraints both on national chauvinism and on the ambitions of hegemonic global elites; what is needed for its functioning is not properly a global state, but "a global community providing protection against the overwhelming power of the nation-state to its citizens and the power of multinational corporations over people's lives." In particularly eloquent language, the constraining as well as enabling role of layered citizenship is emphasized by Richard Falk, who describes cosmopolitans as "citizen pilgrims," that is, as citizens journeying toward a just and peaceful cosmopolis. As he states: "I have used the metaphor of 'citizen pilgrim' to describe the spirit of a sojourner, committed to transformation that is spiritual as well as material, that is promised on the wholeness and equality of the human family."[16]

Institutional Arrangements

Although largely ethical and aspirational, cosmopolitanism cannot entirely ignore the need for institutional arrangements. In this area, supporters of cosmopolitan democracy have advanced numerous proposals aimed at reforming and strengthening existing global institutions. Thus, Richard Falk has made a strong plea for a restructuring of the United Nations, including a reform of the Security Council (to provide for a more equitable representation of the world's major regions), the establishment of a new People's Assembly, and the granting of broader jurisdiction to the World Court. In addition, he has also argued in favor of the extension of "geo-governance" into the domains of environmental protection and global market regulation.[17] Proposals of a similar kind have been sponsored by many international political theorists, like David Held, Daniele Archibugi, and others. David Held, in particular, has introduced a long list of "cosmopolitan objectives" for both the short and the long term, a list whose implementation is designed to lend to cosmopolitanism a measure of institutional concreteness and stability. What one might wish to add to his list is the provision for a global "Truth and Justice" or "Truth and Reconciliation" commission, where peoples and societies would be able to air grievances regarding inflicted wrongs and injustices in the hope of accomplishing a more equitable settlement. What none of the cited sponsors advocate, however, is the erection of a global state or superstate—a modern "Tower of Babel"—endowed with the power of centralized management and control. In Held's words: global democracy "is the only grand or 'meta-narrative' which can legitimately frame and delimit the competing 'narratives' of the good. It is particularly important because it suggests a way of relating 'values' to one another and of leaving the resolution of conflicts open to participants in a political dialogue."[18]

Held's comments are clearly pertinent to our situation "after Babel," throwing into relief the question animating or rather troubling the present pages: Can we or should we reconstruct the ancient tower,

now in the form of a global super-state? Not surprisingly, the sidelining of this option (by defenders of global democracy) is unsatisfactory
and a provocation for international "realists" wedded to the primacy
of "sovereign" power and the imperative of a central command structure. Although frequently advanced as a firm dogma, however, this
primacy has been called into question by a long line of political or
ethical-political thinkers, from Plato and Aristotle to Hegel and beyond. With specific regard to cosmopolitanism, the danger of an imperial despotism (implicit in a global state) has been clearly outlined
by Immanuel Kant in his famous treatise "Perpetual Peace" (which
opted for a lose federation or lateral *Bund*).[19] As is evident already in
its title, Kant's treatise expresses an ethical vision or (what Sacks calls)
a "covenant of hope": a hope predicated on the progressive maturation and transformation of humanity.[20]

At this point, we come back to the notion of *homo symbolicus*
(mentioned at the beginning) and also to Falk's metaphor of "citizen
pilgrims" journeying toward a state of "wholeness" or cosmos in the
world. Seen from this angle, cosmopolis itself is ultimately a metaphor or parable: a parable for a condition of humanity that exists not
only *propter peccatum* (for the correction of evil through force) but
as a projection and anticipation of the good life. Another traditional
metaphor for this condition or cosmos is "Jerusalem" (or else Mecca,
Banares, or "Pure Land"). As the Psalmist says (Psalm 122): "Jerusalem is built like a city, bound firmly together." And he adds: "Pray for
the peace of that city; may they prosper who love you. Peace be within
your walls, and abundance within your towers!" This agrees with an
inspiring line placed over the entrance to the Basilica in Montserrat,
Spain: *Urbs Jerusalem beata dicta pacis visio* (Jerusalem is called the
beautiful vision of peace).

4. Humanizing Humanity

Education for World Citizenship

> It has become appallingly obvious that our technology has
> exceeded our humanity.
>
> —Albert Einstein

This is indeed a momentous gathering: the first "World Humanities
Forum," the first international meeting designed to underscore the
importance of the humanities in our world.[1] And significantly, the
gathering is called and organized by UNESCO, that institutional
branch of the world community whose assigned task is the promotion
of global learning and education. As we read in the charter establishing that world body (in 1946): "The wide diffusion of culture, and the
education of humanity for justice and liberty and peace are indispensable to the dignity of man."[2] To be sure, education whose promotion
is entrusted to UNESCO is not limited to the humanities or to what
we also call the "liberal arts"; however, one can argue—and I shall in
fact argue—that the humanities occupy a crucial and indeed pivotal
place in the educational household of humankind. This has, in part, to
do with the fact that, in many contexts, the humanities are an endan-
gered species. In many colleges and universities today, programs in
the humanities or liberal arts are curtailed if not eliminated in favor of
a focus on technology and narrowly professional training.[3] Such a shift
of focus—I want to argue—comes at a steep price. As we know, our
world today is nearly overrun by atrocities: torture, terrorism, genocide. We have new categories in international law to combat these
atrocities: we speak not only of war crimes but of "crimes against humanity" (where the latter term is equivalent both to "humankind" and

"humaneness"). But how can such crimes be combated or reduced if there is no deliberate cultivation of humanity and humaneness—which is precisely the aim of the humanities?

Looked at from this angle, the frequent charge leveled against the humanities is revealed as utterly baseless: the charge that such education is useless or devoid of tangible benefit. Surely, the reduction of slaughter and mayhem would be of immense benefit to humanity at any time. What is correct about the charge—although not intended as such—is the fact that the humanities do not yield an extrinsic benefit and are not cultivated for the sake of such benefit; to this extent, their cultivation—as Martha Nussbaum has correctly noted—is without profit or "not for profit."[4] Philosophically stated, the yield of the humanities is an "intrinsic" good, in the sense that their cultivation—just like the reading of poetry and flute playing—carries its benefit in itself: namely, in the ongoing transformation and "humanization" of the practitioner. This does not mean, of course, that this benefit may not also have broader social and political ramifications; in fact, in my view, these ramifications—like the reduction of mayhem—are part and parcel of the intrinsic good: the humanizing practice of the humanities. In the following, I want to do mainly three things. First, I shall explore the meaning of the "humanities" by turning to the history of the liberal arts and the so-called classification of disciplines in recent centuries. Next, I want to highlight some of the prominent and distinctive features of the humanities and their educational significance. Finally, I want to discuss the crucial contribution the humanities can and should make to the emergence of a properly humane cosmopolis.

Humanities and the Liberal Arts

The humanities are often also labeled "human studies" because of their primary concern with human life, human conduct and experience. To this extent, Socrates may be called the father of the humanities because of his shift of attention from astronomy and metaphysics to human affairs (*ta anthropina*), including ethics, politics, and social psychology. In a way, Plato continued this shift with his emphasis on the transformational quality of genuine education, leading from random opinion to reflective insight. From Aristotle we have inherited the important division of human knowledge or inquiry into three main branches: "theoretical" science, "practical" inquiry, and "productive" (or constructive-technical) endeavor. While, in the first type, the scientist observes and analyzes phenomena from a detached or neutral standpoint, practical inquiry requires the concrete engagement of the practitioner in human affairs (particularly on the level of ethics and politics); constructive endeavor, finally, involves the fostering of technical "know-how" useful for instrumental purposes. As can readily be seen, among the three Aristotelian types, the practical branch is most closely connected with what today we call the "humanities"—a fact that explains the close affiliation of many "humanists" with the Aristotelian legacy.[5] In a way, what has happened in modern Western thought is a near reversal of the Aristotelian preference scheme, in the sense that theoretical or pure science in combination with instrumental technology has tended to sideline or smother the practical-humanist concerns.

Another term closely connected with the humanities is that of the "liberal arts." The term goes back to the school curriculum established by the Stoics during the Roman Empire—a curriculum that was continued and fleshed out during the European Middle Ages. It was customary at the time to speak of seven liberal arts, with the educational process moving through two stages: from the more elementary *trivium* to the more advanced *quadrivium*—a sequence reflecting distantly the Platonic idea of the transformational quality of human learning.[6] I am not concerned here with the details of the classical curriculum; rather, I want to turn to the employed terminology. Why were the disciplines offered in the classical curriculum called "liberal arts" (*artes liberales*)? One explanation frequently advanced is that these were disciplines fit for the education of "free" citizens rather than slaves (of whom the Roman Empire had plenty). There is probably some grain of truth to this explanation—but it does not account for the persistence of the term in societies devoid of slavery or after slavery had long been abolished. Removed from narrow ideological blinders, the term in fact carries another possible and deeper meaning: the idea that the liberal arts contribute to the liberty or freedom of practitioners, to their liberation from external tutelage and the subservience to materialistic or instrumental benefits. Taken in this sense, the liberal arts clearly resonate with the nonutilitarian and "not-for-profit" character of the humanities; differently put, liberty here is again an intrinsic good of the practice and not an extrinsic project or subsidiary product.[7]

As indicated before, modern Western thought entailed a near reversal of the Greek and Roman concern with practical human affairs (*ta anthropina*). This is curious or surprising in view of the simultaneous ascent of "anthropocentrism" in modern intellectual life. What one needs to take into account, however, is the fact that this ascent was predominantly channeled in the direction of the scientific analysis and control of "external" nature and the technical utilization of this control. One of the leading figures inaugurating the modern shift was the philosopher-scientist Francis Bacon, for whom all study or learning was oriented toward one goal or tangible "profit": the "enhancement of man's estate" and comfortable living. In his *Advancement of Learning* and *Novum Organum*, Bacon dramatically redesigned the traditional (Aristotelian) tripartition of inquiry: namely, by juxtaposing the fields of history, poetry, and scientific philosophy. While history amounted to no more than the gathering of data, and poetry to a mere flight of fancy, scientific inquiry was extolled as the only true path to knowledge proceeding through the investigation of the natural "laws" of cause and effect.[8] Under the impact of Bacon and his followers, the traditional domain of *praxis* or practical thought was either shunted aside or—still more fatefully—transformed into a branch of "theoretical" or scientific knowledge. Thus, ethics was tendentially transformed into the study of psychic affects and aversions and thus into a corollary of empirical psychology. A similarly far-ranging change happened in the domain of "economics," which, for Aristotelians, involved the contributions of the "household" (*oikos*) to the good life. Shifting again radically from *praxis* to theory, modern economics developed into the rational-mathematical calculation of profit in a market largely devoid of any considerations of social well-being or justice.

As one should note in fairness, however, the triumph of the Baconian system in modernity was contested all along by a counter-current or a host of voices remonstrating against the domination of theory over *praxis*. A particularly significant counter-trend was the current of "humanism" extending from the Renaissance through the Enlightenment to the Romantic era. Among Renaissance and post-Renaissance figures special mention should be made of the Italian thinkers Mario Nizolio, Tommaso Campanella, and Giambattista Vico. In sharp contrast to Bacon, Nizolio and Campanella assigned primary significance to the fields of literature and history, treating these fields as rich storehouses of narratives and experiences, in comparison with which the maxims of rational-scientific philosophy are only pale and lifeless abstractions. On the eve of the Enlightenment, Vico boldly proclaimed the preeminence of historical and "human" studies over other sciences, tracing this preferred status to their roots in "practical" knowledge: the fact that history and social life are human activities and thus more readily intelligible (*verum et factum convertuntur*).[9] A bit later, and mainly in response to the pretense of an abstract rationalism, the German philosopher Johann Gottfried Herder issued a plea for the study of different cultures and languages—that is, for a broad study of the "humanities"—arguing that only concrete instances and practical examples could foster the desired "progress" of humankind: the genuine "humanization" of humanity. It was in this connection that Herder formulated the important notion of an upward formation or transformation of humanity (*Emporbildung zur Humanität*)—a notion that can serve as a basic motto for the humanities.[10]

During the subsequent two centuries, "positivism" (the focus on positively useful knowledge) brought increasing pressure on all the disciplines in the "republic of knowledge," seeking to assimilate them to the model of scientific cause-effect analysis. This pressure was felt not only in ethics and economics but also in historiography, linguistics, and even the study of politics, where public conduct was increasingly leveled into quantitative measurement. No doubt, efforts were repeatedly launched to rescue aspects of the social and human sciences from the positivist tentacles. The nineteenth century, in fact, was replete with complex classification schemes seeking to differentiate certain forms of study from the domain of strict scientific inquiry. This is not the place to recount this ongoing "battle of the faculties"; a few comments must suffice. One prominent and widely influential scheme was the distinction between natural sciences and "mental" sciences (*Naturwissenschaften* vs. *Geisteswissenschaften*). For advocates of this scheme, the latter disciplines were anchored in insights generated by the human mind or "spirit"; they all dealt with phenomena available directly to human experience and mental life. Although appealing at a first glance, this distinction was challenged and undermined by the growing inroads of empirical psychology into

mental processes. Another classification scheme relied on the separation between natural science and history, where the former was said
to focus on general laws and the second on particular events (thus
yielding a distinction between "nomothetic" and "idiographic" disciplines). Yet, as long as particular events were not actively interpreted
and understood, historiography could not rise above empirical data
gathering (along Baconian lines).[11] What emerged from these impass-
es, in the long run, was the realization that the "humanities" could
not be rescued or restored without a return to human *praxis* and the
differentiation between two kinds of practical endeavor: the endeavor
either to know and control nature or else to articulate "meaning" in
practical conduct.[12]

The Humanities as Practical Endeavor

In late modern and recent times, the shift toward *praxis*—often inspired by Aristotle's legacy—was promoted by a number of philosophical orientations, including pragmatism, ordinary language philosophy,
and hermeneutics. For the sake of brevity, I shall concentrate here
on the latter and its leading representative, Hans-Georg Gadamer.
As is well known, Gadamer's hermeneutics revolves around interpretation and "understanding," an understanding accomplished through
the dialogical interchange between reader and text, between speaker
and interlocutor. However, what is not always sufficiently recognized
is that "understanding" here is not simply a cognitive exercise, the
acquisition of knowledge by a detached "knower," but always involves
a practical engagement, a close embroilment of thought and *praxis*.
As Gadamer repeatedly emphasizes, entering into dialogical exchange
involves an intellectual as well as an existential risk-taking: one runs
the risk of falling short, of being shown to be wrong, of undergoing
an experience that may transform one's life (not only change one's
"mind"). In his *Truth and Method,* he frequently invokes Aeschylos's
formula *pathei mathos,* which means having learned through suffering or the "hard way," being in the grip of a learning experience that
changes our existence—we might say: an experience that "human-
izes" us.[13] From this angle, learning is "practical" not simply in a utilitarian or instrumental sense; nor does it involve the simple application
of abstract maxims or principles to empirical situations. Rather, it

means taking experience seriously as a presupposition and guidepost to knowledge and ethical conduct. In this broad sense, Gadamer can rightly be considered as an eminent mentor of the humanities.

The title of "mentor" is not an arbitrary designation but follows directly from his work. An important part of *Truth and Method* deals with the "significance of the humanist tradition for the human sciences" (or humanities). To illustrate this significance Gadamer discusses a number of prominent features (or "guiding ideas") of the humanist tradition relevant for the study of the humanities. A central theme is that of *Bildung*, a term that does not simply designate a given empirical culture or way of life, but rather denotes a process of cultivation, a process of "formation" or transformation. As Gadamer notes, the German word *Bildung* derives from *Bild* (image) and thus carries within it the older notion of an *imago Dei* or divine image "in the likeness of which human beings are fashioned and which they must strive to achieve." Thus, what resonates in the word is not just a simple pedagogical recipe, but a complex happening that one might call "humanization as divinization" (or the reverse). The most important aspect stressed by Gadamer is the fact that formation or transformation in this sense does not pursue an extrinsic profit, but carries its value within itself. "It is not an accident," he writes, "that *Bildung* in this respect resembles the Great term *physis*. Like nature (*physis*), *Bildung* has no goals outside itself." Taken in this sense, *Bildung* transcends the mere training of existing talents or aptitudes for occupational or career purposes. Rather, in *Bildung* "that by which and through which one is formed becomes and remains completely one's own."[14]

In the Western humanist tradition, *Bildung* was not a static concept or idea, but involved instead a process of cultivation, of steady reformulation and reinterpretation. Starting from the writings of Renaissance and pietistic thinkers, the term acquired decisive accents or impulses during the Enlightenment and the ensuing period of German classical thought. Herder's contribution was previously mentioned; his immediate interlocutors were the poet Klopstock and Immanuel Kant. For Gadamer, however, a decisive reformulation derives from the work of Hegel. In his *Philosophical Propaideutics* and his *Phenomenology of Spirit*, Hegel clearly insisted on the point that *Bildung* is not limited to the fine-tuning of existing capacities, but involves a movement of self-transgression in response to challenges.

Particularly important in this context is Hegel's notion of "alienation," his insistence that learning has to proceed through otherness, that self-finding can only happen through the encounter with others and the world. In Gadamer's words: "The basic and correct idea is this: To recognize one's own in the alien, to become at home in it—this is the basic movement of spirit (*Geist*) whose essence consists only in returning to itself from and through otherness." One can readily see how fruitful this idea was for the subsequent development of the human sciences, especially the disciplines of history, anthropology, and literature—provided these disciplines remained faithful to the humanist tradition. For, Gadamer states, "what properly constitutes the human studies can be grasped more readily from the tradition of *Bildung* than from the modern canon of natural-scientific method."[15]

Another important feature of the humanist tradition and the humanities is the accent on prudential "judgment" (*Urteil*), in contradistinction from apodictic knowledge and the epistemic claims of strict science. In this respect, the Aristotelian legacy of *phronesis* is decisive, involving the search for the right middle path (*mesotes*) and the cultivation of the ethical ability to weigh carefully the pros and cons of a given situation. Just like the stress on formative *Bildung,* the notion of prudential judgment stands in opposition to, or at lest modifies, the Enlightenment emphasis on universal maxims by requiring attention to particular aspects—an attention that is also characteristic of the English "common-law" tradition, with its reliance on concrete precedents. In Gadamer's words: "Sensible reasoning here is exhibited primarily in the faculty to judge about what is right or wrong, proper or improper, fitting or unfitting. Having sound judgment in this respect does not mean the ability to subsume particular instances under universal rules, but rather the capacity to know what is really important: that is, to judge cases from a right or sound perspective." The latter perspective draws its inspiration from Aristotelian teachings, not from Kantian rationalism—not even from Kant's *Critique of Judgment,* where judging and the weighing of pros and cons remain subordinated to the rule of "categorical imperatives." From the vantage of humanism and the humanities, this kind of subordination is uncongenial and unacceptable because it involves the surrender of *praxis* and practical engagement in favor of abstract knowledge.[16]

Closely connected with the role of judgment, and in many ways the pivot of humanism, is the conception of "common sense" (*sensus communis*). As extolled in the humanist tradition, judgment is not the expression of a purely private or idiosyncratic opinion, but a faculty nurtured in a community or social context, in interaction with other members of that context. To this extent, it is a shared or "public" sense—without ceasing to be amenable to ongoing revision and transformation. An early modern champion of the conception was Giambattista Vico, whose defense of rhetoric and public discourse mounted a challenge to Descartes's celebration of the isolated *cogito* separated from world and society. In Gadamer's account: "A prominent teacher of rhetoric, Vico stands in the humanist tradition dating back to antiquity. Quite clearly, this tradition is important for the self-understanding of the humanities or human sciences." What Vico attempted to do was to give a new direction and a new meaning to modern education and ultimately to the Enlightenment, a direction that would grant primacy not to abstractly universal cognition, but to practical, ethically nurtured experience in a social context. To quote Gadamer again: "For Vico, the wisdom of the ancients, their cultivation of prudence and eloquence, remains indispensable precisely in the face of modern science and its quantitative methodology. For, even now, the most important aspect of education is something else: namely, the cultivation of the *'sensus communis'* which is nurtured not by apodictic truth but by weighing the likely or probable." Seen from this angle, the *sensus communis* is not merely an individual aptitude, but "a sense that founds community or communality (*Gemeinsamkeit*)."[17]

As can readily be seen, common sense here is not simply a set of empirical beliefs, but the emblem of an ethical quest for public virtue (in both the Aristotelian and Stoic sense). The ethical quality of the conception was clearly grasped by Lord Shaftesbury and the entire school of Scottish moralists, from Francis Hutcheson to Thomas Reid and Adam Ferguson. Here one has to take note of the difference between ethical common sense and modern "natural law," the latter entirely committed to abstract rational principles. "What Shaftesbury had in mind," Gadamer comments, "is not so much a universal human capacity captured by modern natural law, but rather a social virtue, a virtue of the heart more than of the head." In Shaftesbury's work, the notion of common sense was closely associated with the social virtue of empathy or "sympathy," functioning as the foundation of his entire metaphysics and as the crucial antipode to the modern glorification of self-interest. In the hands of his followers—especially Hutcheson and Reid—the combination of common sense and sympathy was further developed and fleshed out into the theory of "moral sense," which served as a vital (though ultimately sidelined) counter-current to the liberal individualism of Hobbes and John Locke. To quote Gadamer again: "It was in the philosophy of the Scottish moralists that 'common sense' acquired its truly central systematic significance—a significance which stood polemically against both rationalist metaphysics and its skeptical deconstruction, and which built its own new system on the basis of the original and 'natural' judgments of common sense." At the same time, Scottish moralists never allowed common sense to disintegrate into private preferences. In the words of Thomas Reid, its judgment "serves to direct us in the common affairs of life, where our reasoning faculty would leave us in the dark." Hence, Gadamer adds, the good-sense tradition "not only offers a cure for the 'moon-sickness' of metaphysics, but provides the basis for a moral philosophy that really does justice to social life."[18]

The Humanities and Global Democracy

From historical reminiscences we need to return now to our contemporary situation. As should be clear, the historical excursus was designed primarily to alert us to some key features—like *Bildung*, prudential judgment, and shared sensibility—without which the humanities cannot flourish at any time. In their works, people like Vico, Herder, and the Scottish moralists sought to establish a safe haven or a beachhead for human studies against the onslaught of antihumanist tendencies in modernity. In the meantime, this onslaught has turned into something like a tsunami. Wherever one looks, in the West as well as the non-West, the humanities today find themselves on the defensive in the face of so-called modernizing forces privileging scientific and technological advances; sometimes the defense resembles a "last stand" or nearly abandoned outpost. In lieu of humanizing *Bildung*, we have the increasing stress on career objectives; instead of the cultivation of judgment, we find utilitarian or ideological maxims; in place of common sense, we have the relentless glorification of privatization and private profit. Even some of the traditional custodians of the humanities—like American liberal arts colleges—are increasingly being transformed into corporate businesses. In her book *Not for Profit* (2010), Martha Nussbaum rightly deplores these developments. As she observes, radical educational changes are occurring today: "The humanities and the arts are being cut away, in both primary/secondary and college/university education, in virtually every nation of the world. Seen by policy-makers as useless frills, at a time when nations must cut away all useless things in order to stay competitive in the global market, they are rapidly losing their place in curricula, and also in the minds and hearts of parents and children."[19]

Nussbaum's book provides many concrete examples to back up her claim of a "silent crisis," that is, a crisis that is insidious and pervasive but not fully recognized. In her presentation, what is threatened by this crisis are not only curricula and educational institutions but rather—and this is her most provocative insight—the future of democracy in our world. Here the crucial significance of the humanities for the cultivation of practical judgment and shared sensibility comes to the fore. In her words (which deserve to be quoted in full): "Thirsty for national profit, nations and their systems of education are heedlessly discarding skills that are needed to keep democracies alive. If this trend continues, societies all over the world will soon be producing generations of useful machines, rather than complete citizens who can think for themselves, criticize tradition, and understand the significance of another person's sufferings and achievements. The future of the world's democracies hangs in the balance." Based on this insight, Nussbaum's book delineates two basic models of education, what she calls "education for profit" and "education for democracy," where the former is basically geared toward economic development or growth and the second toward the fostering of humanistic "capabilities" (what I prefer to call the formation or *Bildung* of character, good judgment, and sensibility). As she writes: "Producing economic growth does not mean producing democracy. Nor does it mean producing a healthy, engaged, educated population in which opportunities for a good life are available to all social classes." On the other hand, cultivation of the humanities and liberal arts—properly pruned of older elitist tendencies—can and should form the core of a contemporary "education for democracy."[20]

Significantly, democracy for Nussbaum is not a Western or American prerogative but a global aspiration; accordingly, education for democracy today has to have a global or cosmopolitan cast. One of the most stirring chapters in her book deals with the requisites of a genuinely cosmopolitan *Bildung* or the formation of "citizens of the world." Taking a leaf from Rabindranath Tagore she states that, by contrast to the earlier segregation of continents and cultures, we live today in a world where "people face one another across gulfs of geography, language, and nationality"; hence our problems are "global in scope." To find our way in this context we need more than "the thin norms of market exchange," which are oriented toward private gain; rather, a new pedagogy is needed: "The world's schools, colleges, and universities . . . have an important and urgent task: to cultivate in students the ability to see themselves as members of a heterogeneous nation (for all modern nations are heterogeneous), and a still more heterogeneous world, and to understand something of the history and character of the diverse groups that inhabit it." Among the pioneers of cosmopolitan pedagogy or *Bildung*, Nussbaum mentions above all the Indian Tagore—the founder of Visva-Bharati, with its focus on liberal arts education—and the American philosopher John Dewey, with his commitment to the fostering of global civility and citizenship. Contrary to some narrowly instrumentalist readings, she rightly stresses Dewey's broadly humanist outlook, an outlook that was "capacious and nonreductive" and insisted on "human relationships rich in meaning, emotion, and curiosity." What these and other educational pioneers encouraged was a radical engagement with the pluralism of our world, a "citizen-of-the-world education" as part and parcel of the liberal arts curriculum in schools and colleges.[21]

Nussbaum's *Not for Profit* ends on a sober or sobering note—not a despairing note, but one acknowledging the challenge ahead. The "silent crisis" is not going to go away by itself but requires a courageous response. "If the real clash of civilizations," she writes, "is a clash within the human soul—as greed and narcissism contend against respect and love—then all modern societies are rapidly losing the battle, as they feed the forces that lead to violence and dehumanization and fail to feed the forces that lead to cultures of equality and respect."[22] So there is a struggle going on between humanization and dehumanization. As major resources in the struggle for humanization, the Mahatma Gandhi singled out the commitments to *ahmisa* (nonviolence) and *satyagraha* (the quest for truth and goodness). In terms of its constitution, UNESCO is predicated precisely on this kind of struggle. It seems appropriate in this context to recall the opening sentence of its preamble: "Since wars begin in the minds of men, it is in the minds of men that the defenses of peace must be constructed." To which the preamble adds these statements (partially quoted before): "that the wide diffusion of culture and the education of humanity for justice and liberty and peace . . . constitute a sacred duty which all the nations must fulfill in a spirit of mutual assistance and concern"; and "that the peace must therefore be founded, if it is not to fail, upon the intellectual and moral solidarity of humankind."[23] Let us hope that the present "World Humanities Forum" will foster recognition of this "sacred duty" that all nations must shoulder and thus contribute to the desired cosmopolitan solidarity in our world.

5. Ethics and International Politics

A Response

> Peace cannot be kept by force; it can only be achieved by
> understanding.
>
> —Albert Einstein

It is a privilege and a pleasure to respond to my colleagues and friends.[1]
It is a privilege because my colleagues are distinguished practitioners
in their respective disciplines. It is a pleasure because reading their
papers has broadened my horizons and responding to them enhances
my critical self-understanding. My colleagues pose to me different
questions and approach my work from different angles. However, if
I am not mistaken, I perceive in their papers a common theme or
thematic fabric that links them together: the theme of "ethics and
international politics" (broadly construed). What leads me to this assumption or perception is my understanding of both "ethics" and "international politics" (which I trust is not entirely idiosyncratic). By
ethics I mean a certain endeavor of self-opening or self-transcendence:
a transgression of selfish egotism that happens best in dialogue—
dialogue with oneself, with others (and, if you will, with the "Other").
By international politics or relations I mean a transgression of the
bounds of national self-identity, that is, a transnational or cross-cultural
engagement with other societies, political agendas, and traditions.
Thus, in a rudimentary and purely intuitive sense, one might say that
ethics and the international domain are not alien to each other but
rather linked by a bridge that is already there.

Looked at from this angle, the various paths pursued in my writings are not randomly disjointed but exhibit a certain elective affinity—I mean the paths of dialogue, hermeneutical understanding, comparative political theory, and cosmopolitanism. Of course, the more precise contours have to be fleshed out. Richard Shapcott's essay clearly sees and articulates the connectedness of my endeavors. His main focus is on my engagement with Gadamer's philosophical hermeneutics and on the resulting trajectories of comparative theorizing, bridge-building, and cosmopolitanism. As he notes, my central aim has been "to practice philosophical hermeneutics," which means to put the latter to work in various contexts. In terms of intellectual bridge-building, this aim has spawned first of all the effort to explore "complementarities" among critical theory (Frankfurt), phenomenology and hermeneutics (Freiburg/Heidelberg), and Parisian post-structuralism; somewhat later, the effort was extended to East-West relations, that is, the comparison of Western traditions of thought with traditions prevailing in South Asia (India), East Asia, and also West Asia (Islam). Quite naturally, these inquiries brought me into close contact with practitioners in the areas of comparative philosophy and comparative religious studies—a contact that was deepened by my participation in several meetings of the East-West Center in Hawaii and also by my regular attendance at the annual gatherings of the Society for Asian and Comparative Philosophy (SACP). Inspired by these meetings, the idea arose to launch the project of a "comparative political theory/philosophy," with the deliberate intent of transgressing traditional Western-centric canons of study.

Shapcott first elaborates on my relationship to Gadamer's philosophical hermeneutics. He does it very competently, and there is little I have to add here. Early in my career I was a close witness of the so-called Habermas-Gadamer debate—and it was this experience that prompted me subsequently to find a bridge between Frankfurt and Freiburg/Heidelberg. In that particular debate, Habermas sought to vindicate an objective social science alongside or vis-à-vis Gadamer's "universal" hermeneutics—and this despite his acceptance of the "linguistic turn." For me, Gadamer seemed to have the better point, seeing that even the language of empirical science presupposes a hermeneutical understanding of its concepts. Thus, for purely philosophical reasons, I was drawn toward Gadamer's work. Shapcott's essay lifts up two important points of that work: its dialogical character and its relation to practical ethics. Although acknowledging the role of "prejudgments," hermeneutics does not treat them as incorrigible but opens them up to correction through dialogical encounter. Hermeneutical interpretation accepts neither the sovereignty of the interpreter nor the fixity of the *interpretandum*. It does not unilaterally impose meaning on the world, nor does it submit passively to an external "objectivity" (or absolute "otherness"); rather, meaning arises through dialogical solicitation. This solicitation is precisely at the heart of a practical ethics (pretty much in the Aristotelian sense). As Shapcott correctly notes: hermeneutics is a mode of "practical reasoning" in the sense that "dialogical understanding is oriented toward the question of the good, in dialogue with others."[2]

From hermeneutics Shapcott turns to such offshoots as comparative political theory and cross-cultural dialogues—duly noting the contextual influence of contemporary globalization and other "geopolitical events." Although strongly supported by the latter events, his essay observes correctly that, at least in academic circles, the enterprise of comparative political theory "is still in its infancy, if not gestation." The traditional canon presents a powerful obstacle, and so do engrained geopolitical prejudices. Quite appropriately, Shapcott pays attention both to academic-theoretical and to political issues. Theoretically, comparative study involves an expansion of horizons by shifting our glance "outward and away from the endless focus on the Western canon"; at the same time, and more politically, it corrects an engagement with other cultures, which in the past was driven largely "by instrumentalism and the cultural, political and economic dominance of the West" (one of the important meanings of "Orientalism"). Both the academic and the political aspects are connected, in turn, with a practical-ethical dimension concerned with the issue "how we live together and come to know ourselves and humanity." As Shapcott states, citing one of Gadamer's writings, comparative study responds to the practical task of "reawakening the consciousness of solidarity of a humanity that slowly begins to know itself as humanity." (He also refers briefly to the "methodology" of comparative study—a point to which I shall return later.)

Having traveled this far together, we seem to reach a fork in the road. As Shapcott says, he wants to put some "gentle pressure" on my outlook—a formulation I appreciate. The pressure has to do with the practical yield or output of hermeneutical understanding. Dialogue and comparative political theorizing, he states, have to be "consciously oriented toward questions of 'application' and practice" and must remain "practically engaged in solving or addressing political issues." I have already previously agreed that dialogue and comparison have a practical and not a purely contemplative bent. I hesitate, however, to put them into the harness of "policy studies" and expect them to solve political crises. As I have pointed out elsewhere, for me comparative political theorizing has an ethical orientation: namely, an orientation toward the "good life," possibly a cosmopolitan good life. This orientation implies a striving for justice in the sense that existing grievances are dialogically addressed and if possible redressed, thus making possible shared horizons; and with justice comes peace.[3] However, I am hesitant to bend the orientation in an instrumentalist direction, making it a tool of global social engineering (so that it could tell us "what sort of global community/ies we can build"). For me, the outcome can only emerge from dialogical engagement, with its understandings and misunderstandings. There is no blueprint—such as might be desired by architects or engineers.

What worries me about the desire for blueprints is that it reflects a move beyond the fray: toward a spectatorial overview or a "view from nowhere." I suspect that a move like this is involved when Shapcott urges me to move from comparative or dialogical theorizing to "global political theory." The questions here are immediately: Who is global? What is a global perspective? Where do we find a global language? Questions like these also make me reluctant to embrace the "liberal cosmopolitanism" invoked by Shapcott, especially when it is linked with proceduralism and individualism. Proceduralism is the hallmark of a formal and abstractly "deonotological" moral theory spawned by a certain kind of Enlightenment "universalism." In the absence of a substantive ethics (along the lines, for instance, of an Aristotelian virtue ethics), procedures hang in midair and can always be circumvented (there is no algorithm for the move from procedural rules to practice). This does not mean that rules and procedures do not have practical significance and should not be cultivated as limiting benchmarks. (This is also the significance of legal systems, although laws by themselves do not make people ethical.) It also does not mean that I am ready to abandon rational universalism in favor of a narrow particularism. As Shapcott acknowledges, I resist "the retreat away from universalism," because philosophical hermeneutics is "the medium in which universal and particular are negotiated." To this he adds a statement that I fully endorse: "The dialogic model of comparative political theory and the practical dialogue of civilizations can be understood to involve a form of cosmopolitanism that involves an ongoing process of moving between potential universal values, such as equality, non-domination and freedom, and the particular locations, cultures, cosmologies in which they are expressed." He calls this a "dialogical cosmopolitanism."

Despite this perceptive assessment of my approach, the remainder of Shapcott's paper seeks to apply some more "pressure." Basically, Shapcott invokes a strong version of "liberal universalism," which (he says) "provides a motivating ideal to provoke engagement that goes beyond mutual comprehension." This ideal (he adds) constitutes a "revolutionary moment" that is "subversive of" and "a direct challenge to any particularism." Here we seem to be back to a polarizing and "top-down" agenda. I agree that cosmopolitanism aims at "universal inclusion"; this is so because all those affected by ongoing events must be included in the global dialogue. However, by placing the agenda "beyond mutual comprehension" or dialogical understanding one inevitably accords to it a unilateral and hegemonic character. I realize that Shapcott tries to attenuate this character by presenting universalism as "not indifferent . . . or hegemonic in relation to difference." But then it can also not be indifferent to or "beyond" mutual comprehension. I have some other reservations regarding "liberal universalism" about which I shall be brief. In my view, "liberalism" has been badly tainted—perhaps beyond repair—by its association with neoliberalism, laissez-faire capitalism, and the relentless pursuit of private gain (outside the confines of any possible ethics). The suggestion that liberalism entails "the push to codification, law-making, and procedures" does not particularly endear it to me. Legality and ethics are not synonymous. Moreover, as mentioned before, even the best laws and procedures still need hermeneutical interpretation in order to function in concrete situations.

Different kinds of "pressure" are put on me in Anthony Black's paper. I cannot but relish the beginning, where Black accurately pinpoints the aim of comparative political theorizing. The aim, he writes, is "an existential and philosophical encounter between people of different cultural, religious, and philosophical backgrounds"; it is "a dialogue between persons of all walks of life in a 'global civil society'" amounting to a "globalization from below." This, however, is immediately followed by a first pressure. "Dallmayr," Black observes, "fails to note that in the past there have been many such interactions between cultures." Actually, I have noted it. My book *Beyond Orientalism* surveys a whole series of interactions or encounters, ranging from conquest and conversion to assimilation/acculturation and cultural borrowing to conflict and dialogical engagement. The cases explored range from West to East and from North to South. Black also reminds me that dialogues take place, and have taken place, *"within particular cultures"* between different schools of thought. I too have noticed this. Together with an Indian colleague and friend, I have edited a volume titled *Between Tradition and Modernity: India's Search for Identity*, where we surveyed the complex spectrum of intellectual orientations during the last two centuries. More recently I have undertaken a similar effort with a Chinese colleague in a text titled *Contemporary Chinese Political Thought*, where we explore the diversity of political perspectives in contemporary China.[4]

Thus learning and dialogue clearly take place both within and between cultures. On the issue of cross-cultural encounters, Black credits the "West" with being particularly fond of learning and "perhaps the most persistently learning culture" ever. This may be true for some periods; but at other times the West has preferred teaching and mastering to learning (these are the periods marked by colonialism and Orientalism). As he observes, Westerners have acted as "the acknowledged experts not only on their own history and sociology, but in many cases on those of other peoples." In recent centuries, especially since the Industrial Revolution, however, "nearly all the borrowing" has been by non-Western cultures—which often did not have much choice in the matter. Black wonders whether "other cultures learn from one another" in today's world, and he refers specifically to Muslims and Confucians. Actually, there are close interactions between these two cultures, especially in Malaysia and Thailand and to some extent in mainland China. Probably there is "something to be learned" from Islam and also the Byzantine-Russian tradition, especially in the area of piety and ecopiety. It is in the latter domain that Black finds the "West" most deficient. Western liberal democracy, he writes correctly, "contains no inherent logic limiting people's wholly absurd freedom of consumption"; in a similar vein, Abrahamic monotheism seems to grant humans "the right to exploit the natural world for their own ends"—something resisted in branches of Eastern thought.

In the remainder of Black's essay, the pressures begin to override the shared understandings. For the most part, these pressures come from the side of political realism and an empirical sociological methodology. Black fears that I present "an optimistic, idealistic view" that ignores the looming crises in our world: "the encroaching darkness of diminishing water and food supplies; global organized crime; the insidious advent of global warming," and also the upsurge of political and religious "fanaticism and irrationality," the "polar opposite" of dialogue. Actually, the situation is the reverse. It is precisely my keen awareness of the dark dangers of our time that leads me to champion possible antidotes. What else is the point of my book *Peace Talks—Who Will Listen?* than to serve as a wake-up call in the midst of the relentless war-mongering and hate-mongering poisoning people's minds and lives today? What else is the sense of *In Search of the Good Life* than to summon people to the quest for the common good as a counterpoint to the widespread obsession with power lust and greed? And what is the meaning of *The Promise of Democracy* if not as a clarion call to the cultivation of the ethos of freedom and equality in the face of the reigning ideology of neoliberalism and laissez-faire capitalism, which is ready to sacrifice democracy on the altar of privatization? Yes, these are dark forces indeed, and often our labors seem to resemble the travails of Sisyphos.[5]

A pressure of a slightly different kind derives from considerations of methodology. Here Black appeals to Max Weber and the enterprise of "empirical historical and sociological inquiry." This appeal is meant to correct the hermeneutical emphasis on dialogue and understanding. Following the Weberian method, we are told, we can treat non-Western political thought in the same way we treat Western political thought: namely, "as an object of historical study and analysis." In this manner, we can move beyond a "merely multicultural approach" to a "genuinely comparative approach." I am by no means opposed to historical study or to empirical sociological inquiry in Weber's sense. However, we need to note a few points. First, at least since the "post-empiricist" turn in philosophy, we know that empirical social study also relies on interpretation and understanding. Which "facts" or clusters of "facts" are we going to select for study? What meaning or significance do we assign to these findings? And what is the point of empirical inquiry? Second, Weber himself was ambivalent on the issue of how to relate fact-finding and understanding. Weberian sociology is often (perhaps preeminently) classified as a *Verstehen* approach—which means that hermeneutics is not far afield.[6] For the rest, I agree with Black that we cannot only compare cultures summarily but have to focus on specific topics, such as these: What is the status of human rights in different cultures? What are the respective meanings of justice, law, and even "politics" itself? His closing question to me—"What exactly can we learn from other cultures?"—is in a way answered by the opening paragraph of his paper (cited above). An alternate formulation might be: we learn about the meaning of the good life and how to share it practically in our world.

A pressure from "realist" quarters is also brought to bear on me in Richard Beardsworth's paper—although not instantly, but after a detour through hermeneutical empathy. Beardsworth starts out by giving a perceptive sketch of my intellectual journey or itinerary. The journey starts out (and I cannot but agree) with an engagement with European Continental philosophy, particularly with its phenomenological and hermeneutical tradition (from Husserl and Heidegger to Gadamer, Ricoeur, Derrida, and others). I would only add here one other tradition: that of the Frankfurt School critical theory (from Adorno and Marcuse to Habermas). One of my central intellectual struggles during this period was the attempt to build a bridge between these traditions.[7] The second leg on this journey was my turn to non-Western philosophical traditions and cross-cultural dialogue. My main concern at this point, as Beardsworth points out, was with the philosophical contributions and the lived ethical praxis found in India, East Asia, and the Islamic world. In addition to the texts cited in his paper I would add two edited books: *Border Crossings* (1999) and *Between Tradition and Modernity* (mentioned before). This was also the time of my serious engagement with the thought and practice of Mahatma Gandhi—an engagement that turned out to be permanent. The last leg of the journey, according to Beardsworth, is the increasing involvement with questions of "cosmopolis"—what Shapcott calls my "dialogical cosmopolitanism." It is under this rubric that I would include texts like *Alternative Visions: Paths in the Global Village* (1998), *Achieving Our World: Toward a Global and Plural Democracy* (2001), and *Dialogue among Civilizations* (2002).[8]

Running through these stages, Beardsworth detects a general trajectory that leads from traditional political theory/philosophy (focused exclusively on the Western canon) in the direction of a hermeneutical-dialogical or "comparative" political theorizing. As he points out, this trajectory involves a number of (what he calls) "politico-theoretical responsibilities." Among these responsibilities he lists the need for "mutual learning between individuals and societies" (what I like to call the virtue of hermeneutical openness); the nurturing of a shared humanity and of a "genuine universalism" beyond abstract universalism or liberal proceduralism; and finally the cultivation of a "transformative democratic agency" inspired by Gandhian *satyagraha*, Deweyan pragmatism, and religious and secular republicanism—an agency far removed from domination and imperial hegemony. As Beardsworth adds, these responsibilities are particularly important in the contemporary moment of "deep liberal crisis," a crisis manifest in the recent financial and economic "meltdown," in the climate changes induced by reckless spoliation of natural resources, and in the upsurge of terrorism and counter-terrorism. All these features can ultimately be traced to the doorsteps of a certain domineering or triumphalist Western liberalism or neoliberalism—although care must be taken not to confuse this triumphalism with the genuine search for human freedom, which can only be won in collaboration with others.[9]

Following this friendly prelude, the time has come for pressure or a more agonistic engagement. The title of the paper, "Culture and the Specificity of Politics," pinpoints the issue precisely. For Beardsworth, my work leans toward a "moral politics," while sidelining or bypassing a "responsible politics of power," which is the "appropriate object of international political theory." Differently phrased: I favor a "culturalist notion of political transformation" that neglects "the specificity of the political," thus opting for a "politics of non-violence" in lieu of a "politics of lesser violence." In sum, the issue concerns the relation "between ethics and politics in the political domain." For

Beardsworth, what is particular or "specific" to the political realm is "that it necessarily constitutes a field of differently weighted forces," an aspect that is "all the more important at the international level due to the lack of enforcement mechanisms." The notion of politics as a "force field" or "field of competing forces" is, of course, familiar from the writings of (the early) Foucault, Gilles Deleuze, and to some extent Carl Schmitt. Beardsworth at this point involves me (somewhat surprisingly) in an encounter with Derrida on the issue of "European cultural identity."

As he correctly notes, I have been repeatedly preoccupied with Derrida's *The Other Heading: Reflections on Today's Europe.* What has attracted me is the ambivalence or aporetic complexity of the "other heading" (or heading toward the "other"): the abandonment of self-enclosed identity coupled with a refusal to plunge into abstract universalism or else a complete vacuity. What troubled me increasingly over the years—and this is also what troubled me about a major strand in post-modernism—was the departure from a balanced negotiation of identity/difference in favor of an ever more remote and absolutized "otherness." This was evident for me in Derrida's bending of the possible/impossible doublet in the direction of a "radical impossibility," an "impossible experience," and a "thinking of the event" (the latter construed in near-apocalyptic terms). This move, I felt, tendentially exchanges human capability for human incapacity and ultimately jeopardizes the prospect of democratic *praxis* and "self-rule." In Beardsworth's account, I have tended to endorse "Derrida's understanding of difference and alterity" but have questioned it "politically from the perspective of transformative democratic agency." At this point, the sense of the detour through Derrida becomes clear: my concern with democratic political agency and especially my stress on self-transgression and ethical transformation lead me into a confrontation with Beardsworth's notion of the "specificity of politics."

As previously stated, at stake here is the relation between culture and politics or else between ethics and politics. Beardsworth here reiterates his conception—inspired (as he says) by Machiavelli, Nietzsche, Max Weber, and the "classical realism of Hans Morgenthau"—that politics or "the political" involves "a dynamic force-field of differently weighted, mobile forces." From this angle, the specificity of politics resides not in openness to the other (or others), but in the acceptance that *"limits* constitute the political field." This acceptance, he states, opens up the possibility of a politics that "delimits less violently than more." Nonacceptance, by contrast, leads to radical indeterminacy with all its dangers and ignores the "essentially conflictual structure of the political field." Basically, without determined limits, the field is left open "to the play of more violent forces." Beardsworth realizes, of course, my unwillingness to embrace indeterminacy and my own preference for "more conditioned behavior." In his view, however, "by sitting [still] too close to Derrida," I risk losing the task of "ethico-political responsibility *within* the field of world politics." This leads him into broader reflections on the relation between ethics/culture and politics. Basically, he stipulates a stronger dichotomy between these domains than I would accept. As he writes, somewhat categorically: "In the political field, the direct alignment of peaceful ends with non-violent means is not possible as such." Above all, a Gandhian politics of ethical self-limitation "cannot be embodied by a political ethics of responsible power," and this is due to "the irreducible plurality of forces in the international domain."[10]

Our views on this important issue are clearly divergent. For me, ethics and politics are neither simply identical, nor are they opposed. If confined to the personal level, ethics functions in a more private context, while politics operates on a broader public level; ethics nurtures the personal good life, politics the good life of a larger community. As Beardsworth notes, I have been influenced in this field by a number of thinkers—including Aristotle, and we know that Aristotle wanted us to read his *Ethics* as a gateway to his *Politics.* Apart from Aristotle, my guides have been Montesquieu, Hegel, Schelling, and (among more recent thinkers) Dewey, Gadamer, and Heidegger—and none of them was enamored with a vacuous indeterminacy. All of them assumed that both ethics and politics operate in a contextual field or a network of relationships. In the case of Heidegger especially, his central notion of "being-in-the-world" cannot be construed otherwise than as embeddedness in a net of relations; his stress on human finitude is an acknowledgment of human limits, barring any exit to a "view from nowhere." So, from this perspective, both ethics and politics cannot be "delimited" enterprises. In Gadamer's writings (as previously stated), ethics involves a dialogical engagement that requires the cultivation of "prudence" (in Aristotle's sense) and of "conscience" (in the sense of both Kierkegaard and Heidegger).[11]

The question here becomes how one construes contextual limits. I have used as synonymous such phrases as "network of relationship" or context of "dialogical engagement." Beardsworth prefers phrases like "force field" or "field of dynamically weighted mobile forces." What I find lacking in the latter formulations is the human face, the quality of human agency. Expressions like "force field" are clearly borrowed from physics and electro-mechanics. Here, as physicists, we can observe the interplay of forces as analysts and bystanders. But in the political arena we are agents and not just bystanders. Enmeshed in networks of relationships, we have to ask ourselves how to act, which set of forces to favor and which to oppose, in which direction to bend the force field. By itself, the field will not provide the answers. It is up to us to support the stronger side or the weaker side, the more oppressive or the more liberating and humane side. Here ethical considerations—irrelevant to molecular physics—come into play. As it seems to me, Beardsworth tends to subscribe to the traditional "balance of power" conception, where different powers (mainly states) compete and balance each other as "mobile forces." This conception stands indeed in a respectable European tradition; for an extensive period of time, especially during the so-called Concert of Europe, the arrangement secured a certain containment or limitation of military force (and thus ensured a mode of "lesser violence"). But this was so because the relations between states still could rely on a shared cultural cushion, the underpinning of shared ethics (nurtured by religious and humanist resources). Once this underpinning eroded—as happened in the twentieth century—state relations descended into utter savagery that no mechanism of balancing powers could stop.

In our age of globalization, the cushion supporting the old Concert of Europe—even if it could be restored—is clearly no longer sufficient. Hence there is a need to search for and cultivate a cosmopolitan ethical fabric capable of harnessing the emerging global "force field." Hence ethics today is not less but even more urgent than in past centuries. Here I have to introduce an important caveat to avoid misunderstanding. By marshaling ethical resources I do not mean a simple injection of ethical principles into ongoing politics. As long as the latter is understood as pure power politics, ethics cannot be a ready ally of politics (here their "difference" comes into view). The danger is that politics simply appropriates and instrumentalizes ethics for power-political purposes, using or abusing it for hegemonic aims. Ethics here shares the fate of religion—which also is too often instrumentalized or (what one calls) "politicized" for power-political goals. In the domain of power politics, ethics (like religion) can only have a restraining or limiting and not a supportive role—to avoid co-optation. This is particularly important in international politics, given its proclivity to warfare. Like religious warfare (jihad), "ethical" warfare only intensifies savagery (by demonizing the enemy into an "axis of evil"). Against this background, the notion of a "just war" is deeply problematical, perhaps even an oxymoron, because "war" is almost by definition "unjust" (unless it is waged for narrowly defensive purposes in accordance with the United Nations Charter). Hence, by pleading for a worldwide cushion of ethical sensitivity and responsibility, I do not wish to be misunderstood as wishing to throw a match into the existing powder keg of political ambitions.

These observations lead me back to Beardsworth and his embrace of political "realism" in the international field. Surprisingly, after traveling along very different roads, we arrive at the end at a very similar conclusion: the desire for a limitation of violence or a "politics of the lesser violence." The conclusion is less astonishing once one takes into account that we have read many of the same authors and have wrestled with many of the same problems. In the end, my ethical predispositions are not at odds with a sober kind of "realism" (provided the latter is seen as a counsel of prudence). I agree with Beardsworth when he writes: "With the demise of American 'empire,' and the rapid rise of Asian and other non-Western powers, international liberalism needs to be re-theorized to allow for the possibility of a less violent world." And I fully concur with his concluding statement: "I consider international political theory more responsible to its object, world politics, when it expounds cosmopolitan commitments to humanity, the world and the planet from out of the practical reality of interdependence, of the system of states, and of emerging regionalism." This leads me to a concluding statement of my own. The set of papers and their discussion illustrate perfectly the value of dialogical engagement for purposes of clarification and mutual learning. As it seems to me, dialogue does not always lead to consensus or a "fusion of horizon"; but even if it does not, it is enlightening by revealing the reasons of disagreement. And then, as in this case, it may lead to an agreement for very different reasons (what some have called an "overlapping consensus").

6. Befriending the Stranger

Beyond the Global Politics of Fear

> Do not neglect hospitality to strangers, for thereby some
> have entertained angels unawares.
>
> —Hebrews 13:1

Cosmopolitanism has a difficult relation with borders or boundaries. It cannot completely discard borders or bounded limits—without turning into an extraterrestrial enterprise or a mere flight of fancy. But it can also not blithely accept them, preferring instead to treat them as moving horizons. This dilemma is endemic to human living and thinking. Clearly, our thinking—that is, our attempt to understand the world—inevitably proceeds from certain bounded premises, certain taken-for-granted assumptions or frames of significance—whose precise contours, however, remain amorphous and open-ended. Even if, hypothetically, we should be able to fix or determine the initial framework, we would necessarily have to place ourselves beyond, in order to see the limit as a limit. When encountering alien or unfamiliar life-forms, our initial assumptions are exposed or subjected to testing—a testing that induces a process of transformation navigating precariously beyond affirmation and negation. Hence, our initial understanding or frame of significance can be neither simply discarded nor stubbornly maintained—which attests to the fact that thinking is not a rummaging in finished doctrines but rather a journey or peregrination. Beyond thinking, this insight applies also to our acting and concrete living, that is, to our existential being-in-the-world. This is why some writers describe human life as a continuous mode of "border-crossing," and human agents as *Grenzgänger,* that is, as people criss-crossing multiple borders.[1]

In our world today, border-crossing is under siege, even in danger of being erased. There are two major features marking our present age: the first is the process of globalization, the second the so-called war on terror. The first process is bent on sidelining, perhaps even eradicating, borders in favor of borderless global markets, borderless financial transactions, and digital global communications. The second feature opens up abysmal borders or cleavages far transcending traditional geopolitical divides: the gulf between terror and counter-terror, between "world order" and disorder (or unorder), and ultimately between life and death. As can readily be seen, the war on terror or "terror war" is a strategy affecting not only so-called terrorists but also their opponents and humankind at large. Actually, the phrase "war on terror" is redundant since war itself means the unleashing of terror— with the result that such a war "terrorizes" people on both (or all) sides of the divide. Terror, however, is another expression for intense, overpowering fear. This has as a consequence that terror war, globally pursued, results—not accidentally but inevitably—in a global politics of fear (rather than a politics of dialogue and hope), that is, a politics conducted exclusively under the rubric of security versus insecurity, of the rigid border control between "us" and "them." In the following, I want to examine this ominous development in world politics from a number of angles. First, I want to explore the growing linkage of politics with terror war by tracing its roots ultimately to the friend-enemy distinction. Next, I want to discuss the shortcomings of the terror war syndrome, by turning to some prominent critics of this ideology. Finally, I want to examine possible ways pointing beyond this ideology, enlisting for this purpose a number of theologians and intellectuals, to arrive again at the promising notions of "thinking with(out) borders" and political-existential *Grenzgänger.*

The Politics of Fear

The great English philosopher Thomas Hobbes described himself, in an autobiographical vein, as a child of fear. The reason for this description is that, at the time of his birth (in 1588), the mighty Spanish Armada was sailing toward England. One can plausibly argue that fear, or the sense of fear, never left the philosopher and, in fact, came to overshadow his entire work. As is well known, Thomas Hobbes's theory has human beings move from an initial "state of nature" via a social contract to a "civil state" or commonwealth; but fear is present from the beginning to the end. Given that the natural human condition is marked by aggressive selfishness engendering the prospect of a "war of all against all" (*bellum omnium contra omnes*), the dominant and overpowering psychic condition at that stage is the fear of violent death. However, even after people contract with each other and establish a civil state, fear does not come to an end. Now fear is due not to the aggressive conduct of the contracting agents, but to the awesome power of the sovereign who is above and beyond the contract and rules not by reason or persuasion but by political might (*auctoritas non veritas facit legem*). Hence, order and peace in a commonwealth are predicated not on social custom or on the intrinsic virtue of citizens, but on the general fear of sovereign retribution. As Hobbes stated, articulating the perennial watchword of political "realism": words or arguments "without the sword" are empty slogans incapable of securing civic order.[2]

In many ways, the Hobbesian formula of sovereign power became the bedrock of the modern (Western) state; even when softened or outwardly repudiated, its harsher features continue to hover in the background. Although reformulating the notion of sovereign prerogatives, John Locke's approach retained many aspects of the earlier formula: especially the accents on contract and self-centered competition (readily giving rise to violent conflict in crisis periods). From Locke's time forward, this soft version of Hobbesianism served to buttress—overtly or covertly—the agenda of modern liberal politics and public (state-centered) policy. Under the impact of steadily intensifying economic (or class) conflicts and culture wars, the Hobbesian background features moved progressively into the foreground. One of the most prominent spokesmen of neo-Hobbesianism in the twentieth century is the German legal and political theorist Carl Schmitt. Taking the English philosopher as his mentor, Schmitt deliberately centerstages the primacy of sovereign power over all forms of public deliberation or civic cohesion. As he states famously at the very start of his book *Political Theology*: "Sovereign is the one who decides on the case of the exception." The state of exception is not an ordinary condition manageable by ordinary procedures; rather, it is an "exceptional" or extranormal state, one that opens up an abyss or breach where only sovereign power can secure order. Although in a way abnormal, the exceptional state for Schmitt is not marginal but penetrates deeply into the very fabric of politics or political life, namely, by pinpointing a decisive divide or division: the division between friend and enemy, between "us" and "them," between inside and outside. As he writes in another famous text, *The Concept of the Political*, the very meaning of "the political" must be found in a "specific political distinction," namely, the division or difference "between friend and enemy." This distinction, he adds, denotes "the utmost degree of intensity of a union or separation, of an association or dissociation" (where union applies to friends and separation to enemies).[3]

For Schmitt, the friend-enemy distinction was not just a rhetorical formula but a criterion of war and peace—in the sense that (according to his repeated statements) the enemy is someone who can be killed. Thus, in the guise of legal-conceptual language, the Hobbesian fear factor powerfully returns: fear of the sovereign and fear of violent death. Without any familiarity with the textual sources, many prominent political leaders in our time have appropriated the Schmittian formula for their own purposes. According to a distinguished American senator, America (meaning the United States) today lives in an "either-or" world and cannot achieve its objectives "by being inoffensive." What many well-meaning observers tend to brush aside or forget is a basic feature of international reality today: namely, "the difference between America's friends and America's enemies."[4] In the wake of these pronouncements, the Hobbesian fear factor reasserted itself, with unmitigated intensity, in the linkage of enmity and warfare. In the aftermath of September 11, traditional warfare was supplemented and deepened by the spread of seemingly unlimited "terror wars," by the upsurge of a Manichean division of the world into friends and enemies, into supporters of Western-style "freedom" and devotees of an infernal "axis of evil."

For present purposes, a crucial implication of the Schmittian formula is its erection of a basic divide or unbreachable boundary. At the site of the friend-enemy distinction, border-crossings and the role of *Grenzgänger* are deemed to be impossible or impermissible. In the face of enmity, borders are meant to be solidified, fortified, and militarized. From this results a peculiar feature of our presumably globalizing and ultimately "borderless" world: the return to fences, checkpoints, and dividing walls. Just a few decades after the dismantling of the infamous Berlin Wall—inaugurating or accompanying the demise of the Cold War—we witness today the ominous resurgence of dividing barriers: the fence between the United States and Mexico, the gates between Europe and North Africa, and the wall between Israel and Palestine. By themselves, the barriers are only physical constructs; but their presence testifies to deep-seated motivations: the prevalence of fear and distrust; the desire to exclude the unfamiliar or alien; and the obsession with being free from intrusions. Another term for fear is *phobia*—and the world today is inundated with phobias, among which "Islamophobia" probably tops the list. More than other phobias, Islamophobia is closely connected with violence and the (Hobbesian) fear of violent death—which today means fear of "terror." In this respect, while unsettling traditional (national) boundaries, Islamophobia opens up new borders or fissures of horror on both domestic and global levels. Against this background, the frequently voiced question "How can a nice boy from Brooklyn become a terrorist?" reveals a deep and unsettling shift in the friend-enemy formula.

In less dramatic form, the fear of Islamic strangers comes to the fore in the battles over the wearing of veils or burqas and the building of minarets that recently have agonized many European countries. A more amorphous but no less widespread type of fear today is "xenophobia," which in many cases has the character of an economic phobia, fear over the loss of job security due to the influx of migrant workers or immigrants. Almost everywhere in the West today, one finds an insistence—among both right-wing and left-wing political movements—on new immigrant legislation and a tightening of border controls. A prominent example in this area is the new law enacted in the state of Arizona that allows police to investigate the legal or illegal immigrant status of suspicious people—a law that not unexpectedly has led to widespread protests and demonstrations. In the context of Europe, recent surveys and analyses have shown that major sources of exclusion or distrust are primarily economic and no longer (or not exclusively) cultural and religious. In the words of one prominent researcher, Albena Azmanova: "In contrast to the old version in which hostility to foreigners was cast in terms of the protection of cultural and political sovereignty (national chauvinism), the foundation of xenophobia is now often economic. It is related to the perceived threats to socio-economic well-being, especially job loss, brought about by the open border policies of globalization." This development obviously has profound implications for the conception of borders and the prospect of border-crossings. As Azmanova adds: "'Closed border' attitudes are grounded on the emerging culture of individual responsibility for economic survival which has redefined the legitimacy relationship between public authority and citizens in recent years. The more individuals [have to] accept responsibility for their own economic well-being in a context of economic uncertainty, the more they are averse to otherness—as they see the other as [hostile] competitor, rather than as a 'significant' other."[5]

Countering Terror Wars

Although unprecedented in their scope and intensity, today's terror wars have distant precursors in the religious wars of seventeenth-century Europe. As previously indicated, Hobbes's congenital fear was based on the approach of the Armada, that is, Spain's military attempt to extend its Catholic empire—an attempt that was only a prelude to the devastating religious conflicts of subsequent decades (and also to the English civil war between royalists and Puritans). These conflicts exacted a horrendous price in terms of human lives and civil culture, but somehow a sense of decency survived. In the midst of bloody conflagrations and displays of terror, a few European intellectuals stood out as mediators and models of political restraint. One was the great Dutch humanist Erasmus, who did not cease to urge moderation on all contending religious parties and also on the conflictual relations between Europe and the "Turks."[6] Another major figure was the French essayist Michel de Montaigne, who experienced and reacted to the bitter feud between French Catholics and Huguenots. Both figures, Erasmus as well as Montaigne, sought to mitigate and, if possible, resolve the prevailing enmity—the friend-enemy polarity—without necessarily endorsing a bland compromise neglectful of just aspirations. In the words of social theorist Bryan Turner, Montaigne presented an argument "that gave priority to *humanité* as the basis for mercy and sympathy because *humanité* moderates vengeance and resentment." Properly applied, Montaigne's ethics—stressing "forgiveness, clemency, talking it out rather than fighting it through"—was able to "make men behave more humanely to one another, perhaps lead his countrymen out of their civil war, and restore conditions of justice."[7]

In our own time, do we still have moderating mediators of this kind? Can we still find public intellectuals attuned to, and living up to, the tradition of Erasmus and Montaigne? To be sure, there are some outstanding religious leaders—like the Dalai Lama and Bishop Tutu—willing and able to resist the prevailing politics of fear (I shall return to this point a bit later). When we look elsewhere, however, the situation is more bleak. Faced with the accelerating terror wars after September 11, members of the academy in the West have for the most part maintained silence—even deafening silence. Preoccupied with careers within professional borders, academic philosophers and literary intellectuals have by and large been unwilling, or else unable, to challenge the predominance of the Schmittian formula. The task itself, to be sure, is challenging and daunting—mainly because of the globalization of that formula. Basically, in contrast to earlier, mainly domestic conflicts, terrors wars in our time have both a national and a transnational or global character; as such, they hover uneasily between domestic and international warfare and, more precisely, between civil war and interstate war. While, in modern times, interstate wars have precariously been regulated by international norms, nonstate conflicts are typically subject to police control—a control that comes to an end in outright civil war (including global civil war), which inaugurates a state of total normlessness and savagery spawning intense fear of violent death.

Given the complexity of terror wars, few intellectuals have stepped into this arena in a properly humanist spirit; a major exception (in my view) is the international relations scholar Richard Falk. In his book *The Great Terror War,* published at the onset of the invasion of Iraq (2003), Falk lucidly pinpointed the character of the newly emerging friend-enemy division. "Unlike most past radical movements that were embedded in a specific society whose ruling structure was being challenged," he writes, "al-Qaeda exemplifies the organizational form of the current era of globalization: a network that can operate anywhere and everywhere, and yet is definitely situated nowhere," that is, a network "without an address." Falk in this context introduces the term *megaterrorism* to characterize the elusiveness of the new warfare with respect to normative limits and especially with regard to the borders between civilians and combatants. "Megaterrorism," he notes, "is violence against civilian targets that achieves significant levels of substantive as well as symbolic harm, causing damage on a scale once associated with large-scale military attacks under state auspices, and thus threatening the target society in a warlike manner that gives rise to a defensive urgency to strike back as effectively as possible." Conceived under the rubric of "terror war" or war against "terrorism," this "defensive urgency" takes on the same amorphous character that marks the network launching the 9/11 attack. Hence, Falk notes in a critical vein, the generalizing of terrorism "misdirects the American-led response, weakening the commitment to struggle specifically against the al-Qaeda network, while distracting the needed energies from an appropriately conceived 'war.'"[8]

What particularly troubles Falk is the fact that the broad rhetoric of terror war or war against terrorism extends or generalizes the resort to violence, while weakening or blurring the distinction between state actors and nonstate actors, that is, between interstate and civil war. In his words: "I believe that the over-generalized American approach to the megaterrorist challenge is dangerously serving to exempt state violence and policies from being regarded *as* terrorism—even when their violence is deliberately directed at civilian society." This exemption allows governments everywhere "to rely on large-scale violence against their own and other civilian populations, and to avoid the stigma of terrorism, while at the same time tending to taint all *reactive* violence from oppressed peoples . . . as terrorism." For Falk, the only chance to make headway in the present politics of fear is to restrict the focus to very specific targets, rather than extending it to global networks, and thereby to rein in the danger of indiscriminate global mayhem or war on civilian populations. By proceeding in this manner, the traditional normative standards applicable (however loosely) to interstate warfare are bound to be strengthened, while the normlessness of civil strife can hopefully be curbed. On the other hand, terror warfare is liable to be "lost" or a losing strategy through an overindulgence in violence and also by treating attacks "in isolation from their social, political, and cultural contexts." The likelihood of failure is prone to be increased by unilateralism and the relentless pursuit of global hegemonic designs, a pursuit "pushing the world into a new phase of strategic [friend-enemy] rivalry" while being undertaken "behind the smokescreen of the war on global terror."[9]

As one should note, Falk does not entirely reject a military response to terrorist attacks—as long as the politics of fear is not allowed to trump or obliterate the politics of hope and global cooperation. Faced with the threat of megaterrorism, he writes, "the rationale for *limited* war seems to me persuasive, provided the focus on al-Qaeda is not superseded by more expanded war aims—which lamentably seems to be happening as a matter of deliberate choice by American political leaders" (at least during the Bush administration). As a student of global politics, Falk finds our world precariously lodged at the cusp between two paradigms: the "Westphalian" paradigm based on military state power and an (emerging) paradigm of global interdependence. "We find ourselves in a situation," he states, "that *both* calls for reliance on war to achieve tolerable levels of security . . . and [calls for] an emphasis upon the minimization of disruptive violence and a receptivity to post-Westphalian alternatives."[10] In the meantime, since 2003, the paradigm of military warfare has continued, while shifting its accent from Iraq to Afghanistan (and possibly Iran). Despite the ongoing relocation of geographical focus, however, a basic feature of terror wars has remained unchanged: the intermingling of state war and civil war, that is, of violence against armed forces and against civilian populations. In the case of Afghanistan, the use of unmanned "drones" illustrates in a particularly dramatic fashion the confluence of combatants and noncombatants. As we are reliably told, although ostensibly directed at terrorist cells, drone attacks in many cases have resulted in a bloodbath of entire civilian families and village clans. Outrage and resentment are the inevitable result. As we read in one of Falk's subsequent publications, large numbers of people in the Islamic world are prone to end up with the conclusion that their "sufferings and grievances" do not count and are "the result of the abusive ways in which America uses its power and wealth in the world."[11]

Falk is not the only prominent international relations expert willing to examine and challenge global terror wars. Among some others in this field, I want to single out especially Joseph Nye—author of such well-known texts as *The Paradox of American Power* and *Soft Power*—and also some writings of Andrew Linklater.[12] Their voices have been ably seconded and reinforced by the renowned Malaysian student of global politics Chandra Muzaffar. In a book penned after the invasion of Iraq—and the reelection of the president guiding that invasion—Muzaffar reflected on the deeper sources or motivations of these events. "Fear," he comments, "had probably a great deal to do with [the president's] electoral triumph." In the aftermath of 9/11, the American public's "overwhelming concern" was with "security," which is thought to provide a bulwark against the onslaught of terror. At the end of the day, this concern with security, in Muzaffar's view, was "more important to voters" than all the problems surrounding the war in Iraq, including the pretended weapons of mass destruction, the burgeoning military budget, Abu Ghraib, and the rest. Fear of terror and the resulting concern with security provided the West with the rationale, or better: the excuse, to extend its military reach or hegemony throughout the Middle East and around the globe. Like Falk and other observers, Muzaffar does not attribute the politics of fear exclusively to September 11 but lists a number of other contributing factors, including "the quest for identity, the upsurge of ethnic consciousness, political antagonisms and animosities, and economic instability and upheaval."[13]

Beyond the Politics of Fear

When searching for a more just and peaceful global order, as an alternative to the politics of fear, attention shifts almost inevitably to religious-spiritual as well as moral or ethical resources and traditions. Both Falk and Muzaffar are eloquent in invoking and articulating these resources. Addressing the "growing evidence of geopolitical hubris" evident in the militarization of the globe, Falk stresses the counter-strategy of geopolitical self-limitation and interdependence nurtured by a sense of religious and ethical "humility." As he states, humility in this setting would mean "adopting the narrowest war aims possible, identifying limits, seeking closure, and exploring alternatives to war-based security politics"—alternatives designed to "promote and sustain the well-being of all peoples on the planet." In his turn, Muzaffar finds the "root cause" of the ills of our time in the neglect of spiritual and ethical legacies or teachings that could provide a remedy to the fear-inspired focus on security. "The question we have to ask at this point," he writes, "is this: should we—as inhabitants of the planet Earth—not look for the metaphysical causes, the spiritual cures for the ailments that afflict us?" Indeed, has the time not come for modern people "to develop a deeper understanding of what really lies behind the colossal challenges of our age"—and thereby to garner glimpses of a more peaceful, less fear-inspired global politics?[14]

When consulting the scriptures or traditions invoked by Falk and Muzaffar, we are not at a loss. All the spiritual and ethical teachings emphasize an alternative to self-centered fear and security: the alternative of self-transcendence, self-opening, and border-crossing. In the so-called Abrahamic traditions, the key teaching is found in Deuteronomy and Leviticus, in passages stressing the two commandments (which in the end are one): to love or open ourselves to God with all our being and to love our fellow-beings in the same way (Deuteronomy 6:5, Leviticus 19:18). The teaching was taken over almost verbatim by Jesus when he identified the core of religious faith with the enactment of these two modes of love (Matthew 22:37–40; Luke 10:27–28; Mark 12:29–31). However, as is well known, Jesus added to this dual plea a new and hitherto unheard-of commandment: the plea to "love your enemies" (Matthew 5:44; Luke 6:27). By all accounts, this is the plea that is most disturbing and even unacceptable to international "realists" preoccupied solely with fear and security. In his *The Concept of the Political*, Carl Schmitt seeks to circumvent Jesus's commandment by employing a deft form of verbal casuistry, namely, the distinction between private and public enemy (*inimicus* and *hostis*). As he writes: "An enemy exists only when, at least potentially, one fighting collectivity of people confronts a similar collectivity. The enemy is solely the public enemy" and not "the private adversary." In Schmitt's construal of Christ's exhortation, "no mention is made of the political enemy"—with the result that, against the latter, warfare and killing remain altogether legitimate and permissible. As it happens, of course, no such private/public distinction is made anywhere in the gospels.[15]

As mentioned before, several religious leaders in our time have stepped forward critiquing or denouncing the dominant focus on fear and terror wars;[16] fortunately, their pleas have not been isolated or ignored. Following September 11, a number of Christian theologians and religious scholars have pondered the challenge posed by megaterrorism and megafear—reflections collected in a volume titled *Strike Terror No More: Theology, Ethics, and the New War.* As can readily be seen, for theologians and Christian believers, fear and especially the fear of violent death cannot have the central status it tends to have for nonbelievers or agnostics; above all, fear cannot provide a ready-made license for counter-fear or counter-terror. Seen in the light of biblical teachings, death no longer possesses final authority but is inserted into a redemptive story and the vision of "final days." In the words of theologian Stanley Hauerwas (of the Duke Divinity School), Christians as a community are "shaped by the practice of baptism that reminds us there are far worse things that can happen to us than dying." Unfortunately, the indiscriminate leveling of Christians into the secular American "way of life" is an indication "that the Christian 'we' of baptism has been submerged in the American fear of death." In the wake of September 11, what Christians can and should do—in Hauerwas's view—is to escape from fear and terror in favor of an alternative possibility and pathway. For what Christians have learned and can show to others, he writes, is "that the worst thing that can happen to us is not death, but dying for the wrong thing." After all, Christians have been instructed, by their Lord's example, "that we must prepare for death exactly because we refuse to kill in the name of survival."[17]

For theologians like Hauerwas and others, the main point is not simply to resist the fear syndrome but to lay the groundwork for another scenario where fear would give way to trust, cooperation, and redemptive care. At this juncture, the instructions of Deuteronomy and Leviticus as well as Jesus's new commandment are of crucial importance. In a section in the same volume titled "Do Christians Have Anything Distinctive to Say?" John J. Cobb Jr. (from the Claremont School of Theology) turns precisely to these teachings for support. In the face of our dark horizons, he comments, it cannot be the proper Christian response to resort to "us-versus-them" formulas and to endorse policies "that harm them for our gain." Especially in situations of danger when fear is trying to overwhelm us, it is crucial to remember and enact the biblical instructions and, above all, Jesus's new commandment. This does not mean that we condone or approve of terrorism or fail to bring terrorists to justice, if possible; but it *does* mean that we do not simply retaliate and repay terror with terror, enmity with torture and Abu Ghraib. In a similar vein, Walter Wink (from Auburn Theological Seminary) pleads for the exercise of non-violence—at least to the greatest possible extent—as an alternative to blind retaliation or revenge. "The church," he writes, "is called to nonviolence—not in order to preserve its purity, but to express its fidelity. . . . The gospel is not in the least concerned with our anxiety to *be* right; it wants to see *right done*." As he adds, nonviolence of this kind in the final analysis is "not a matter of legalism but of disciple-ship. It is the way God has chosen to overthrow evil in the world."[18]

In remonstrating against terror wars (including counter-terrorism), theologians can also find assistance—apart from biblical passages—in ethical-philosophical teachings of the past, including the traditional theory of "just war." Thus, John Milbank (who teaches philosophical theology at the University of Virginia) aptly points to the compatibility—within certain limits—between biblical faith and clas-sical philosophical insights. As he writes: "Both empty secular power and arbitrary theocratic power, in their secret complicity, show us no way forward." Rather, what we need to reconsider is the "Platonic-Aristotelian" legacy and its resonance in all three monotheistic reli-gions. "We should ponder ways," he states, "in which this legacy may provide us with a certain common vision and practice, while at the same time respecting social and cultural spaces for exercised differ-ence." In this manner, we might glimpse how "human wisdom can imitate, imperfectly but truly, something of an eternal order of jus-tice." Appealing explicitly to the "just war" tradition, Max Stackhouse (from the Princeton Theological Seminary) reminds us first of all that "God wants everyone to live in peace and to be nonviolent toward the neighbor near and far." Recognizing that, among imperfect hu-man beings, violence sometimes has erupted and continues to erupt in history, just war theory lays down normative principles designed precisely to keep violence in check. First of all, resort to violent means (*jus ad bellum*) must be for defensive reasons only, undertaken as a last resort (after all alternatives have been exhausted), and guided by a legitimate authority (not a bunch of mercenaries). Second, during warfare (*ius in bello*), care must be taken to distinguish between com-batants and civilians, to use only proportionate force, and to treat en-emies "as human." Finally, the entire course of war must be oriented toward its end, that is, conducted in such a way as to render possible final reconciliation and a just peace.[19]

To be sure, the struggle against the politics of fear cannot be left to theologians and religious leaders alone. There are major tasks left for political leaders and policy makers: tasks like reforming the United Nations, strengthening regional organizations, building new cross-cutting alliances, and reducing the stockpiles of nuclear weapons and other armaments. Given that the focus on terror and counter-terror is ultimately destructive of peace as well as democracy, it is also important to consult political theorists and philosophers on this point. In this context, it is fruitful to remember the work of the Baron Montesquieu, which—in the modern Western tradition—constitutes the perfect antidote to the fear paradigm of Thomas Hobbes. In his *The Spirit of Laws,* Montesquieu pinpointed the underlying motivation or "spirit" of different political regimes. Tellingly, his work associated the motive of fear with tyranny or despotism, while democracy or a republican regime was necessarily linked for him with the spirit of "love," more specifically the "love for equality" (or equal dignity) among all citizens or participants. In Montesquieu's view, such love cannot be legislated or imposed by political force but is a civic virtue that needs to be cultivated through an ethics of openness and generosity toward follow-beings.[20] The great American philosopher of democracy John Dewey would have fully agreed with him in this respect. As is well known, democracy for Dewey was not a finished product but on ongoing process requiring the constant openness of participants to new learning experiences, new border crossings, and the diligent cultivation of ethical sensibilities capable of fostering the common good. Accordingly, he called democracy "a form of moral and spiritual association."[21]

All this does not imply a neglect of fear and of the danger of violence and terror wars, but an insistence on vigilance to keep this danger at bay or at a minimum to prevent it from crowding out the prospect of cooperation and peace. In this regard, Dewey was clearly more than a "realist," adopting the perspective of (what one may call) a "utopian realist" or a "realistic idealist" willing to "befriend" strangers and even enemies. As he wrote in one of his famous texts on democracy (in the spirit of both Montesquieu and Gandhi): "To take as far as possible every conflict which arises—and they are bound to arise—out of the atmosphere and medium of force, of violence as a means of settlement, into that of discussion and of intelligence is to treat those who disagree—even profoundly—with us as those from whom we may learn and, insofar, as friends."[22]

7. The Body Politic

Fortunes and Misfortunes of a Concept

> The humane person regards Heaven and Earth and all
> things as one body.
> — Ch'eng Hao, *Ech-Ch'eng i-shu*

> The body is not yours, nor does it belong to others.
> — *Samyutta Nikaya* (Buddhist scripture)

Looking at contemporary humanity, one can hardly avoid the impression of a huge body or organism ravaged by multiple diseases and even catastrophes.[1] Even without detailed diagnosis, it is not hard to trace these ailments to a set of underlying factors or causes: political oppression or domination; radical inequality between rich and poor; xenophobia sometimes resulting in genocide; terrorist violence; and the abuse of religions and ideologies. If such ailments occurred on a small scale or in a limited group of people, efforts would quickly be made to find remedies to combat the existing ills. However, if they happen on a large scale—in nations or in the global community—fatalism often takes over, backed up by the argument that ills of this magnitude must be the work of inscrutable "nature" or else divinely ordained. What is correct about this argument is that the cited ailments are not merely "mental" phenomena or matters of opinion, but sufferings inflicted on multitudes of people seen as concretely "embodied" human beings. Here might be the beginning of a "natural" philosophy of politics, a philosophy taking seriously the notion of politics occurring in a "body politic."[2]

In ancient times, human societies were typically seen as tightly

101

knit, homogeneous entities or organisms dominated by a supreme king or ruler representing divine power. From this angle, kings or rulers were seen as embodiments of a godlike agency, while the people at large were a passive body under the sway of destiny. During the Christian Middle Ages, Western societies were governed by a combination of worldly and spiritual rule; Ernst Kantorowicz speaks appropriately of "the king's two bodies" as the emblem of royal absolutism.[3] During the Renaissance and Enlightenment, the people at large slowly awakened from the "slumber of tutelage" (to use Kant's phrase) and began to discover their own role as agents and not merely passive victims of political events. The result was a series of dramatic social-political changes and revolutionary upheavals. This sequence of changes is often interpreted as a process of "secularization" involving the growth of agnostic disbelief; however, this reading is lopsided and misleading. What happened in modernity or the modernizing process was rather that political agency was predominantly (mis)construed as instrumental fabrication, as the construction of the "body politic" as an artificial body through contractual design. Here we have the signature conception of modern Western political thought, which views the political community or "state" as an artifact created through a social contract—a conception that has taken several shapes.

In the following I shall, in a first step, discuss this modern conception of the "body politic" as it was developed by a string of leading thinkers, from Thomas Hobbes to Rousseau. In a second step I show how, during the nineteenth century—and chiefly under the influence of positivism and natural "scientism"—politics and political agency were increasingly construed as an empirical process subject to quasi-scientific natural or biological laws. By way of conclusion, I turn to more recent developments in the twentieth century, when—partly under the impact of phenomenology, hermeneutics, and neo-Aristotelianism—efforts were made to overcome the conceptions of the "body politic" as either a willful construct or a purely physical organism. What emerges or what is rediscovered at this point is the notion of the political community as an interactive body, that is, as a shared "embodied praxis" or an affective "interbody."

The Body Politic as Artifact

One of the crucial presuppositions of ancient and classical thought was that human beings are social or political creatures and that hence political communities are at least to some extent "natural" bodies or organisms. During the Middle Ages, Thomas Aquinas translated the Aristotelian notion of "political animal" (*zoon politikon*) into "social animal"—but without a significant change of meaning. It was the rise of antiessentialism and voluntarism during the late Middle Ages that began to undermine this traditional conception. The decisive step in this respect was taken by Thomas Hobbes, who took direct aim at the Aristotelian legacy. His book *De Cive* (*The Citizen,* 1642)—antedating by nearly a decade the *Leviathan*—uses bold and uncompromising language. "The greatest part of those who have written about commonwealth," the opening chapter declares, "either suppose or require or beg us to believe that man is a creature born fit for society. The Greeks called him *zoon politikon,* and on this foundation [or axiom] they built up the doctrine of civil society"—an axiom that "though received by most, is yet certainly false and an error proceeding from our too slight contemplation of human nature." For Hobbes, those who inquire more deeply into the reasons why people gather in societies "shall easily find that this happens not because *naturally* it could not happen otherwise, but by accident" (or deliberate design). Although human inclinations—especially desire and fear—have something to do with the fact that people gather together, the actual establishment of the body politic requires an act of mature will and decision, which as such is contingent.[4]

Somewhat disarmingly, Hobbes acknowledges a certain "performative contradiction": the fact that his argument proceeds in a societal context from which it abstracts or claims to be aloof. He even speaks of a "wonderful kind of stupidity" seemingly involved in the strategy of placing at "the very threshold" of his argument this "stumbling block" of denying that human beings are "born fit for society." Deftly, Hobbes at this point shifts the accent from man's "social nature" to the nature or character of presocial, segregated individuals, and he finds the wellspring of the behavior of such individuals in pleasure and pain: that is, in the striving for individual benefit or advantage and the fear of resulting consequences. Basically, the relentless striving for individual gain or utility leads human beings into conflict and violent strife—which Hobbes, in defiance of the entire Aristotelian tradition, calls the "state of nature"—and the fear of the consequences of this conflict (the likelihood of violent death) leads human beings back into society by means of a deliberate and rationally designed agreement or contract. In Hobbes's stern, antitraditional language: human beings "do not by nature seek society for its own sake" (meaning that social life for humans is not *autoteles,* or an intrinsic good). Rather they seek society for an extrinsic purpose so that "they may receive some honor or profit from it"; hence honor and profit "we desire primarily," but social life only "secondarily." However, unless restrained, striving for benefit does not lead to social harmony but rather to the "war of all against all"—which is the source of fear: "We must therefore resolve [conclude] that the original [motive] of all great and lasting societies consisted not in the mutual good will men had toward each other, but in the mutual fear they had of each other."[5]

The motivations leading to the construction of social and political life are developed and fleshed out more clearly in *Leviathan* (1651). The first part of that text is devoted to the study of "man" (human nature) and especially of the "interior beginnings" of voluntary motions commonly called "passions." Hobbes here reaffirms the basic division of passions into desires or appetites and fears or aversions, where the former mean a movement "toward something which causes it" and the latter a motion "fromward [away from] something." This division, in the next step, is shown to be the engine driving human beings into society and the formation of the body politic. The impulse would be negligible if human desire were limited, but this is not the case: "I put forth a general inclination of all humankind, a perpetual and restless desire of power after power that ceases only in death." The restlessness of desire—manifest in boundless competition, in diffidence, and glory seeking—leads to the well-known result of violent strife: "Hereby it is manifest that during the time men live without a common power to keep them all in awe [that is, in the state of nature], they are in that condition which is called war, and such a war as is of every man against every man." Hobbes describes this condition of strife in stark language and vivid images, images that seem to derive from his experiences in the English civil war: There is then "no place for industry," "no culture of the earth," "no instruments of moving," "no arts, no letters, no society"; but what is worst of all, there is "continual fear and danger of violent death." The horror of this situation convinces human beings caught in this conflict at last that a better arrangement must be possible, an insight that—supported by fear of violent death and the desire for more "commodious living"—drives them into a contractual settlement designed to procure peace. In this settlement or compact all participants mutually agree to relinquish their unlimited freedom to do as they please, that is, to "lay down their right to all things" (*ius ad omnia*); at the same time they confer this right to a supreme or "sovereign" power able to enforce the terms of the contract.[6]

With this installation of supreme power, a new body comes into existence: a commonwealth, an artifact or artificial body that Hobbes in his vivid Baroque language calls "Leviathan." As we read in the text's introduction: "Nature (the act whereby God has made and governs the world) is by the art of man, as in many other things, so also in this imitated that it can make an artificial animal." This "art" or technical capacity is shown in "automata" and engines of many kinds. Yet art goes even further, namely, by "imitating that rational and most excellent work of nature, man." For "by art is created that great *Leviathan* called a commonwealth or state (in Latin *civitas*) which is but an artificial man, though of greater stature and strength than the natural for whose protection and defense it was intended," and "sovereignty is an artificial soul as giving life and motion to the whole body." In the section of the text dealing with the "commonwealth," Hobbes makes it clear that the compact undergirding the body politic is not merely a harmonious order such as one finds sometimes among animals in nature; rather, it erects a unified structure or body, "which is artificial." What unifies this body is a supreme and common power that is based not on sympathy or mere good intentions, but on will or willpower. "The only way to erect such a common power," we read,

> is to confer all their [participants'] power and strength upon one man or upon one assembly of men that may reduce all their wills, by a plurality of voices, unto one will: which is as much as to say to appoint one man or assembly of men to bear their person . . . and to submit their wills everyone to his will, and their judgments to his judgment. This is more than consent or concord; it is a real unity of them all, in one and

the same person, made by covenant of every man with every man.[7]

The metaphysical and even theological premises of this construction are not left in doubt. Behind the constructed edifice stands the image of divine omnipotence: a God characterized not so much by insight, love, or compassion, but by supreme will, whose power has been transferred (as Carl Schmitt has rightly observed) to the political sovereign—and subsidiarily to the citizens who construct the edifice by conferring to the sovereign their power or unbounded freedom. As Hobbes continues in the same section of the *Leviathan:* "This is the generation of that great *Leviathan* or rather (to speak more reverently) of that mortal God, to which we owe under the immortal God our peace and defence." For by this authority, given to him "by every particular member in the commonwealth," the sovereign has "the use of so much power and strength conferred on him, that by terror thereof he is enabled to form the will of them all."[8] Employing the language of his contemporary Spinoza, one might say that the sovereign embodies the supreme *natura naturans* (deriving from God's omnipotence), a capacity that enables him to reduce citizens to mere "subjects" (*natura naturata*)—although the latter retain a residue of *natura naturans* through the transfer of their wills to the sovereign will (and the retention of their freedom in case of the sovereign's malfunction). Deviating from earlier philosophical and theological traditions, however, the driving motor behind this distribution of functions is not wisdom or practical virtue but willpower—a capability manifest above all in the construction (and possible deconstruction) of an artificial body called the state or commonwealth.[9]

The Hobbesian formula of technical construction became the dominant or canonical model of political life at least until the French Revolution—although repeated attempts were made to modify or else moderate the harshness of the Hobbesian design. A particularly noteworthy attempt was undertaken by John Locke, often styled as the founder of modern Western "liberalism," especially in his *Second Treatise on Government.* In an accommodating and irenic fashion, Locke there combined aspects of the Aristotelian legacy with the Hobbesian artifact—but the former were hardly able to camouflage the radical break or rupture. Together with Hobbes, Locke started his argument from the premise of an original, hence presocial "state of nature" composed of separate individuals endowed with perfect liberty to pursue their self-interest. In his words, the "natural" condition of human beings is "a state of perfect freedom to order their actions and dispose of their possessions and persons as they think fit . . . without asking leave or depending on the will of any other man." For Locke—echoing Aristotle or rather the "judicious" Anglican Hooker—the perfect freedom of humans in the original state was hemmed in by "the bounds of the law of nature" and thus apparently involved some sociable dependence. Yet, again with Hobbes, Locke's *Treatise* concurs that "the execution of the law of nature in that state is put into every man's hands, whereby everyone has a right to punish the transgressors of that law to such a degree as may hinder its violation." Curiously, although likely to be clouded by human self-interest, individual execution of the natural law for Locke does not result in serious conflict or dispute and certainly not in a Hobbesian state of war, which would be "a state of enmity and destruction." In fact, Locke's *Treatise* stipulates that there is a "plain difference between the state of nature and the state of war, which however some writers have confounded."[10]

On the basis of these premises, the subsequent steps are equally ambivalent. For Locke, the move from the natural to the civil state and the construction of the body politic is prompted not by overwhelming fear (especially fear of violent death), but rather by lingering defects or "inconveniences" of the original condition. As he writes: "Civil government is the proper remedy for the inconveniences of the state of nature, which must certainly be great where men may be judges in their own case, since it is easy to imagine that he who was so unjust as to do his brother an injury will scarce be so just as to condemn himself for it." Hence, instead of being driven by fear, human beings are moved into social life more gently by the desire for comfort and sociality—but the move is effected again through contract or deliberate design. For we read, "to supply those defects and imperfections which are in us [in the original state] . . . we are naturally induced to seek communion and fellowship with others," and this can happen only by people's "own consent" whereby "they make themselves members of some politic society." The actual character of the contract and the resulting construction of the commonwealth are not very different from the Hobbesian model. Through the joining of individual wills a new supreme will is generated: "Wherever any number of men so unite into one society as to quit everyone his executive power of the law of nature and to resign it to the public, there and there only is a political or civil society," a society that makes "one people one body politic under one supreme government." With this move the original "state of nature" comes to an end and makes room for a "commonwealth," which sets up "a judge on earth with authority to determine all the controversies and redress the injuries that may happen to any member of that commonwealth."[11]

In addition to the denial of a possible Hobbesian state of war, Locke's *Treatise* exhibits another curious ambivalence: the simultaneous assertion of the end of the state of nature and its preservation in the commonwealth. Although admitting that the erection of the body politic terminates the original state and "puts men out of the state of nature into that of the commonwealth," this admission is nearly reversed in the chapter on "the beginning of political societies." As Locke states there in a famous passage: this beginning happens "by [each] agreeing with other men to join and unite into a community for their comfortable, safe, and peaceable living one amongst another, in a secure enjoyment of their properties and a greater security against any that are not [part] of it." The crucial passage here concerns the "secure enjoyment of their properties." Although it is in the state of nature that "man" has by nature "a power to preserve his property, that is, his life, liberty, and estate," and defend it against injury by any means, the formation of the body politic apparently makes no dent in this original power. Probably one of the most fateful aspects of Locke's text is his doctrine of the "naturalness" of human property and its undisturbed maintenance in the commonwealth, that is, the equation of private de facto possession with a de jure public property (an equation that Hobbes would have been loath to accept). The naturalness of property is announced in the *Treatise* in the so-called labor theory of value, which states: "Though the earth and all inferior creatures be common to all men, yet every man has a 'property' in his own 'person.' . . . The 'labor' of his body and the 'work' of his hands, we may say, are properly his." More specifically, "whatever he removes out of the state that nature has provided and left it in, he has mixed his labor with it and joined to it something that is his own and thereby makes it his [exclusive] property." As is well known, the *Trea-*

tise, to Locke's credit, does not advocate the unlimited accumulation of private property; rather, reflecting the conditions of an agrarian society, it adds the notion of "spoilage": "As much as anyone can make use of to any advantage of life before it spoils, so much he may by his labor fix a property in."[12]

Seen as a doctrine and influential political ideology, the "liberalism" inaugurated by Locke has always exhibited the noted ambivalence: the tension or rather antinomy between nature and artifact, between unlimited natural freedom and the body politic. This antinomy was intensified by developments that happened after Locke's period: the progressive transformation of an agrarian into an industrial society, the replacement of barter by the market, of the primacy of agricultural goods by money or capital, and hence the removal of "spoilage." In the course of these developments, "liberal" Western societies were increasingly revealed as a conflicted or antinomian body: a body riveted between unlimited desire (for accumulation) and fear (of loss), between private freedom of will and external constraint. In terms of the "body politic," the oscillation is between a radical laissez-faire regime (in which the rich dominate the poor) and the Hobbesian *Leviathan* (styled as "security state")—an oscillation that, in times of crisis, always tilts toward the Hobbesian side.

This basic tension was both recognized and attempted to be removed by Jean-Jacques Rousseau in his *Social Contract.* As the opening passage of that text declares: "Man was born free, and everywhere he is in chains. . . . How has this change come about? I do not know. What can render it legitimate? I believe that I can settle this question." Together with Hobbes and Locke, Rousseau starts from an original condition of freedom in which every individual is in charge of his/her self-preservation. As in the case of Locke, the hazards and inconveniences of that condition prompt individuals to enter into a social pact or contract with the (Lockean) aim to create "a form of association which may defend and protect with the whole force of the community the person and property of every associate, and by means of which each, coalescing with all, may nevertheless obey only himself, and remain as free as before." To accomplish the latter feat, Rousseau takes refuge in the Hobbesian notion of sovereignty—with the important twist that the latter is lodged not in an individual ruler, but in the collectivity of all members embodying their "general will."

In this manner, Lockean liberalism is transformed in the direction of a "people's republic" (or a popular *Leviathan*).[13]

Positivism and Naturalism

The model of the body politic as an artifact erected by social contract is the signature formula of modern Western political thought, and its effects lingered on long after the demise of its founders. This does not mean that ensuing years did not bring radical changes or reformulations that steadily pushed the standard model into the background, reducing it to a residual resource. What particularly was eclipsed was the notion of a "state of nature" as an arena of radical freedom coupled with the constructive device of a social contract. Although treated by the founders more as a hypothetical premise than as an actual occurrence, these ideas were bound to collide with the empirical-scientific temper of the nineteenth century. What chiefly chagrined devotees of that temper were lingering "metaphysical" traces inherited from the Baroque and Enlightenment periods: traces accentuating the rational autonomy of human beings and their spontaneous constructive or engineering capability. For natural scientists as well as empirical utilitarians, all these traces were "ghosts in the machine" that could be exorcised by a rigorous reliance on cause-effect explanation. In the famous words of Jeremy Bentham, the idea of a "state of nature" replete with natural rights was simply "rhetorical nonsense on stilts." Once these stilts are removed, the underlying mechanism of all human affairs comes to the fore: the mechanism of pleasure and pain, desire and fear—which equally governs both natural and artificial (or political) bodies.[14]

During the nineteenth century, the spirit of the scientific age was carried forward especially by a movement or orientation called "positivism" because of its stress on positive-empirical knowledge to the exclusion of all metaphysical or rationalistic premises. According to one prominent student, positivism involves "a philosophical tendency oriented around natural science and striving for a unified view of the world of phenomena, both physical and human, through the application of the methods and the extension of the results whereby the natural sciences have attained their unrivaled position in the modern world." What the movement aimed at was the universal triumph of the empiricist method, which alone can grant "positive" knowledge of "the facts and things of immediate perception as well as the relations and uniformities which inquiry may discover without transcending experience."[15] By common consent, the leading sponsor of the movement was Auguste Comte, who gained prominence through his *System of Positive Polity* (1851–54) and *The Catechism of Positivism* (1852). In these and related texts, Comte developed a new discipline or science that he first called "social physics" and later simply "sociology." The new science for him involved two branches: "social statics" and "social dynamics," where the former deals with the existing network of practices, customs, and ideas, while the latter examines the development or evolution of society through the three stages of theology, metaphysics, and science. After having overcome the first stage, the hallmark of the Enlightenment for Comte was the invention of such "fictions" as the "state of nature," "natural rights," the "social contract," and "popular sovereignty." The new and dawning period, however, heralded the erasure of these fictions in favor of knowledge: "The true *positive* spirit consists in substituting the study of the invariable laws of phenomena for their so-called [hidden] causes, in a word, in studying the *how* instead of the *why*."[16]

In the domain of evolution, the positivist-scientific agenda was implemented by the biologist Charles Darwin, whose *Origin of the Species* (1859) traced the organic development in physical nature not to some intentional design or purposive will, but to a process of "natural selection" in which the more "fit" type of species advances at the cost of the weaker organisms. Although initially confined narrowly to the biological domain, some of Darwin's ideas were soon transferred to the social and political arena, where they gave rise to such doctrines as the "social struggle for survival" and the "survival of the [socially] fittest." This transfer was accomplished chiefly by the British theorist Herbert Spencer, in whose writings evolution was shown to be a process of complex differentiation and recoordination, a quasi-mechanical process devoid of intent and applicable across the board from physics to politics. In Spencer's words: "Evolution is an integration of matter and concomitant dissipation of motion"—a movement where "matter passes from a relatively indefinite, incoherent homogeneity to a relatively definite coherent heterogeneity" and where "retained motion undergoes a parallel transformation." In order to leave the evolutionary development as undisturbed as possible, and thus to promote the survival of the socially fittest, Spencer's texts advocated minimal governmental interference, largely in tune with the "liberal" (laissez-faire) maxim that the regime that governs least governs best. On the motivational level, his work endorsed the pleasure-pain principle—and again across the board from physics to social life, in the sense that pleasurable sensations were assumed to accompany acts promoting survival and painful sensations acts detrimental to survival.[17]

In the latter respect, Spencer could rely on a psychological doctrine that by then was already well established: "utilitarianism," as articulated chiefly by Jeremy Bentham. In formulating the so-called utilitarian calculus, Bentham drew inspiration from a string of Baroque and Enlightenment thinkers who—without always presenting a full-fledged theory—had insisted on the central role of pleasure and pain as the governing engine of human conduct (in both private and public life).[18] In his famous *Introduction to the Principles of Morals and Legislation* (1789), Bentham had stated his basic premise in clear terms: "Nature has placed mankind under the governance of two sovereign masters, *pain* and *pleasure*. It is for them alone to point out what we ought to do, as well as to determine what we shall do." Pleasure and pain, he added, are the sensations that provide us with the "standard of right and wrong," while nature anchors those sensations in a "chain of causes and effects." As previously indicated, Bentham had scant or no respect for the Enlightenment ideas of state of nature, natural rights, or natural justice. It is pleasure itself that has to be seen as "good," pain itself as "bad" or "evil." In terms of political arrangements, early utilitarianism anticipated Spencer's laissez-faire agenda. Shunning the idea of a common good (or the "good life"), social or public life for Bentham was simply the summation of private individual interests. As a corollary, the role of government was basically negative, and the glory of citizenship was negative freedom (from government): "Every law is an evil, because every law is a violation of liberty."[19]

Although contested by other orientations (some favoring social collectivism), positivism and utilitarianism became the dominant paradigms of the nineteenth century, whose ramifications and offshoots penetrate deeply into more recent times. My purpose here is not to dwell on all these offshoots; rather, I limit myself to implications for the "body politic." As can readily be seen, by focusing on external (or externally induced) sensations and mechanisms, the two paradigms treat the body politic basically as a physical organism that is sensual but devoid of ethical sensibility. (Invoking again Spinozist language, the accent seems to be entirely on *natura naturata,* while *naturans* is reduced to a mystery removed from cognition.) For present purposes I want to draw attention briefly to traces or remnants of positivism that (perhaps surprisingly) can be found in some recent "post-modern" writings. In particular, I lift up for discussion a recent text called *Political Physics* (2001), whose title clearly evokes Comte's idea of a "social physics."

In this text, the author John Protevi focuses on the work of two leading post-modern thinkers, Jacques Derrida and Gilles Deleuze, with the aim (he says) of exploring "their respective approaches to the question of the *body politic."* Let me leave open the question whether the two thinkers are well chosen for Protevi's purpose. My concern here is simply with the interpretive slant. Among the two thinkers, the author acknowledges, Derrida is less helpful and at best provides a gateway to "political physics" properly speaking. Although "destroying the self-evidence" of the various traditional systems, he writes, Derrida can only "prepare the way for the radicality of Deleuzian historical-libidinal materialism: the principles guiding the empirical study of forceful bodies politic in their material production." What Derrida's "deconstructive" agenda is good for is its ability to "move us from the pretensions of metaphysics or phenomenology as the self-grounding of a rational, meaningful sign system . . . to the inscription of marks in a world of force and [textual] signification." After deconstructing the social contract and other metaphysical premises, however, his body politic remains "an inarticulate ('mystical') other." Thus, while demolishing the metaphysics of politics, his work cannot "offer us an empirical research program for exploring the [political] text and the material bodies formed therein."[20]

Deleuze's work, in Protevi's reading, brings the potential contained in Derrida's approach to positive (or positivist) fruition. Positive fruition here means the disclosure of the "principles guiding the empirical study of forceful bodies politic." In a manner distantly akin to the notions of "bio-power" and "micropolitics" (employed by Michel Foucault), Deleuzian analysis is said to engage "all the powers of contemporary physics and biology" to study "sectors of the contemporary global system which gleefully embrace difference and flow." For Protevi, three main ideas are at work in this enterprise: those of "forceful bodies," of "anti-hylomorphism," and of "material self-ordering." The first notion—clearly the centerpiece—refers to "particular force-arrangements of chemical, biological and social bodies," which are themselves force-constellations and hence "forceful bodies politic." The denial of "hylomorphism" means the rejection of purposely designed artifacts (or artificial bodies), that is, of "the imposition of an architect's vision of form on chaotic matter." The last notion, of "material self-ordering," refers to the immanent, nonpurposive arrangement of elements in accord with recent "complexity theory."[21] Although impressive in its radicality and its display of neopositivist terminology, *Political Physics* in the end is bound to leave the reader puzzled or at sea. Where in all this array of forces is there room for human beings with their joys and sufferings? Are they simply cogs (*naturata*) in a self-propelled mechanism? How does complexity theory deal with the whims of political power? How do "forceful bodies" protect us against injustice, corruption, oppression, and torture?

Politics as Embodied Praxis

The issues of injustice, corruption, and oppression bring to the fore aspects of political life that no theory of politics (no matter how scientifically sophisticated) can safely ignore—especially in our time. More than any other modern period, our age has been afflicted with a deluge of injustice, oppression, and corruption—ills accompanied by extensive mayhem and violent atrocities. To a greater or lesser extent, all the major modern worldviews or ideologies have contributed to these afflictions. Although seemingly benign in its focus on freedom and "natural rights," modern liberalism has been a frequent accomplice of imperialism and colonial domination—on the pretext of bringing the blessings of liberty and progress to "underdeveloped" populations. Its later offshoot—laissez-faire liberalism—has sponsored the private accumulation of wealth to such an extent that societies have become split into the two bodies of the rich and the poor, with the former (a minority) exploiting the masses of the latter. On the other hand, while seeking to correct this division, social collectivism has tended to produce its own calamities and disasters: primarily those of totalitarian coercion under either nationalist or communist auspices. To compound this series of afflictions, all the modern worldviews—from liberalism and socialism to positivism and utilitarianism—have been wedded to the unlimited pursuit of "positive" science and the technological exploitation of nature: a pursuit whose trajectory conjures up the dual calamities of nuclear holocaust and ecological destruction.

To be sure, the picture of modernity given here is simplified and overdrawn. Throughout the modern period we find recessed counter-movements or counter-tendencies that challenge the focus on self-indulgence, on individual or collective self-interest. A prominent counter-movement of this type was the group of Scottish moralists—from Francis Hutcheson to Adam Ferguson and Thomas Reid—who sought to counterbalance self-interest with the motivation of compassion and the role of transformative education. Another counter-tendency was the vogue of German classical literature (Goethe, Schiller) and philosophy (Kant, Hegel, Schelling), a vogue continued and modified by later Romanticism (from Schlegel and Hölderlin to Wordsworth and Shelley).[22] In more recent times, other valuable resources for a counter-perspective are provided by American pragmatism (James, Dewey), European phenomenology and hermeneutics (Heidegger, Gadamer, Merleau-Ponty), and the worldwide renewal of Aristotelian "virtue ethics" (MacIntyre, Du Weiming). What emerges from this confluence of currents is a reassessment of the meaning of politics, above all the meaning of the "body politic." If these currents are taken seriously, the body politic can no longer be viewed as a mere artifact constructed for extrinsic, instrumental purposes (such as national glory, economic wealth, or security). Nor can that body be seen as a mere assemblage of physical nerves and corpuscles held together by "complexity." Although not reducible to a mental idea, the body politic is also more than just a "libidinal" body—if by "libido" is meant the unilateral desire for appropriation and self-gratification. A better way to describe the body politic would be to call it an affective, solicitous, or "caring" body where all members are linked through mutual ethical engagement and a shared commitment to justice and general well-being.

A body of this kind was clearly involved in Aristotle's treatment of the political community as an arena of ethical practice, a practice geared not toward the achievement of extrinsic aims, but toward the intrinsic good of political practice: the formation or transformation of human beings into responsible citizens. As Aristotle pointed out in his ethical writings, civic virtues are not simply innate qualities but need to be practiced like other human abilities in a concrete public context; and like piano playing or flute playing, the practice carries within it its own good or reward: in this case, the achievement of public happiness and peace. Thus, virtues need indeed to be "embodied"—not in a machine or a selfish libidinal organism, but in a shared, responsive, and affectionate body that Aristotle called "civic friendship."[23] Another valuable insight regarding the public body comes to us from Montesquieu's *Spirit of the Laws.* According to that text, political societies or communities regularly are held together by a set of laws, rules, and procedures. But what is decisive is not so much the static set of rules, but the dynamic motivations and aspirations—the *natura naturans*—undergirding these rules, which he termed the "spirit" of laws. In the case of republics or democracies, Montesquieu singled out one central requisite or required affectionate commitment: namely, the "love of equality"—where equality does not signify a numerical sameness, but a qualitative bond of respect and sympathy. (I have indicated before how far contemporary "democracies" have traveled from this requisite.) In talking about this qualitative bond, one must also not forget the work of Spinoza, whose writings on politics brought closely together *natura naturans* and *naturata,* emphasizing that the former engenders that affective ethical bonding of members without which the body politic cannot subsist.[24]

Among more recent thinkers, glimpses of an affective body politic can also be found, I believe, in some of the texts of Merleau-Ponty and Martin Heidegger. For the former, the human body was never an isolated cauldron of libidinal impulses, but always an "interbody" carefully negotiating the crossroads between self and other, sameness and difference, familiarity and strangeness. For this reason, the body—including the body politic—was never a finished product, but always a "becoming" body, a body undergoing the process of formation and transformation. His posthumously published text *The Visible and the Invisible* speaks intriguingly of the "flesh" of the world characterized by intertwining and reversibility, a passage showing that "there is neither me nor the other as 'positive' subjectivities," but rather there are "two caverns, two opennesses, two stages where something will take place." Accordingly, "flesh" for Merleau-Ponty is not the objective (physical) body or the body posited by the cogito as its property; rather, it is sensuality or sensibility "in the twofold sense of what senses and what one senses."[25]

Similar glimpses can also be gleaned from the writings of Heidegger—provided his central notion of "Being" (borrowed from Aristotle) is not seen as an abstract category, substantive, or noun, but rather as a verb, with the result that being is always a "becoming," an enabling potency (or *naturans*) that allows all beings to be ("letting-be"). In the same way, human *Dasein* or "being-in-the-world" is likewise involved in continuous becoming or formation—a process, moreover, that is accompanied by affect or mood (*Stimmung*), which in turn is anchored in the central wellspring of "care" and "solicitude" (*Sorge* and *Fürsorge*). It is true that Heidegger himself did not fully work out the implications of his thought for politics or the body politic (in some ways he even hindered this endeavor). But some recent scholars have taken promising steps in this direction. Thus, commenting on Heidegger's overcoming of the mind-body dualism, Frank Schalow refers to the "incarnality of being" in Heidegger's thought, a notion applying with equal force to individual embodiment and to the communal body politic (and even to the cosmos seen as body).[26]

If the political community is really embodied, then all its members share in the happiness or flourishing of that body, but also in its sufferings, calamities. As indicated before, political communities in recent times have been exposed to a particularly grievous battery of calamities and even catastrophes. On the domestic level, societies have been subjected to the yoke of ruthless domination and exploitation—either by private corporate elites or by agencies of the state—and frequently also to the plague of torture, genocide, and ethnic cleansing. Under the aegis of globalization, these ills have been magnified and extended to the level of the global community or cosmopolis. If these are the major calamities—and I believe my diagnosis is not far off the mark—then what are the needed remedies or cures? Fortunately, in these matters we are not entirely left ignorant or at sea. We have the teachings of Plato and Aristotle but also the teachings of great thinkers in other cultures, like al-Farabi, Ibn Rushd, Confucius, and Mencius. What all these teachers counsel is a turnaround or *metanoia:* a turning from the radical pursuit of self-interest to the search for the "common good" or the "good life"; for all of them, this turning requires the steady practice of civic virtues. By way of conclusion, I want to invoke the marvelous remedies proposed by Mahatma Gandhi, which he called *ahimsa* and *satyagraha*. *Ahmisa* here means not just the noninfliction of violence, but the steady practice of nonviolence in the sense of the cultivation of solicitude, compassion, and care. *Satyagraha*, in turn, means the pursuit of lived (or living) truth, ethical goodness or justice, and embodied sensibility (or beauty). These, I am convinced, are the guideposts whose observance yields social peace and well-being and whose neglect yields misery and destruction.[27]

8. A Secular Age?

Reflections on Taylor and Panikkar

Why do you stand looking into heaven?

—Acts 1:11

At least in the Western context, our age is commonly referred to as that of "modernity"—a term sometimes qualified as "late modernity" or "post-modernity." Taken by itself, the term is nondescript; in its literal sense, it simply means a time of novelty or innovation. Hence, something needs to be added to capture the kind of novelty involved. To pinpoint this innovation, modernity is also referred to as the "age of reason" or the age of enlightenment and science—in order to demarcate the period from a prior age presumably characterized by unreason, metaphysical speculation, and intellectual obscurantism or darkness. Seen in this light, modernity for a large number of people—including supporters of scientific and social progress—is a cause for rejoicing, celebration, and unrelenting promotion. As is well known, however, this chorus of support has for some time been accompanied by discordant voices pointing to the dark underside of modernity, evident in what Max Weber called the "disenchantment" of the world and others (more dramatically) the "death of God" or the "flight of the gods." More recently, discontent has given rise to claims regarding an inherent "crisis" of modernity manifest in the slide toward materialism, consumerism, irreligion, and a general "loss of meaning."[1]

For present purposes I want to lift up for consideration two highly nuanced and philosophically challenging assessments of our modern condition: Charles Taylor's *A Secular Age* (2007) and Raimon Panikkar's *The Rhythm of Being* (2010). As it happens, both texts are strongly revised versions of earlier Gifford Lectures (presented respectively in 1999 and 1989). Before proceeding, a word of caution: neither of the two thinkers belongs to one of the polarized camps—which means that neither is an uncritical "booster" or else a mindless "knocker" of the modern age.[2] Both thinkers share many things in common. Both complain about certain glaring blemishes of the modern, especially the contemporary period; both deplore above all a certain deficit of religiosity or spirituality. The differences between the two authors have to do mainly with the details of their diagnosis and proposed remedies. In Taylor's view, the modern age—styled as the "secular age"—appears marked by a slide into worldly agnosticism, into "exclusive humanism," and above all into an "immanent fame" excluding or marginalizing theistic "transcendence." Although sharing the concern about "loss of meaning," Panikkar does not find its source in the abandonment of (mono)theistic transcendence; nor does he locate this source in secularism or "secularity" per se—seeing that, in view of its temporality, faith is necessarily linked with a given age (or *saeculum*). Instead of stressing the dichotomy between immanence and transcendence, Panikkar focuses on the pervasive "oblivion of being" in our time, an oblivion that can only be overcome through a renewed remembrance of the divine as a holistic happening in a "cosmotheandric" mode.

A Secular Age

At the very beginning of his massive study, Taylor distinguishes among three kinds of secularity or "the secular": "secularity 1" involves the retreat of faith from public life; "secularity 2" denotes a diminution or vanishing of faith among certain people; and "secularity 3" involves the erosion of the very conditions of possibility of shared faith. While in the first type, public spaces are assumed to be "emptied of God, or of any reference to ultimate reality," and whereas in the second type secularity consists "in the falling off of religious belief and practice, in people turning away from God," the third type involves a more pervasive change: namely, "a move from a society where belief in God is unchallenged and indeed, unproblematic, to one in which it is understood to be one option among others, and frequently not the easiest to embrace." Taken in the third sense, secularity means more than the evacuation of public life or else the loss of a personal willingness to believe; rather, it affects "the whole context of understanding in which our moral, spiritual or religious experience and search takes place." Viewed on this level, an age or a society would be secular or not "in virtue of the conditions of experience of and search for the spiritual." As Taylor emphasizes, the focus of his study is on the last kind of secularity. In his words: "So I want to examine our society as secular in this third sense, which I could perhaps encapsulate in this way: the change I want to define and trace is one which takes us from a society in which it was virtually impossible not to believe in God, to one in which faith, even for the staunchest believer, is one human possibility among others. . . . Belief in God is no longer axiomatic."[3]

In seeking to flesh out the meaning of secularity as a mode of modern experience, Taylor's text very quickly introduces the notion of "exclusive humanism" or "self-sufficient humanism," characterized by a neglect of transcendence. An important criterion here is the notion of a "fullness of life" and whether this fullness can be reached by human resources alone or requires a step "beyond" or "outside." "The big obvious contrast here," we read, "is that for believers the account of the place of fullness requires reference to God, that is, something beyond human life and/or nature; where for unbelievers this is not the case." Typically, for believers fullness or completion is received as a gift, whereas for unbelievers the source of completion resides "within." Appeal to internal resources can take many forms. In modernity, the appeal is frequently to the power of reason and rational knowledge. However, self-sufficiency can also be predicated on a "rigorous naturalism." In that case, the sources of fullness are not transcendent but are to be "found in Nature, or in our own inner depths, or in both." Examples of such naturalism are provided by "the Romantic critique of disengaged reason, and most notably certain ecological ethics of our day, particularly deep ecology." Other forms of self-sufficiency or internal self-reliance can be found in versions of Nietscheanism and existentialism, which draw empowerment "from the sense of our courage and greatness in being able to face the irremediable, and carry on nonetheless." A further modality can be detected in recent modes of post-modernism, which, while dismissive of claims of self-sufficient reason, yet "offer no outside source for the reception of power."[4]

In subsequent remarks the distinction between inside and outside ("within-without") is further sharpened by the invocation of the binaries of immanence/transcendence and natural/supernatural. "The shift in background, or better the disruption of the earlier background," Taylor writes, "comes best to light when we focus on certain distinctions we make today: for instance, that between the immanent and the transcendent, the natural and the supernatural. . . . It is this shift in background, in the whole context in which we experience and search for fullness, that I am calling the coming of a secular age, in my third sense . . . [and] that I want to describe, and perhaps also (very partially) explain." In general terms, modernity for Taylor assumes the character of a "secular age" once priority is granted to immanence over transcendence and to a self-sufficient humanism over divine interventions. "The great invention of the [modern] West," he writes, "was that of an immanent order of Nature whose working could be systematically understood and explained on its own terms." This notion of immanence involves denying, or at least questioning, "any form of interpenetration between the things of Nature, on the one hand, and the 'supernatural,' on the other." Seen from this angle, he adds, "defining religion in terms of the distinction immanent/transcendent is a move tailor-made for our culture." From a humanist perspective, the basic question becomes "whether people recognize something beyond or transcendent to their lives."[5]

At the core of the modern secular shift, for Taylor, is the issue of human fulfillment or "flourishing," that is, the question of "what constitutes a fulfilled life." At this point, an intriguing radicalism comes to the fore: in the sense that not only are the secular goals of fulfillment chastised, but the very idea of human flourishing is called into question. In earlier periods, he comments, it was still possible to assume that the best life involved our seeking "a good which is beyond, in the sense of being independent of human flourishing." In that case, the highest, most adequate human striving could include our aiming "at something other than human flourishing." Under the aegis of an exclusive or self-sufficient humanism, the possibility of such higher striving has atrophied and even vanished. Differently phrased: "secularity 3" in Taylor's sense came along together with the possibility and even probability of exclusive humanism. In fact, he states, one could offer this "one-line description" of the difference between earlier times and the secular age: "a secular age is one in which the eclipse of all goals beyond human flourishing becomes conceivable." Here is the crucial link "between secularity and a self-sufficing humanism." In traditional religion, especially in Christianity, a different path was offered: namely, "the possibility of transformation . . . which takes us beyond merely human perfection." To follow this path, it was needful to rely on "a higher power, the transcendent God." Seen in this light, Christian faith requires "that we see our life as going beyond the bounds of its 'natural' scope between birth and death; our lives extend beyond 'this life.'"[6]

It cannot be my ambition here to recapitulate Taylor's complex and lengthy tome; suffice it for present purposes to draw attention briefly to a central chapter dealing with the noted binary tension: the chapter titled "The Immanent Frame." At this point, the notion of an exclusive humanism is reformulated in terms of a "buffered self." According to Taylor, what modern secularity chiefly entails is "the replacement of a porous self by the buffered self," a self that begins to find "the idea of spirits, moral forces, causal powers with a purposive bent, close to incomprehensible." Buffering here involves "interiorization," that is, a withdrawal into "an inner realm of thought and feeling to be explored." Examples of this inward turn are said to be Romanticism, the "ethic of authenticity," and similar moves prompting us to "conceive ourselves as having inner depths." A corollary of this turn is "the atrophy of earlier ideas of cosmic order" and the rise of individual self-reliance and self-development, especially of an "instrumental individualism" exploiting worldly resources to its own exclusive benefit. Aggregating the various changes or mutations occurring in secular modernity, Taylor arrives at this succinct formulation: "So, the buffered identity of the disciplined [self-reliant] individual moves in a constructed social space, where instrumental rationality is a key value and time is pervasively secular [as clock time]. All of this makes up what I want to call 'the immanent frame.'" There is one important background feature that also needs to be taken into account: namely, that "this frame constitutes a 'natural' order, to be contrasted to a 'supernatural' one, an 'immanent' world, over against a possible 'transcendent' one."[7]

As Taylor recognizes, the boundary between the two "worlds" is not always sharply demarcated. Although ready to "slough off the transcendent," the immanent order occasionally makes concessions to the former. This happens in various forms of "civil region" and also in vaguely spiritual movements or expressions like Pentecostalism or "Romantic forms of art." However, such concessions are at best half-hearted and do not basically challenge or impede the "moral attraction" of immanence, of this-worldliness, of materialism and naturalism. As Taylor remarks with regard to the latter: "We can see in the naturalistic rejection of the transcendent . . . the ethical outlook which pushes to closure" in immanence, especially when the rejection is coupled with wholesale trust in modern natural science and associated technologies. Undergirded by this trust, the entire growth of modern civilization can be seen "as synonymous with the laying out of a closed immanent frame." To be sure, the text insists, the "moral attraction" of immanence is not absolutely compelling or preordained; it only prevails as a dominant pull or possibility, leaving room for other recessed alternatives. Resisting the dominant frame, some individuals find themselves placed in the cauldron of competing pulls—a cauldron giving rise sometimes to the striving for a radical exodus, accomplished through a stark (Kierkegaardian) "leap of faith." However, this personal experience of cross-pressures does not call into question the basic structure of secular modernity. What his study is trying to bring to the fore, Taylor concludes, is the "constitution of [secular] modernity" in terms of the emphasis on "'closed' or 'horizontal' worlds" that leave little or no place for "the 'vertical' or 'transcendent.'"[8]

Without doubt, Taylor's *A Secular Age* is an intellectual tour de force, as well as a spirited defense of religious faith (seen as openness to a transcendent realm). In an age submerged in the maelstrom of materialism, consumerism, and mindless self-indulgence, his book has the quality of a wake-up call, of a stirring plea for transformation and *metanoia*. Nevertheless, even while appreciating the cogency of this plea, the reader cannot quite escape the impression of a certain one-dimensionality. Despite repeated rejections of a "subtraction story" (treating modernity simply as a culture minus faith), the overall account presented in the book is one of diminution or impoverishment: leading from a holistic framework hospitable to transcendence to an "immanent frame" hostile to it. Surely, this is not the only story that can be told—and probably not the most persuasive one. In Taylor's presentation, immanence and transcendence, this world and the world "beyond," seem to be immutable binary categories exempt from change. Clearly, there is the possibility of another (more compelling) narrative: a story where immanence and transcendence, the human and the divine, encounter each other in ever new ways, leading to profound transformations on both (or all) sides. Curiously, Taylor's own earlier writings had been leaning more in that direction. One of his best-known earlier works, *Sources of the Self*, narrated the development of human selfhood from antiquity to modernity in a nuanced manner not reducible to a slide from porousness to buffered closure. Very little of this story remains in *A Secular Age*. In a similar manner, the "ethics of authenticity" (highlighted in one of his earlier books) now seems the be just another synonym for modern buffering and self-sufficiency. Even the move toward personal religiosity—celebrated earlier in the case of William James—now seems to be relegated to a marginal gloss on the "immanent frame." Hardly an echo seems to be left of the "thanks to Voltaire and others"—extended in his "Marianist Lecture"—for "allowing us to live the gospel in a purer way," free of the "often bloody forcing of conscience" marking previous centuries.[9]

As it seems to me, one of the more curious and troubling aspects of the book is the determined privileging of the "vertical" or "transcendent" dimension over the lateral or "horizontal worlds." Even if one were to grant the atrophy of transcendence, modernity styled as a "secular age" surely has witnessed important "horizontal," social-political developments by no means alien to a religious register: the demolition of ancient caste structures, the struggles against imperialism, the emancipation of slaves, the steady process of democratization promising equal treatment for people without regard for gender, race, and religion. Strangely, in a book seeking to distill the essence of Western modernity, these and similar developments occupy a minor or shadowy place, being eclipsed by the accent on verticality (heavily indebted to certain monotheistic creeds). The accent is all the more surprising in the context of a largely Christian narrative, given the traditional linkage of that faith with embodiment and "incarnation."[10] The downgrading or relative dismissal of the horizontal has clear repercussions with regard to "humanism" and the divine-human relationship. The conception of an "exclusive humanism" seems to leave ample room for a more open and nonexclusive type. Yet, despite an occasional acknowledgment of the possibility of nonexclusiveness, the point is not further developed or explored. Equally bypassed or sidelined is the possibility of a symbiosis of the divine, the human, and "nature"—a triadic structure requiring resolute openness on all sides. At one point, Taylor ponders the deleterious impact of a certain "non-religious anti-humanism" (associated mainly with Nietzsche and his followers). However, his own privileging of verticality conjures up the specter of a radically religious antihumanism—a specter bound to be disturbing in the context of the current vogue of fundamentalist rhetoric.[11]

The Rhythm of Being

To some extent, the preceding paragraph can serve as a gateway to the work of Raimon Panikkar, the renowned Spanish-Indian philosopher and sage (who passed away on August 26, 2010). Among many other intellectual initiatives, Panikkar is known for his endorsement of a triadic structure of Being—the so-called cosmotheandric conception—in which God (or the divine), human beings, and nature (or cosmos) are linked in indissoluble correlation or symbiosis. Seen from the angle of this conception, the radical separation or opposition between transcendence and an "immanent frame" seems farfetched if not simply unintelligible. It is fairly clear that Panikkar could not or would not have written a book titled *A Secular Age* with a focus on immanentization. For one thing, the two terms of the title for him are synonymous—seeing that "age" is equivalent to the Latin *saeculum.* More important, the divine (or transcendent) in Panikkar's view cannot be divorced from the temporal (or "secular") without jeopardizing or destroying the intimate divine-human relation and thereby the mentioned triadic structure. The distinctive and unconventional meaning of secularism or secularity is manifest in a number of his early writings that remain important in the present context. Thus, his book *Worship and Secular Man* (1973) put forward this provocative thesis: "Only worship can prevent secularization from becoming inhuman, and only secularization can save worship from being meaningless." To which he added this equally startling comment: "Now, what is emerging in our days, and what may be a 'hapax phenomenon,' a unique occurrence in the history of humankind, is—paradoxically—not secularism, but the sacred quality of secularism."[12]

Panikkar has never abandoned this provocative thesis; it still pervades powerfully his later writings, including *The Rhythm of Being*. As he notes in the preface to that book (written on Pentecost 2009), the original title of his Gifford Lectures was "The Dwelling of the Divine in the Contemporary World"—a phrase surely not far removed from the notion of sacred secularity. Although for various reasons the original title was changed, the "leading thread" of the book—he adds—"continues to be the same." What characterizes this "leading thread," despite textual revisions, is the idea of a radical "relationality" or "relativity" involving the three basic dimensions of reality: cosmos (nature), human beings, and God (or the divine)—where each of these dimensions is seen not as a static essence, but as an active and dynamic participant in the ongoing transformation of reality or "Being." As Panikkar states, what he intends to convey in his book is a new sense of *creatio continua* in which each one of us, in St. Bonaventure's phrase, is a "co-creator." A crucial feature of the intended relationality is the close linkage between the "temporal" and the "eternal," or between time and Being. "Time," we read, "is not an accident to life, or to Being. . . . Each existence is *tempiternal* . . . and with this observation we have already reached our topic of the 'Rhythm of Being,' which is ever old and ever new." Instead of bogging down in irremediable ruptures and dichotomies, this rhythm proceeds in the modality of mediation (*utrum*, both, as well as) and thus in "the *advaitic* language."[13]

Along with other ruptures and dichotomies, *The Rhythm of Being* also refuses to accept the split between the "vertical" and "horizontal" dimensions of reality. In fact, despite its basically philosophical and meditative character, the book elaborates more explicitly on present-day social-political ills than does the Canadian political thinker. For Panikkar, dealing with the "rhythm of Being" cannot be a mode of escapism but involves a struggle about "the very meaning" of life and reality—a struggle that has to be attentive to all dimensions of reality, even the least appealing. "In a world of crisis, upheaval, and injustice," he asks, "can we disdainfully distance ourselves from the plight of the immense majority of the peoples of the world and dedicate ourselves to 'speculative' and/or 'theoretical' issues? Do we not thereby fall prey to the powers of the status quo?" In language that becomes ever more urgent and pleading, he continues:

Can we really do "business as usual" in a world in which half of our fellow-beings suffer from man-made causes? Is our theory not already flawed by the praxis from which it proceeds? Are we not puppets in the hands of an oppressive system, lackeys to the powers that be, hypocrites who succumb to the allure and flattery of money, prestige, and honors? Is it not escapism to talk about the Trinity while the world falls to pieces and its people suffer all around us? . . . Have we seen the constant terror under which the "natives" and the "poor" are forced to live? What do we really know about the hundreds of thousands killed, starved, tortured, and *desapericidos*, or about the millions of displaced and homeless people who have become the statistical commonplace of the mass media?[14]

For Panikkar, we cannot remain bystanders in the affairs of the world but have to become involved—without engaging in mindless or self-promoting activism. In a disjointed and disoriented world, what is needed above all is a genuine search for the truth of Being and the meaning of life—which basically involves a search for justice and the "good life" (or the goodness of life). "We are all co-responsible for the state of the world," Panikkar affirms. In the case of intellectuals or philosophers, this responsibility entails that they "ought to be incarnated in their own times and have an exemplary function," which in turn means the obligation "to search for truth (something that has saving power) and not to chase after irrelevant verities." Genuine search for truth of life, however, proceeds from a lack or a perceived need that provides the compelling motivation for the quest: "Without this thirst for 'living waters,'" Panikkar writes, "there is no human life, no dynamism, no change. Thirst comes from lack of water." On this level, we are not dealing with epistemological, logical, or purely academic questions. Quest for life and its truth derives ultimately from "our existential thirst for the reign of justice," not from a passing interest or curiosity: "We are dealing with something that is more than an academic challenge. It is a spiritual endeavor to live the life that has been given us."[15]

The quest for life and its meaning, in Panikkar's presentation, is not simply a human initiative or an individual "project" (in Sartre's sense); nor is it an external destiny or a fate imposed from on high. The reason is that, in the pursuit of the quest, the human seeker is steadily transformed, just as the goal of the search is constantly reformulated or refined. This is where Panikkar's "holistic" or nondualistic approach comes into play, his notion of a constantly evolving and interacting triadic structure. As he writes: "I would like to help awaken the dignity and responsibility of the individual by providing a holistic vision," and this can only happen if, in addition to our human freedom, we remain attentive to the *"freedom of Being* on which our human and cosmic dignity is grounded." From a holistic angle, the different elements of reality are not isolated fragments but interrelated partners in a symphony or symbiosis where they are neither identical nor divorced. "Each entity," Panikkar states, "is not just a part, but an image or icon of the Whole, as minimal and imperfect as that image may be." Holism thus stands opposed to the Cartesian dualistic (subject/object) epistemology, without subscribing to a dialectical synthesis where differences are "sublated" in a universal (Hegelian) system. Importantly, holism does not and cannot equal "totalism" or "totalitarianism" because no one can have a grasp or overview of the totality or the "Whole." "No single person," we read, "can reasonably claim to master a global point of departure. No individual exhausts the totality of possible approaches to the real." For Panikkar, the most adequate idiom in which to articulate such holism is the Indian language of Advaita Vedanta: "*Advaita* offers the adequate approach . . . [because it] entails a cordial order of intelligibility, of an *intellectus* that does not proceed dialectically." Different from rationalistic demonstration, the *advaitic* order is "intrinsically pluralistic."[16]

By overcoming Cartesian epistemology, *advaitic* holism inaugurates a close relation between human mind and reality, or (in different language) between "thinking" and "Being." In this relation, thought not only thinks *about* Being (as an external object), but Being penetrates thinking as its animating ground. As Panikkar states pointedly: "The underlying problem is that of thinking and Being." What is conjured up by this problem is the Vedantic conception of *atman-braham* or else the Thomistic formula *anima quodammodo omnia.* Another, more general idiom is that of ontology. In Panikkar's words: "The consecrated word for what we were pondering about the Whole is precisely 'Being'—and we shall not avoid this word any longer." At this point, the text offers a passage that is not only evocative of but directly congruent with Heideggerian formulations. *"Thinking 'thinks Being,'"* we read. "Being begets thinking; one might even risk saying: Being 'beings thinking'" (in line with Heidegger's phrase that Being "calls forth" thinking). "Thinking is such only," the passage continues, "if it is permeated by Being. Thinking is an activity of Being. Being thinks; otherwise thinking would be nothing." This does not mean, of course, that human thinking can ever exhaust Being—which would result in "totalism" or totalization. Rather, thinking and Being are responsive to each other in a rhythmic "complementarity" or a spirited embrace: "The vision of the concrete in the Whole and the Whole in the concrete is, in fact, another way of saying that the relationship is rhythmic. Rhythm is not an 'eternal return' in a static repetition . . . [but] rather the vital circle in the dance between the concrete and the Whole in which the concrete takes an ever-new form of the Whole."[17]

For human beings, participation in this dance means not only lighthearted entertainment but involvement in a transformative struggle to overcome selfishness or possessive self-centeredness. Panikkar speaks in this context of a "purification of the heart," which is needed in order to join the dance. He quotes at this point the words of Hugo of St. Victor: "The way to ascend to God is to descend into oneself"; and also the parallel statement by Richard of St. Victor: "Let man ascend through himself above himself." What is involved here is not merely an epistemic principle, nor a purely deontological duty, but "an ontological requirement." As Panikkar stresses, the issue here is not an esoteric or private whim but simply this: that we shall not discover our real situation, collectively as well as individually, "if our hearts are not pure, if our lives are not in harmony within ourselves, with our surroundings, and ultimately with the universe [Being] at large." The text here adds a passage that can serve as the passkey to Panikkar's entire vision: "Only when the heart is pure are we in harmony with the real, in tune with reality, able to hear its voice, detect its dynamism, and truly 'speak' its truth, having become adequate to the movement of Being, the Rhythm of Being." The passage refers to the Chinese *Chung Yung* (in Ezra Pound's translation), saying: "Only the most absolute sincerity under heaven can effect any change," and adds: "The spiritual masters of every age agree that only when the waters of our spirit are tranquil can they reflect reality without deforming it."[18]

What becomes clear in this context is that some of Panikkar's key notions—like the "cosmotheandric" vision or "sacred secularity"—are not simply neutral-descriptive devices but are imbued with a dynamic, transformative potency. As one should note, however—and this is crucial—his notions do not reflect a bland optimism or trust in a "better future" but are based on "hope": which is a hope "of the invisible," a hope for a promised possibility. With regard to "sacred secularity," this possibility is not an empty pipe dream but is supported by a novel phenomenon (a *novum*) in our time: "This *novum* does not take refuge in the highest by neglecting the lowest; it does not make a separation by favoring the spiritual and ignoring the material; it does not search out eternity at the expense of temporality." Differently phrased: the *novum* consists in a growing attentiveness to holism in lieu of the customary polarities (of *this* world and the *other* world, the inner and the outer, the secular and the divine). A still further way to express the *novum* is the growing awareness of the "Rhythm of Being" and the growing willingness to participate in that rhythm. What is becoming manifest, we read, is that "we all participate in Rhythm," and that "Rhythm is another name for Being and Being is Trinity." The last formulation refers again to the triadic or "cosmotheandric" structure of reality. For, Panikkar states, "rhythm is intrinsically connected with any activity of the gods, men, and nature." In more traditional language, one might say that rhythm is "the cosmotheandric order of the universe, the *perichoresis* (*circuminsessio,* mutual in-dwelling) of the radical Trinity."[19]

As in the case of Taylor's *A Secular Age,* it cannot be my aim here to submit Panikkar's entire volume to reflective review and scrutiny. A few additional points must suffice. One point concerns the traditional conception of monotheism. The notion of *perichoresis*—coupled with the accent on the "metatranscendental" status of Being—does not seem to accord well with monotheistic "transcendence." In fact, Panikkar's text subjects the conception to strong critique. As he writes at one point: "I suspect that the days of unqualified theisms are not going to be bright." What troubles Panikkar, apart from philosophical considerations, is the implicit connection of monotheism with a heteronomous command structure ("God, King, President, Police"). "The titles of King and Lord," we read, "fit the monotheistic God quite well, and conversely, the human king could easily be the representative of

God, and his retinue a copy of the heavenly hierarchies." This is the gist of "political theology" (so-called). To be sure, traditional hierarchies no longer prevail—despite recurrent attempts at constructing "theocracies." What is required in the context of modern democracy is a radical rethinking of the monotheistic command structure. In Panikkar's words: "Regardless of certain forms of fundamentalism, both Christianity and Judaism clearly show that human freedom and love of neighbor belong to the *kernel* of their message." This means that any "revealed" monotheism must ultimately acknowledge its intrinsic reference to its "human reception" (and hence to *circuminsessio*). Differently phrased: divine revelation "has to fall on human grounds in order to be a belief for humans." This belief is "a human experience, humanly interpreted, and humanly received into the collective consciousness of a culture at a given time." Summarizing his view, Panikkar writes: "My position . . . is neither naively iconoclastic nor satisfied with a reformed monotheism. It recognizes the valid insight of belief in God, but at the same time it acknowledges that God is not the only symbol for that third dimension we call the Divine, and it attempts to deepen the human experience of the Divine by formulating it more convincingly for our times."[20]

In a central chapter of the book, titled "The Dwelling of the Divine" (capturing the originally intended title of the Gifford Lectures), Panikkar returns to the central meaning of the triadic structure understood as mutual in-dwelling. As he reaffirms, one-sided theisms "no longer seem to be able to satisfy the most profound urges of the contemporary sensibilities." What is coming into view instead is *perichoresis,* seen as radical relationality, where "everything is permeated by everything else." Seen from this angle, "man is 'more' than just an individual being, the Divine 'different' from a Supreme Lord, and the world 'other' than raw material to be plundered for utility or profit." This view can be grasped neither in the language of transcendence nor in that of immanence, because "we cannot even think" one without the other. Thus, where does the Divine dwell? "I would say," Panikkar states, "that the space of man is in God in much the same way as the space of God is in man." From this perspective, man and God are not two separable, independent substances: "There is no real *two* encompassing man and God . . . , but they are not *one* either. Man and God are neither *one* nor *two*." This, again, is the language of "*advaitic* intuition" (perhaps of

Heideggerian *Unterschied*). *Advaita,* we are told here, does not simply mean "monism," but rather "the overcoming of dualistic dialectics by means of introducing love [or wisdom] at the ultimate level of reality." Regarding the trinitarian structure, Panikkar takes pains to broaden the conception beyond traditional Christian theology. Both "esoteric Judaism and esoteric Islam," he notes, are familiar with the threefold structure of the Divine. Thus, Philo of Alexandria interpreted the vision of Abraham and his three "visitors" in a trinitarian fashion. The Muslim mystic Ibn Arabi was even more explicit when he wrote: "My beloved is three / —three yet only one; / many things appear as three / which are no more than one." And the Chinese Taoist Yang Hsuing explained the "great mystery" as constituting simultaneously "the way of Heaven, the way of Earth, and the way of Man."[21]

Toward the end of his book, Panikkar returns to the relation of meditation and praxis, of thinking and doing in a transformative process. As he writes: "The task of transforming the cosmos is not achieved by a merely passive attitude nor by sheer activism." What is needed is a "synergy" in which human beings are seen neither as designing engineers nor as victims: "The world does not 'go' independently from us. We are also active factors in the destiny of the cosmos. Otherwise, discourse about the dignity of man, his 'divinization' or divine character is an illusion." Seen from an *advaitic* angle, "man" is a "microcosmos" and even a "microtheos." Hence, human participation in the rhythm of the cosmos means "a sharing in the divine dimension" or what is sometimes called "salvation history." Participation in this dynamism is indeed a striving for a "better world"—but a striving where the latter is "neither the dream of an earthly paradise nor [a retreat into] the inner self alone," but rather a struggle for "a world with less hatred and more love, with less violence and more justice." For Panikkar, this struggle is urgent because the situation of our world today is "tragic" and "serious enough to call for radical measures." Ultimately, the struggle involves a quest for the "meaning of Life," which will never be found through selfish exploits or violent conquest but only "in reaching that fullness of Life to which [*advaitic*] contemplation is the way." As Panikkar finally pleads: "Plenitude, happiness, creativity, freedom, well-being, achievement etc. should not be given up but, on the contrary, should be enhanced by this transformative passage" from man-made history to a triadic redemptive story.[22]

Concluding Comments

The passage just cited highlights an important difference between Taylor and Panikkar. Basically, *The Rhythm of Being* is an affirmation and celebration of "life" in its deeper *advaitic* meaning. Panikkar uses as equivalents the terms *plenitude, happiness, creativity, freedom,* and *well-being;* another customary term is *flourishing* (often used to translate Aristotle's *endaimonia*). At another point, he introduces the word *life* "at the level of Being, as a human experience of the Whole"; the term here means "not only *anima,* animal life, but *physis, natura, prakriti,*" referring to "reality as a Whole." On this issue, *A Secular Age* appears astonishingly (and unduly) dismissive. As Taylor notes in his introduction, in modernity "we have moved from a world in which the place of fullness was understood as unproblematically outside or 'beyond' human life, to a conflicted age in which this construal is challenged by others which place it . . . 'within' human life." For Taylor (as mentioned before), the basic question raised by the modern secular age is "whether people [still] recognize something beyond or transcendent to their lives," that is, whether their highest aim is "serving a good which is beyond, in the sense of independent of human flourishing" or involving "something other than human flourishing." The truly believing or devout person is said to be marked by readiness "to make a profound inner break with the goals of flourishing in their own case"; unwillingness to do so is claimed to be the hallmark of "self-sufficient humanism." In sum: "A secular age is one in which the eclipse of all goals beyond human flourishing becomes conceivable."[23]

Taylor's comments here are puzzling—and also disturbing. They are disturbing in a time when many presumably religious people are ready to throw away their lives in the hope of gaining quick access to the "beyond." They are puzzling by jeopardizing the very meaning of faith. For most believers, salvation (or *moksha*) signifies precisely the highest level of flourishing and the ultimate fulfillment of life. What, then, does it mean for believers to seek something "outside or 'beyond' human life," or something "transcendent to their lives"? Commonly, the antithesis of life is said to be death. Is God (the monotheistic God) then a God of death or of the dead? Clearly, this cannot be the case if we listen to Isaiah's words: "The dead shall live, their bodies shall rise" (Isaiah 26:19). It becomes even less plausible if we recall Jesus's provocative saying: "Follow me, and leave the dead to bury their dead" (Matthew 8:22), or his admonition that "the Father raises the dead and gives them life" (John 5:21). As it happens, Taylor himself wavers on this point and has to resort to ambivalent language. "There remains a fundamental tension in Christianity," he writes. "Flourishing is good, nevertheless seeking it is not our ultimate goal. But even when we renounce it, we re-affirm it." And he adds: "The injunction 'Thy will be done' is not equivalent to 'Let humans flourish,' even though we know that God wills human flourishing."[24]

Rather than pursuing the contrast between the two thinkers, however, I want to emphasize here a commonality. While differing in many ways, neither Taylor nor Panikkar shows sympathy for theocracy or for any kind of religious triumphalism. Being turned off by the megalomania and massive power plays of our world, both thinkers are sensitive to new modes of religiosity—quite outside impressive spectacles and miraculous events. As it seems to me, one of the distinctive features of our age is not so much the "death of God" or the lack of faith, but rather the withdrawal and sheltering of the divine in recessed, inconspicuous phenomena of ordinary life. The Indian novelist Arundhati Roy has caught this aspect in her book *The God of Small Things*. Inspired by the Indian text, I tried to capture the sense of (what I called) "small wonder" in one of my earlier writings. Here are some lines:

> For too long, I fear, the divine has been usurped and co-opted by powerful elites for their own purposes. . . . For too long in human history the divine has been nailed to the cross of worldly power. However, in recent times, there are signs that the old alliance may be ending and that religious faith may begin to liberate itself from the chains of worldly manipulation. Exiting from the palaces and mansions of the powerful, faith—joined by philosophical wisdom—is beginning to take shelter in inconspicuous smallness, in those recesses of ordinary life unavailable to co-optation.[25]

The change in religious sensibility is vividly displayed in modern art, especially in modern and contemporary painting. As we know, in medieval art the presence of the divine or the sacred was expressed symbolically by a golden background and the haloes surrounding sacred figures. Modern art cannot honestly, or without caricature, imitate or replicate this mode of expression. This does not mean that the sense of sacredness has been lost or abandoned. As it seems to me, that sense resurfaces in less obvious, more subdued ways: for example, in the miniature paintings of Paul Klee or else in a still life by Paul Cézanne. Viewed from this angle, modern secularism has a recessed meaning that is actually the very reverse of the popular "secularization thesis" (meaning the triumph of this-worldliness). The French philosopher Maurice Merleau-Ponty—a strong admirer of Cézanne—had a phrase for it: "the invisible of the visible." Seen against this background, the relation between the two books reviewed here—*A Secular Age* and *The Rhythm of Being*—acquires a new meaning. Perhaps, one might conjecture, the "secular age," as portrayed by Taylor, functioned and functions as wholesome conduit, a clearing agent, to guide a more mature and sober humanity to the appreciation of the "rhythm of Being." If this is so (at least in approximation), then it may be propitious to remember Hölderlin's lines: "But where there is danger, a saving grace also grows."[26]

9. Post-Secularity and (Global) Politics

A Need for Radical Redefinition

> I will put my law within them, and I will write it upon
> their hearts.
>
> —Jeremiah 31:33

In recent intellectual discussions, the term *post-secularity* has acquired a certain currency or prominence. Like other hyphenated terms (post-modernism, post-metaphysics), the word exudes a certain irenic quality, in the sense that the harsh features of traditional conflicts—between faith and reason, religion and agnosticism—are presumably mitigated if not laid to rest. Unfortunately, this hope may be mistaken. Like many similar labels, the term *post-secularity* papers over disputes of interpretation that cannot be brushed aside. For some interpreters—clinging to the prefix *post*—the term signals the end of a loathed or despised aspect of modernity, its lapse into irreligion and agnostic "secularism," thus heralding a return to old-style religious orthodoxy (possibly under clerical auspices). Seen from this angle, the hyphenated expression means the correction of an errancy, an outgrowth of what Gilles Kepel has called "the revenge of God."[1] For another type of interpreter—attached to secularity or secularism—the phrase is a concession to the Zeitgeist, to the inevitably multicultural and multidimensional character of contemporary democracy. Averse to dogmatism and stirred by their "liberal" conscience, secular agnostics are willing to accommodate or tolerate deviant nonconformists, including religious people—provided their conduct and utterances submit to the dominant language game.

Thus, underneath the seemingly irenic phrase, the older animosities and resentments still persist; behind the facade of a hyphenated term, traditional culture wars continue. In some fashion, for both sides of the dispute, the terms *secularism* and *secularity* designate a "worldly" domain basically immune from "other-worldly" intrusion, a realm of "immanence" categorically opposed to religious "transcendence." The two sides differ in placing their evaluative preference respectively in opposing domains; the hyphenated phrase reflects mainly a pragmatic compromise. The question remains, however, whether the stipulated dichotomy—often styled "two-world" theory—can really be maintained. At a closer look, the dichotomy is quickly thrown into disarray. On a purely logical level, the two terms—*immanence* and *transcendence*—presuppose each other as mutual conditions of possibility—which means that they cannot be radically separated. More important, as mentioned in the preceding chapter, simple etymology contests such separation. Deriving from the Latin *saeculum* (age/century), secularism basically refers to the necessary time dimension of human experience—a temporality that inevitably permeates both reason and faith, both "worldly" cognition and religion (thus undercutting their presumed contrast). In the following I want to pursue these issues further. In a first step, I review the persisting conflict within "post-secularity," that is, the conflict between post-secular "secularists" and post-secular (or post-modern) religious traditionalists. What this review yields, I believe, is a basic commonality: namely, the shared and inevitable reliance on interpretation or hermeneutics—a point developed in a second step. By way of conclusion, I want to indicate the genuine relevance of "post-secularity"—properly interpreted—for both domestic democracy and the emerging global cosmopolis.

Secularity versus Faith

In mainstream liberal-democratic theory, the political regime is supposed to be removed from, and hence basically neutral toward, religion(s) or what are called "comprehensive worldviews." This conception was formulated most famously in the early writings of philosopher John Rawls. In subsequent years, however, this formula of sequestering religion in a private faith, removed from the public domain, was found to be too rigid and also not quite compatible with democratic standards (mandating the "free exercise of religion"). Hence, religion was allowed—within limits—to reenter the public realm, provided certain conditions regarding public conduct and linguistic discourse were met.[2] It is at this point that Jürgen Habermas—one of the originators of the term *post-secularity*—joins the debate. In several writings published during the past decade, he has sought to pinpoint clearly the conditions under which religion might reenter the public sphere. Thus, in an essay published in 2008 entitled "An Awareness of What Is Missing," Habermas stressed the stark distance separating modern enlightened reason from religious faith, a distance that also reflects stages of historical development. "The philosophically enlightened self-understanding of modernity," we read, "stands in a peculiar dialectical [conflictual?] relationship to the theological self-understanding of the major world religions which intrude into this modernity as the most awkward element from its past." From the angle of modern reason, both religion and traditional metaphysical worldviews have an ambivalent status: they are rejected in their present validity though (grudgingly) accepted as historical precursors. While acknowledging metaphysics "as belonging to the prehistory of its own emergence," modern thought "treats revelation and religion as something alien and extraneous." As Habermas insists, "the cleavage between secular knowledge and revealed knowledge cannot be bridged"—although secular or "post-metaphysical" reason may concede "the shared origin of philosophy and religion in the revolution of the Axial Age."[3]

In his essay, Habermas clearly accepts the Rawlsian formula regarding the relation between the public and private domains. "The constitutional state," he writes, "must not only act neutrally towards worldviews but it must rest on normative foundations which can be justified neutrally towards worldviews—and that means in post-metaphysical [i.e., secular] terms." This formula clearly imposes a heavy and primary burden on faith. "The religious communities," he adds, "cannot turn a deaf ear to this normative requirement." In fact, "the content of religion must open itself up to the normatively grounded expectation that it should recognize, for reasons of its own, the neutrality of the state towards worldviews. . . . This is a momentous step." Following the more "liberal" or accommodating arguments of the later Rawls, however, the essay also seeks to ease the burden imposed on religious belief: "Conversely, the secular state . . . must also face the question of whether it is imposing asymmetrical obligations on its religious citizens. For the liberal state guarantees the equal freedom to exercise religion not only as a means of upholding law and order, but also for the normative reason of protecting the freedom of belief and conscience of everyone." The upshot of this argument is the compromise that the state "may not demand anything of its religious citizens which cannot be reconciled with a life that is led authentically 'from faith.'" What is presupposed in this compromise, however, is the availability and maintenance of a common language in the public field, and this requisite brings into the foreground the issue of translation.[4]

From a secular or post-secular vantage point (that of Habermas), the situation is not only that the "cleavage" between secular reason and revelation "cannot be bridged," but that there are two different languages or discourses whose sharp contrast cannot be overcome except through an effort of translation—an effort designed to render religious idioms publicly available. The assumption here is that there is a standard public discourse whose language is readily accessible, while religious language is odd, obsolete, and esoteric—although secular citizens are exhorted "not to treat religious expressions as simply irrational" (which is a widespread temptation). If modern liberal democracy is to function, Habermas affirms, a common language is required, and for this requisite to be secured, "two presuppositions" must be fulfilled: "The religious side must accept the authority of 'natural' reason as the fallible result of the institutionalized sciences and the basic principles of universalistic egalitarianism in law and morality. Conversely, secular reason may not set itself up as the judge concerning the 'truths' of faith—even though in the end it can accept as reasonable only what it can translate into its own, in principle universally accessible, discourses." What this means is that modern secular discourses are self-contained and wholly accessible or intelligible on their own terms, without the need of translation or interpretation—whereas the very opposite is the case for religious language. The self-contentment of secular reason even seems to shield it against philosophical or interpretive questioning. Modern science, Habermas asserts, enables modern rationality to break with all "metaphysical" issues: "With this advance in reflection, nature and history became the preserve of the empirical sciences, and not much more is left for philosophy than the general competences of knowing, speaking, and acting subjects."[5]

About a year later, at a conference held in New York, Habermas reiterated and fleshed out further his views on the role of religion in the "public sphere." After touching on a number of issues (including Carl Schmitt's notion of "the political"), he returned there to the Rawlsian formula mentioned before and its limitations. As he pointed out, Rawls's formula had met the critique that "many citizens *cannot* or *are not willing* to make the required separation between contributions expressed in religious terms and those expressed in secular language." Moreover, the formula suffers from a democratic deficit given that a liberal regime "also exists to safeguard religious forms of life" and hence cannot excise religious language. It is at this point that the translation proposal recurs. "According to this proposal," Habermas states, "all citizens should be free to decide whether they want to use religious language in the public sphere"—with the crucial proviso that "were they to do so, they would have to accept that the potential truth contents of religious utterances must be translated into a generally accessible language before they can find their way into the agendas of parliaments, courts, or administrative bodies." Fine-tuning his proposal, Habermas introduces the further distinction between formal and informal language, a distinction monitored by a screening filter: instead of requiring citizens to cleanse their comments of religious rhetoric, "an institutional filter should be established between informal communication in the public arena and formal deliberations of political bodies that lead to collectively binding decisions." In this manner, a "universally accessible language" is secured in the public sphere, while "the 'monolingual' contributions of religious citizens depend on the translational efforts of cooperative fellow citizens (if they are not to fall on deaf ears)."[6]

The emphasis on translation efforts and complex filtering devices attests to the presumed distance between religion and modern rationality—what Habermas earlier called the unbridgeable "cleavage between secular knowledge and revealed knowledge." What this means is that religious people and secular rationalists are divided not only by different beliefs but by a linguistic gulf that is as deep as (and maybe even deeper than) the gulf between English and Chinese. Presumably, adepts of religion are proficient in some kind of "metaphysical" or "other-worldly" language, whereas secularists are fluent in vernacular or "this-worldly" language. Clearly, what surfaces here in new guise is the old "two-world" theory, now couched in linguistic vocabulary. Together with that theory, we also encounter again the ancient conundrum that has variously been termed the rift between "Athens and Jerusalem" or (more simply) between knowledge and faith. Curiously, in our contemporary period, the rift is affirmed not only by secularists—including those favoring translation devices—but also by radical religious thinkers thoroughly opposed to secularism and modernity. In the latter case, the *post* in post-secularity acquires a very different meaning: namely, that of a farewell or demise. Insisting on the stark distance between "this" world and the next, an assumption has recently emerged in various quarters that extols the radical "otherness," transcendence, and unintelligibility of the sacred or divine—thereby reviving the famous dictum of Tertullian: "What has Jerusalem got to do with Athens?"[7]

Once the division is construed as cleavage, the sacred or divine can enter the "worldly" domain—including the domain of human understanding—only by way of irruption, interruption, or disruption—which amounts to a form of violence or violation. My concern here is not with the different ways in which this conception is expressed in our time. On a popular level, we are only too familiar with such modes of religious extravagance as the celebration of "rapture" and the speedy arrival of Armageddon. On a more recessed and sober level, traces of exuberance can also be found among some "post-modern" thinkers, especially supporters of a "transcendentalist" phenomenology and a radical type of post- or anti-hermeneutics. Despite differences of accent, what is common to these tendencies is the stress on divine incommensurability, on the nonreciprocity or nonrelational character of the sacred and secular realms. Occasionally, sacred intervention is styled as a divine largesse or "gift"—but with no ability granted to recipients to recognize divine largesse "as" a gift. Carried to an extreme and transferred to a linguistic register, the separation of worlds implies not only a difference of language games but their actual nontranslatability. On this and similar issues I find it preferable to follow Italian philosopher Gianni Vattimo, who counsels us to be "suspicious of an excessive emphasis on the transcendence of God, as mystery, radical alterity, and paradox" and to return to the simplicity of the gospels.[8]

Religion and Ordinary Language

Vattimo's counsel, to be sure, applies not only to exuberant post-modernists but also—with equal force—to secular "post-secularists" championing the integrity of modern rational discourse. As presented by Habermas, modern discourse—as used by rationalist thinkers as well as by legal courts and parliaments—is claimed to be readily and universally accessible, whereas religious discourse is the opposite: mysterious and urgently in need of translation. But how persuasive is this argument? Are modern rationalist texts—from Kant to Carnap, Quine, and Rawls—not exceedingly difficult texts constantly in need of interpretation and reinterpretation and hence of translation into more accessible language? And what about courts? Do the judgments of courts not always involve the interpretation, application, and thus practical translation of earlier legal texts, precedents, and judicial opinions? And do members of parliament not always claim to interpret, apply, and hence translate the will of the "people" (or at least of their constituents)? And where is there an end to such interpretation and translation, that is, the effort to distill the meaning of texts, utterances, and events and thus to render them accessible to understanding? As recent "post-empiricist" epistemology attests, the range of interpretation extends even to scientific paradigms and the findings of natural science. As it seems to me, these comments only confirm the truth kernel of the hermeneutical claim of "universality"—a claim prominently articulated by Hans-Georg Gadamer (but side-stepped or neglected by Habermas).[9] No doubt, the demand for interpretation also applies to religious teachings; but as I shall try to show, the demand here may be less urgent and involve not so much a strictly linguistic translation but a translation into lived practice.

The one-sided or lop-sided character of the Habermasian translation proviso has been noted by several observers but especially by Charles Taylor. In his 2009 response to the former, titled "Why We Need a Radical Redefinition of Secularism," Taylor takes issue with the assumption shared by Rawls and Habermas that modern secular reason is "a language that everyone speaks and can argue and be convinced in," whereas religious languages "operate outside this discourse by introducing extraneous premises that only believers can accept." In the case of Habermas, this distinction amounts not just to a linguistic difference but to an "epistemic break" between secular reason and religious thought, "with the advantage on the side of the first." In a somewhat provocative vein, Taylor speaks here of "a myth of the Enlightenment" where the legitimate demand for the use of reason is transformed into a shibboleth and shielded against any intrusions or transformative horizons. In the same context, he links this shibboleth with the "principle of self-sufficient [or self-contained] reason" (which, in turn, seems to be connected with what he elsewhere calls the "buffering of the self" in modernity). For all their differences, he adds, Rawls and Habermas "seem to reserve a special status for non-religiously informed reason (let's call it 'reason alone')," assuming that such reason is able to resolve moral-political issues in a way "that can legitimately satisfy any honest, non-confused thinker"; by contrast, both find it necessary to "restrict the use of religious language in the sphere of public reason" by circumscribing this use with various translation and filtering devices. Summing up his discussion of this issue, Taylor concludes: "This distinction in rational credibility between religious and non-religious discourse seems to me utterly without foundation"—or else to rest on a rationalist "foundationalism" (stemming from Descartes) that is no longer credible.[10]

At this point, I want to push Taylor's argument a bit further by calling into question the notion of an "epistemic break" between modern secular reason and religious faith. In Habermas's account, both modern reason and religious faith seem to have the character of an epistemic or cognitive paradigm, each equipped with a *magisterium* designed to guard the integrity or correctness of the respective discourse. But this assumption seems to be implausible and the result of a misplaced "intellectualism." As it appears to me, at least the so-called Abrahamic religions are not at all anchored in an epistemic premise or a claim to special knowledge. The basis of these religions is rather found in Deuteronomy (6:4–6), in the famous "Shema Israel." What does "Shema" here mean? It is an invocation to the listeners to open their ears, not to harden their hearts or to become "buffered selves." What are they to hear? Only this: that the Lord God is one and that "you should love the Lord with all your heart, with all your soul, and with all your might" and that this plea should dwell "upon your heart." So the appeal here is to the heart rather than the head, to the whole human being rather than the knowing "subject." This appeal or plea is extended in Leviticus (19:18), where listeners are exhorted to love neighbors (or fellow beings) "as yourself." As we know, Jesus explicitly accepted these two kinds of love—which ultimately are one—and even affirmed that on these two pleas "depend all the law and the prophets" (Matthew 22:40). Clear echoes of the great "Shema," however, can also be found in the Qur'an, which speaks of the need for humans to love the divine and to extend a similar love to each other. Likewise, the Hindu text Bhagavad Gita exhorts followers to bond with the divine through *yoga* and also to implement this bonding through interhuman service. And in Buddhism, compassion and ethical-spiritual service are meant to assist in the "awakening" of all creatures even beyond the interhuman domain.[11]

Given their concrete "existential" appeal, the language commonly used in religious texts is an ordinary language readily accessible to people in all walks of life and at all times; it is not a highly esoteric idiom tailored for theologians and hence in need of vernacular filtering. As it happens, this aspect was emphasized by Moses at the very time when he announced the divine laws. "This commandment which I command to you this day," he said (Deuteronomy 30:11–14), "is not too hard for you, nor is it far off. It is not in heaven, that you might say: 'Who will go up for us to heaven and bring it to us, that we may hear it and do it?' Neither is it beyond the sea, that you might say: 'Who will go over the sea for us and bring it to us, that we may hear it and do it?' But the word is very near you; it is in your mouth and in your heart, so that you can do it." Large portions of the Hebrew Bible are historical accounts—and these are surely accessible to ordinary readers without special expertise. And what about the Psalms? They seem to be addressed to the joys and sorrows, the delights and sufferings of "everyman" (or every person). Uplifting and brazing—and beyond the need for filtering devices—are the words of the first Psalm: "Blessed is the man [person] who walks not in the counsel of the wicked . . . but his delight is in the law [teaching] of the Lord." And everyone who has experienced trouble or misery in life is surely touched by the words of Psalm 23: "The Lord is my shepherd, I shall not want; he makes me lie down in green pastures. He leads me beside still waters; he restores my soul."

The Christian (or "New") Testament is likewise filled with many stories or narratives, and especially the central story of the birth, ministry, and suffering of Jesus. Throughout his ministry, Jesus himself tells many stories, usually in the form of parables accessible to ordinary listeners. What filtering device is really necessary to understand the parable of the "good Samaritan" (Luke 10:29–37): the story where two Jewish priests (of all people) piously pass by a person who was robbed and brutally beaten—but where that victim is picked up and cared for by a traveling Samaritan (who was not even a member of the Jewish community)? To be sure, the story was not told for mere entertainment, but for instruction—on the question "who is my neighbor?" And what about the story of the rich man who will have difficulty entering the "kingdom of God" (Matthew 19:23)—a story told again not for entertainment but instruction? In his ministry, Jesus never proclaimed a doctrine or epistemic paradigm but simply taught by practical example. When, after Golgotha, two men encountered him and followed him to Emmaus, they did not recognize him through an epistemic formula, but in the simple breaking of bread (Luke 24:30–31). And what is one to say about the Sermon on the Mount and the great "beatitudes"? Where in modern moral theory—from utilitarianism to Kantianism—can one find similarly stirring words, like these (Luke 6:20–22): "Blessed are you poor, for yours is the kingdom of God. Blessed are you that hunger now, for you shall be satisfied. Blessed are you who weep now, for you shall be comforted"?

If, in these words, there is a need for translation, it is not so much a linguistic as rather a practical translation, that is, the transfer of teachings into human and social life. Here the letter of James is exemplary, and again it is written in generally accessible language. Elaborating on the great "Shema" in Deuteronomy, James emphasizes that hearing or listening cannot just be a passive receptivity but require active following. As he states: (James 1:22–25): "But be doers of the word and not hearers only, deceiving yourselves." For, he adds, someone who remains entirely passive is like a person who glances at an image and soon forgets what s/he has seen. But someone who looks into divine teachings and their message—which is "the law of liberty"—and perseveres in an active fashion "shall be blessed in his doing." In an effort to underscore this point, James continues (2:14–17): "What does it profit if someone says he has faith but has no works? Can faith alone save him?" His letter, to be sure, does not say that action without faith is sufficient or commendable; rather, hearing and doing should go together. Giving an example, he adds that "Abraham our father was justified by his works"—although one should better say that "his faith was active in or along with his works, or faith was completed by his actions." Returning to the role of religious faith in action, James offers a memorable definition (1:27): religion that is "pure and undefiled" means simply this: "to visit orphans and widows in their affliction, and to keep oneself unstained from the world."[12]

Post-Secularity and Politics

Going back to Habermas's essay of 2008, one can now see fairly clearly "what is missing": it is an awareness of the primacy of lived experience over cognition, of ordinary language over epistemic paradigms, or (more simply) of doing or practice over knowing. This lacking awareness leads to the postulate of a self-enclosed (or "buffered") epistemic grid that is immune from disturbing experiences. This deficit has practical-political implications. In a somewhat disarming way, Habermas's essay acknowledges the deficit, stating that "enlightened reason loses its grip on the images, preserved by religion, of the moral whole—of the Kingdom of God on earth—as collectively binding ideals." The consequences of this loss are far-reaching. Under the sway of the modern rational paradigm, "practical reason [too] fails to fulfill its own vocation when it no longer has sufficient strength to awaken, and to keep awake, in the minds of secular subjects, an awareness of the violations of solidarity throughout the world, an awareness of what is missing, of what cries out to heaven." Unfortunately, Habermas's own carefully guarded epistemic grid provides few if any resources to remedy the acknowledged deficit.[13]

Against this background, it seems appropriate and desirable to take another look at "post-secularity." Maybe the time has come to redefine the term in such a way as to extricate it from the grip of both secular rationalists and religious anti-secularists. As it seems to me, once the latter is done, a new meaning of post-secularity comes into view: namely, a social-political meaning endowed with a transformational quality. At this point, post-secularity comes to designate a move beyond a corrupt kind of secular or "worldly" politics oriented solely toward such aims as power, wealth, and selfish interest; by correcting these aberrations, the *post* of post-secularity becomes a goalpost pointing toward the pursuit of justice and the good life (which are the intrinsic aims of politics). In his 2009 response in New York City, Charles Taylor seems to gesture in this direction when he speaks of a "new moral order" (what I would prefer to call an ethical mode of public life) embracing such qualities as the rights and liberties of members, the equality of status among them, and the consensual legitimacy of public rule. If this general orientation is kept in mind, he writes, then what are called secularist or post-secularist regimes should be conceived "not primarily as bulwarks against religion but as good faith attempts to secure" the qualities mentioned before. And this means that contemporary regimes have "to shape their institutional arrangements not just to remain true to a hallowed tradition but to enhance the basic goods of liberty and equality between basic beliefs" and their adherents.[14]

At this point, I believe, one needs to take a few more steps beyond Taylor's recommendations—which still cling too closely to "liberal" conventions in celebrating universal maxims and cognitive "beliefs." In view of the enormous ills besetting political regimes today—large-scale economic corruption, media manipulation, and exploitation—it appears timely to envisage a still more "radical redefinition of secularism" that resonates more fully with a prophetic idiom—of which religious tradition is replete. Returning again to the book of Deuteronomy, we find this exhortation (16:20): "Justice and only justice you shall follow, so that you may live." And the psalmist proclaims in a similar vein (37:28): "For the Lord loves justice; he will not forsake his saints." And if we turn again to the Qur'an, we find these lines: "O ye believe! Stand out firmly for justice as witness to God" (Sura 4:135) and "Be just, for that is next to piety" (Sura 5:8). Although couched in somewhat different (nonprophetic) language, similar exhortations can readily be found in non-Abrahamic religious traditions in South and East Asia. As the Malaysian scholar Chandra Muzaffar has correctly remarked: "Justice is the real goal of any religion. It is the mission of every prophet and the message of every scripture." Nor is the call to social justice narrowly restricted to "religious" texts: it figures prominently in classical and modern philosophical teachings about civic "virtues." In the words of Aristotle—words echoed in the writings of al-Farabi, Avicenna, and Mencius: "What we call just is whatever produces and maintains happiness or blessedness (*eudaimonia*) for the whole of a political community and its parts." And as Aristotle importantly adds: justice and other virtues are practiced not for an external benefit or profit, since happiness or well-being is "choiceworthy in itself."[15]

This redirection or redefinition of secularism has implications also for the general meaning of "post-secularity." Viewed under social and political auspices, post-secularity is no longer the monopoly of secularists with a troubled conscience or else of anti-secularists but becomes available as a term designating all people—religious or not— with a public conscience, a conscience stirring them toward justice and social reform. From this angle, cognitive beliefs of whatever kind become secondary or subordinated to *orthopraxis*. In this respect, I completely concur with religious scholar Karen Armstrong when she states: "I say that religion is not about believing things. It's ethical alchemy: it is about behaving in a way that changes you, that gives you intimations of holiness and sacredness." In making this statement, Armstrong has the support not only of upright proponents of secular praxis but also of passages in sacred scripture, passages that sketch a development radically different from the well-known positivist trajectory (religion to metaphysics to science): namely, a path leading from cognition to practice, and from head to heart. The main passage can be found in Jeremiah (31:31–34), but its gist is repeated elsewhere:

> Behold, the days are coming, says the Lord, when I will make a new covenant with the house of Israel and the house of Judah, not like the covenant which I made with their fathers. . . . And this is the covenant: I will put my law within them, and I will write it upon their hearts, and I will be their God, and they shall be my people. And no longer shall each man have to instruct his neighbor and brother saying "know the Lord," for they shall know me, from the least of them to the greatest.[16]

What this and similar biblical passages suggest is a slow maturation or seasoning: a willing turn of people toward social justice and truth without doctrinal inculcation or creedal manifestoes. What is involved here is a patient learning process through concrete experience, an educational transformation that Paolo Freire has aptly called a "pedagogy of the heart." Such a process does not lend itself to political platforms or ideological proclamations and certainly cannot rely on coercion or make common cause with "top-down" interruption or disruption. People involved in this process are not condemned to passivity or apathy, but their practice cannot be rash or violent and must be seasoned by the virtues of tolerance, forbearance, and goodwill—and above all by the yearning for justice and social well-being. In our time, this yearning can no longer be restricted to one locality, one society, or one nation but must extend to humanity seen as a global community of interactive and ethically engaged people. In this manner, the contours of a "post-secular" cosmopolis come into view—a condition in which the differences among cultures, creeds, and customs would not be erased but subordinated to a shared striving for justice and well-being. This cosmopolis would not be a superstate or a military-industrial complex but only the emblem of a hope or promise sustaining ordinary human lives: the promise of the "city of peace."[17]

10. Political Self-Rule

Gandhi and the Future of Democracy

> To see the universal spirit of truth face-to-face one must
> be able to love the meanest of creation as oneself.
> —Mahatma Gandhi, *Satyagraha*

For students and friends of Gandhi, 2009 was an important year.[1]
As we know, it was a hundred years ago, on a long sea voyage, that
Mohandas Gandhi penned his book *Hind Swaraj* or *Indian Home
Rule*—a text justly famous because it has stood the test of time. The
book was Gandhi's opening salvo in his attack on colonialism and imperialism and his first public plea for Indian independence, freedom
or liberation from foreign domination. Surely, there is ample reason
for commemorating and celebrating this anniversary. Yet celebration
here cannot just mean a nostalgic retrieval of the past or a rummaging in literary archives. What is urgent and imperative today is an
effort to recover the guiding spirit of the text, the message pervading
its pages. And this spirit or message is not confined to 1909 or to the
twentieth century. It is as relevant today as it was then, and it will
remain relevant and even gain in salience in the present century and
future years.

In my view, the significance of the text can be found on two levels: one overt and directly accessible, the other more recessed and
of *longue durée*. The first level has to do with India's struggle for independence and subsequent struggles more or less directly inspired
by Gandhi's example. It is this level that tends to capture immediate
political attention. In a sense, Gandhi's *Hind Swaraj* can be seen as a
"classic" of anti-imperialist literature, a handbook of struggle not only

151

for Indians but for oppressed and colonized people around the world. The handbook has galvanized people in many continents and led ultimately to the demise of the traditional European empires. It also became a primer in America for African Americans involved in the civil rights struggles led by Martin Luther King Jr. It served as an inspiration for the struggle against apartheid in South Africa, as well as for several "velvet revolutions" in Eastern Europe against Soviet imperialism. As one needs to add right away, this level of significance is by no means exhausted or obsolete. In the words of the Palestinian American Edward Said, imperialism or imperial ambitions have not come to an end but only resurface in new guises or constellations. What mainly characterizes such ambitions today in comparison with earlier empires, Said writes, is "the quantitative leap in the reach of cultural authority" and "the unprecedented growth in the apparatus of the diffusion and control of information."[2]

The other level is more recessed or shielded from view, mainly because of its ethical and even ontological (or metaphysical) connotations. As I shall argue in these pages, Gandhi's *Hind Swaraj* captures the basic meaning or idea of democracy—a meaning that is not restricted to subjugated or colonized people but to friends of democracy everywhere. Basically, his text formulates a conception of "self" and "self-rule" (*swaraj*) that is constitutive for genuine democracy or democratic politics—in contradistinction from forms of monarchical, aristocratic, or theocratic tutelage. While constitutive in this sense, the conception also differs sharply from prevalent reductions of democracy to individual self-seeking or the unhampered pursuit of private self-interest. What surfaces behind this contrast is a different or starkly revised understanding of democratic "freedom" or the status of "being free." In the following I proceed in three steps. First, I shall discuss Gandhi's notion of "self-rule" (*swaraj*) and its connotations. Next, I shall delineate the political implications of Gandhi's conception, chiefly by distinguishing it from current ideologies of liberalism and neoliberalism (what I call "minimalist democracy"). Finally, I shall highlight the central contributions that Gandhi's conception makes to political theory or philosophy in our globalizing age.

Gandhian Swaraj

Gandhi's text ranges over a number of issues, all discussed in dialogue form (between an "editor" and a "reader"). For present purposes, it must suffice to highlight briefly passages relating directly to self-rule or *swaraj*. Following a discussion of the present condition of India— the state of ferment and unrest pervading the subcontinent due to British imperial rule—*Hind Swaraj* turns immediately to the central issue of self-rule, finding it mired in perplexity and confusion. Addressing himself to his interlocutor, Gandhi observes that "you and I and all Indians are impatient to obtain *swaraj*, but we are certainly not decided [agreed] as to what it is." In the opinion of many people, self-rule consists simply in driving the English out of India; but "it does not seem that many have properly considered why it should be so." For Gandhi, the goal of *swaraj* could not be obtained by simply replacing British rulership with Indian rulership, British power with Indian power; the problem was much deeper and more complex, involving a change in the very meaning and character of rulership. Those people wedded to simple expulsion, he notes, seem to want "English rule without the Englishman" or "the tiger's nature but not the tiger." Successful pursuit of this policy would "make India English, and when it becomes English, it will be called not Hindustan but Englistan. This is not the *swaraj* that I want."[3]

The problem with British rulership, in Gandhi's view, is that it reflects some unenviable and defective features of British civilization and ultimately of modern Western civilization in general. Apart from outlining a number of specific defects in British politics, *Hind Swaraj* reviews a host of Western customs and ordinary living practices that together testify not to steady civilizational progress but to a spreading malaise or decay. What links and unifies these diverse phenomena is one central feature: the upsurge of self-indulgence and self-centeredness, at the cost of ethical (or spiritual) civic commitments. Gandhi is not unaware that Western modernity has brought greater freedom for many people, including political freedom in democracies. This freedom, however, is tarnished by its misuse. In his words, the gist of modern civilization lies in the fact that "people living in it make bodily [or material] welfare the sole object of life." What is lacking in this kind of civilization is sustained ethical responsibility, responsiveness, and unselfish striving involving self-transformation. In the stark language of *Hind Swaraj:* "This civilization takes note of neither morality (*niti*) nor religion (*dharma*). . . . [It] seeks to increase material comforts, and fails miserably even in doing so."[4]

The remedy proposed in Gandhi's text for the spreading cultural malaise is self-rule or *swaraj*—a notion that requires close examination. As Gandhi points out, self-seeking or the rampant pursuit of self-interest may be an ingrained human impulse, but it conflicts with the dictates of moral and spiritual rightness (which is one sense of *dharma*). It is also at odds with the teachings of practically all the great religions of the world—including, next to Hinduism, Islam, Buddhism, Christianity, and Zoroastrianism. What all these religions try to teach us, Gandhi observes, is "that we should remain passive about worldly [or material] pursuits and active about godly [or ethical-spiritual] pursuits; that we should set a limit to our worldly ambition, and that our religious ambition should be unlimited." Despite differences of accent or detail, all religions and spiritual paths can thus be seen as "different roads converging on the same point." People following these paths or teachings are liable to achieve not a spurious or flawed kind of civilization, but a genuine civilization fitting for upright and free human beings. Here is Gandhi's terse formulation: "Civilization is that mode of conduct which points out to human beings the path of duty. Performance of duty and observance of morality [*niti*] are convertible terms." Observance of moral or spiritual standards requires self-restraint and the curbing of unbridled self-seeking or self-interest. The chief implication of this view is a new and transformative understanding of self-rule or *swaraj*. In a section titled "How can India become free?" Gandhi proceeds to offer a concise definition of the term as he sees it: "It is *swaraj* when we learn to rule ourselves."[5]

Swaraj as self-rule, as rule over oneself—clearly a difficult and demanding enterprise. It is surely the opposite of "selfish" rule or rule by the self over others, in the sense of tyranny or domination. To this extent, it points to the core meaning of democracy. In his new edition of *Hind Swaraj*, Anthony Parel writes that "Gandhi draws a subtle distinction between *swaraj* as ethical self-rule and *swaraj* as [political] home rule"; but he also adds that the good state or good self-government is possible only if Indians acquire a capacity for "self-rule" and that political *swaraj* requires people "who rule themselves."[6] (To this extent, Gandhi clearly was not a supporter of the "moral man/

immoral society" formula.) In my own interpretation, I like to draw individual and public *swaraj* close together: public *swaraj* or *swarajya* means self-government or genuine democracy, but democracy in turn needs people who are able to rule themselves, that is, people who are not captive to selfish addictions, to the lust for power, the greed for wealth, the impulse for destruction (all of which are forms of violence or *himsa*). As one can see, we are here on a steep incline. *Swaraj*, as Gandhi sees it, means basically an ethical ascent or transformation: a willingness to shed all forms of *himsa* in favor of *ahimsa*—where the latter denotes not just abstention from overt violence but a commitment to fostering goodness or the "good life" in all dimensions.

In a way, *swaraj* for Gandhi was part, and even the essence, of *karma yoga*—which, in the Hindu tradition, is a "soteriological" path. As we know, Gandhi explicitly described himself as a *karma yogin*—which does not mean a mindless activist or social busybody, but one who in his actions follows a path, an invitation, a calling (and thus is almost inactive or passively receptive). The path of *karma yoga* is delineated in the Bhagavad Gita as one of the prominent pathways—*margas* or *yogas*—on the way to redemption (*moksha*). Seen against this background, *karma* (action) is not synonymous with instrumental design or social engineering. Among many other things, the Gita distinguishes between different kinds of action: selfish or self-seeking action and unselfish or self-giving action; it also distinguishes between different notions of selfhood: a captive, self-imprisoned ego and a free or liberated self (we might perhaps use the terms *inauthentic* and *authentic* self). Following in the footsteps of the Upanishads, the Gita intimates that, by overcoming selfishness or self-centeredness, the human being comes to realize its freedom, its genuine self or *atman*—which ultimately merges with *brahman* (or the divine ground of being). Seen in this light, *karma yoga* cannot be a form of fabrication or human self-aggrandizement and certainly not a mode of industrial productivity. Above all, freedom (*swaraj*) as the goal of self-transformation cannot be willfully engineered but constitutes an experiential task that needs to be patiently and almost passively shouldered and undergone. In Gandhi's own words, freedom is not an instant boon or acquisition but is "attained only by constant heart-churn" or self-suffering.[7]

In his book *Self and Society: A Study in Gandhian Thought*, Ramashray Roy thoughtfully connects *karma yoga* with self-giving, sacrifice, and even sanctification, stating that Gandhi "equates action with *yajña* (sacrifice), that is, the performance of action as sacred duty. This sacred duty lies, for Gandhi, in exerting oneself to the benefit of others, that is, service."[8] This statement resonates again with the teachings of the Gita, where we read (4:32): "In many ways men sacrifice, and in many ways they go to *brahman.* Know that all sacrifice is holy work, and knowing this thou shalt be free." Viewed from this angle, achievement of self-rule or *swaraj* involves self-transcendence and a diligent training in the ways of freedom. In a manner akin to Aristotelian ethics, pursuit of soteriological paths demands steady practice and habituation; again in an Aristotelian vein, such practice revolves around the nurturing of a set of virtues—which Gandhi reformulated under the rubric of "vows" (*yamas*). Transferred to the political realm, *karma yoga* means the cultivation of civic virtues conducive to a free democratic regime. Here one needs to take seriously Gandhi's comments that *swaraj* has to be "experienced by each one for himself" and that "independence must begin at the bottom." Basically, for Gandhi, democratic self-government cannot be imposed on people from above—neither by a foreign power nor by the modern nation-state (an institution he always regarded with suspicion). Rather, democratic *swaraj* must first be nurtured, through education and example, on the local or village level and then be encouraged to spread out into larger communities and the world through a series of (what Gandhi called) "oceanic circles."[9]

Swaraj *and Liberal Democracy*

As one can see, Gandhian *swaraj* is quite different from modern "liberal-individualist" democracy—at least as the latter has developed in recent times. As one will recall, modern liberalism in the West had its origins in the Glorious Revolution and the work of John Locke—but at that time it still functioned as an adjunct or corollary of a monarchical regime. Following the French Revolution, liberalism came into contact, or became affiliated, with various republican or democratic regimes—but in such a manner that the latter would be progressively trumped by a liberal-individualistic agenda (a development in which the rise of capitalism played a significant role). What emerged, as a result, was a minimal or "minimalist" form of democracy; according to nineteenth-century liberals, the role of government, including democratic government, was meant to be minimal: seen chiefly as protectors of private property, political regimes were said "to govern best when governing least." The dismal experiences of the twentieth century with populist and totalitarian governments have reinforced the preference for political or public minimalism—despite occasional concessions to "welfare" programs during times of economic hardship. Due to these experiences and developments, the notion of individual "freedom" has come to be equated preponderantly with "negative liberty" (to use Isaiah Berlin's phrase)—with only limited or grudging allowance made for active or "positive liberty."[10]

If one compares Gandhian *swaraj* with the liberal laissez-faire agenda, the contrast is obvious. What one discovers right away is the distance separating *swaraj* from prevalent conceptions of freedom, especially those of "negative" and "positive" liberty. In this binary scheme, negative liberty basically designates the freedom to be left alone (that is, liberalism's retreat into private self-satisfaction), whereas positive liberty denotes the unhampered pursuit of collective goals—a pursuit sometimes shading over into social engineering on behalf of ideological panaceas. As can readily be seen, neither of these options shows kinship with Gandhian *swaraj*. Even when highly spiritualized, negative liberty still bears traces of individual self-centeredness, while the positive type—in stressing worldly activism—seems ignorant of self-restraint and nonattachment to the fruits of action. This distance is clearly pinpointed by Ramashray Roy. As he observes, negative liberty insists on social aloofness, on the retreat into a private realm often coinciding with selfishness or the wanton "satisfaction of desires." On the other hand, while emphasizing social and political engagement, positive liberty sidesteps the task of self-curtailment and self-transformation by extolling the benefits of collectively chosen goals. For Roy, it was "Gandhi's genius" to have squarely faced this dilemma and have shown an exit from this dilemma. The central point of Gandhian *swaraj*, he notes, was the emphasis on self-rule as a transformative process—whereby people are able to rule not so much over others as over themselves.[11]

The arguments regarding freedom or liberty can readily be transferred to the basic meaning of democracy. The difference between

Gandhian *swaraj* and the liberal-minimalist conception of democracy has been highlighted by numerous writers, especially the Gandhi scholar Ronald Terchek in his essay titled "Gandhi and Democratic Theory." Right at the outset Terchek states the crux of the matter: that democracy for Gandhi was not merely "procedural" or minimal but "substantive," in the sense of being grounded in a nonoppressive way of life. He cites Gandhi himself to the effect that, under democracy, "the weakest should have the same opportunity as the strongest. And this can never happen except through [political, social, and psychological] non-violence."[12] Basically, he notes, for the Mahatma democracy is not a regime organized or imposed "from the top down" (or from the state down), but one nurtured "from the bottom up." This explains his emphasis on village life and village self-government (through councils or *panchayats*), as well as on economic decentralization and local industries. In Terchek's presentation, Gandhi believed that the means of production (at least of the basic necessaries of life) should remain ultimately in the hands of the people—and not be relinquished or alienated to corporate elites. In contrast to the rampant competition unleashed by the capitalist market, he stressed the need to cultivate cooperative dispositions so that the brute "struggle for survival" would be transmuted into a "struggle for mutual service" or "mutual existence."[13]

The central point of Terchek's essay is the differentiation of the Gandhian approach from (what he calls) "the dominant model of democracy today," which relies on the unhampered pursuit of self-interest and, politically, on competitive elections where voters choose delegates maximally committed to promoting their interests.

An argument along similar lines has been presented by the Indian political theorist Thomas Pantham, in his article "Beyond Liberal Democracy: Thinking with Mahatma Gandhi." As Pantham points out, Gandhi repeatedly criticized the liberal-democratic model—its "objectification and technocratization of the political" (in the state) and its concomitant "alienation of the people's political rights" (by reducing such rights to private interests). The alternative he put forward was that of *swaraj*, which, in addition to self-rule, can also be translated as "participatory democracy," where the gulf between "subject and object," between ruler and ruled, is erased. For Gandhi, modern liberal thought was based largely on a "one-dimensional conception" of human beings as self-contained and self-seeking creatures whose pursuit of selfish ends could only be tamed by power and nonmoral force. The escape route he proposed was reliance on "truth-doing" (*satyagraha*) and nonviolence (*ahimsa*) as "the most important moral norms"—norms that are "not cloistered virtues" but are to be discovered and formed through "the ordinary activities of life" in the social, economic, and political spheres.[14]

Swaraj *and Recent Political Philosophy*

As it happens, the critique of political minimalism or minimalist democracy is not restricted to Indian intellectuals or writers directly influenced by Gandhi. On the contrary, some of the most eloquent critical voices have been precisely Western theorists and philosophers. Just a few years ago, the American political theorist Michael Sandel issued a plea for a renewed "public philosophy" that would re-connect ethics and politics. What stands in the way of such a renewal, in his account, is the predominance of (what he calls) the "voluntarist conception of freedom," that is, the laissez-faire ideology of untrammeled self-seeking that dispenses with the "difficult task" of cultivating civic dispositions. As an antidote to this ideology, Sandel pleads in favor of a "formative politics" concerned with the formation of ethical civic attitudes and practices; for (he says) "to share in self-rule requires that citizens possess, or come to acquire, certain civic virtues."[15]

Apart from Sandel, a host of Western political thinkers have focused on the issue of democratic freedom and sought to clarify or reformulate its meaning. One of the most prominent and innovative initiatives was undertaken by Hannah Arendt in a string of her writings, especially in *The Human Condition*. Rupturing the inner/outer or negative/positive binaries, Arendt placed human freedom not in a sphere of self-centered inwardness, but rather in the open arena of human interaction in practical political life—what she called the *vita activa*. During the classical period, she affirmed, Greeks on the whole took it for granted that "freedom is exclusively located in the political realm"—whereas physical need fulfillment and technical production were seen as "pre-political" phenomena. Only by interacting and communicating in an open space or "public sphere" were humans thought to be capable of showing free initiative and displaying their unique talents. For Arendt, public freedom in this sense decayed in subsequent centuries and reached a nadir in late-modern times when the *vita activa* was steadily submerged in the pursuit of need fulfillment and economic productivity. A corollary of these developments has been the atrophy of active political life and the truncation of freedom through its confinement to private self-seeking and self-interest.[16]

Challenging this late-modern trajectory, Arendt endeavored to revitalize the worldly or embedded character of freedom, as distinguished from individual thought or will. As she noted in an essay on the meaning of *freedom,* modern individualistic liberalism, "its name notwithstanding, has done its share to banish the notion of liberty from the political realm." What was needed in this situation was a change of outlook and focus: "We first become aware of freedom and its opposite in our intercourse with others, not in the [private] intercourse with ourselves." Before being transmuted into "an attribute of thought or a quality of the will," she emphasized, freedom needs to be understood as a synonym for "being free" or "the free man's status" in active public life. To salvage this legacy, everything depended for Arendt on the recuperation of public space as a platform for human agency: "Without a politically guaranteed public realm, freedom lacks the worldly space to make its appearance."[17]

Together with Arendt, Charles Taylor has sought to recapture political freedom from the snares of a purely subjective privacy; like Arendt, he has thereby transgressed the negative/positive binary (outlined by Berlin). As he wrote, in an attack on this binary, negative liberty is untenable since freedom cannot just denote "the absence of external obstacles, for there may also be internal ones." Once this is recognized, freedom must mean not only the removal of external impediments but also the ability to deal with "emotional fetters" and to channel and transform human inclinations. In appealing to motivational guidance and self-rule, Taylor places the accent not just on action but on its ethical quality and significance—thus preserving the classical (and Hegelian) linkage between ethics and politics, between moral self-rule and self-government. As he writes at one point, "The nature of a free society is that it will always be the locus of a struggle between higher and lower forms of freedom. . . . Through social action, political change, and winning hearts and minds, the better forms can gain ground, at least for a while."[18]

Probably the strongest American voice against the derailment of democracy into laissez-faire minimalism has been John Dewey. In all his writings, Dewey was relentless in critiquing a reckless individualism and in upholding social "relationism" and the need for civic bonds. As one should note well, his animus was directed not against liberalism as such, but against a minimalist version incompatible with democratic self-rule. Likewise, his target was not individual liberty (or individual selfhood) per se, but only its imprisonment in the Cartesian fortress of the *ego cogito*. Above all, what needs to be remembered is that, for Dewey, democracy is not a finished state, but an ongoing process of democratizing pointing toward rich untapped horizons. Democracy, he states at one point, is "an end that has not been adequately realized in any country at any time. It is radical because it requires great change in existing social institutions, economic, legal and cultural." To this might be added his observation that, under democratic auspices, "the supreme test of all political institutions and industrial arrangements shall be the contribution they make to the all-round growth [or better: flourishing] of every member of society."[19]

Returning to the theme of self-rule or *swaraj*, it is clear that growth or flourishing cannot mean simply the enlargement of power or managerial control. Rather, to be ethically tenable, democratic self-rule has to involve a practice of self-restraint and self-transformation capable of instilling the habit of nonviolence (*ahimsa*) and generous openness toward others. As Dewey once remarked, in a very Gandhian spirit: "To take as far as possible every conflict which arises . . . out of the atmosphere and medium of force, of violence as a means of settlement, into that of discussion and of intelligence is to treat those who disagree—even profoundly—with us as those from whom we may learn and, insofar, as friends."[20] This disposition toward nonviolence, however, does not come easy. For Dewey, as we know, such a disposition or civic habit is not a readymade "natural" endowment, but a human potentiality requiring continuous struggle and lifelong educational cultivation. Treated as such a potentiality, self-rule or *swaraj* opens up the horizon of a possible future democracy on both the domestic and the cosmopolitan levels.

11. Radical Changes in the Muslim World

Whither Democracy?

History defies linearity. In a time when, at least in the Western world, major issues appeared to be settled and some even predicted the "end of history," drama has suddenly erupted elsewhere—and especially in the Muslim world. A political arena that in many respects seemed relatively stagnant has unexpectedly been gripped by radical turmoil and revolutionary fervor. This does not mean that such turmoil is ever completely unprepared or unmotivated. Contrary to their portrayal (by some academics) as near-apocalyptic interruptions beyond intelligibility, revolutions have precursors or conditioning factors; usually they are the product of a deep social malaise, of the decay of shared meanings and public discourse in a society.

The historian Arnold Toynbee has famously depicted historical developments not in terms of linear progress or regress, but as an interplay of "challenge and response," of provocation and rejoinder. As long as the interplay is carried on with mutual respect and civic decency, a measure of stability is likely to prevail; but when dialogue gives way to exploitation and abuse, the torn social fabric calls for dramatic remedies. This notion of interplay can clearly be observed in the Muslim world. During the last few centuries, Western modernity presented itself to the Muslim world as a challenge or provocation and was experienced as such. In this situation, three (ideal-typical) responses are possible: cooptation, meaning the absorption into the Western model; rejection, meaning the negation of that model coupled with "fundamentalist" retreat; and balanced mediation. In large

162

measure, the first response characterized the Kemalist reforms (bordering on revolution) in Turkey, the second the Islamist revolution in Iran, and the last (and most promising) the recent democratic uprising in Egypt (as part of the "Arab Spring").[1]

Apart from exhibiting three different responses to Western modernity, the three cases illustrate different forms of the relation between religion and politics. In the first, Kemalist model, the public domain was entirely "laïcized" or purged of religious traces—with the result that faith (to the extent it persisted) was "privatized" or forced to find refuge in inner life. In the Iranian case, religion was allowed to conquer and eventually dominate the public space—with the result that faith was "politicized" in the form of a quasi-theocracy. By contrast to these two examples, the recent revolution in Egypt initially aimed neither at the elimination nor at the public enthronement of Islam, but rather at a genuine democratic renewal in which faith would find its rightful place in a free and pluralistic civil society open to believers and nonbelievers alike. In my view, only this third model promises a proper reconciliation of Islam and democracy. While, by enforcing laïcism, the Kemalist agenda inhibited the democratically required free exercise of faith, the theocratic model—by imposing religion from above—prevents precisely the "freedom" of belief (and nonbelief).[2]

In the following, I shall sketch the chief characteristics of the three models, with particular attention to their democratic potential. As will become clear, all three models were responses to challenges presented by the modern age. While, emulating the West, Kemalism aimed to correct the deficit of secularism in traditional Muslim society, Iranian theocracy sought to remedy the deficit of religion prevalent in the West (and Westernized Persia). By contrast, what provoked Egyptian revolutionaries was neither the presence nor the absence of religion, but rather the lack of democracy. To remedy this lack they had to overcome first of all a basic hurdle: the fear of autocratic power.

Kemalism

As is well known, modern Turkey emerged after World War I from the ruins of the Ottoman Empire. Its formal institutions took shape slowly during the protracted "war of independence" and were finalized with the Treaty of Lausanne and the establishment of the republic in 1923. Its first president was a military officer, Mustafa Kemal, who had earlier served as a commander in the Ottoman army and subsequently held leading positions in the provisional government during the independence struggle. His chief ambition was to establish a modern nation-state patterned on the examples of France, Sweden, and Switzerland, that is, a state separated from feudal traditions of the past by the trademarks of a uniform legal system and a strictly secular or nonreligious state apparatus. In the latter regard, the French example was particularly influential, above all the French revolutionary tradition of "laïcism" (or anticlerical secularism).

The actual implementation of the European model was not an instantaneous event, but rather a slow process stretching over several years. Yet although slow and drawn out, the substance of the transformation was profoundly radical and touched on virtually every aspect of social life. In March 1924, the Caliphate was abolished—an institution that had been the unifying center of (Sunni) Islam since the time of the "righteous caliphs" after the Prophet's death. In the same year, the system of education was radically reformed by placing all schools under the supervision of a national Ministry of Education, a change that effectively terminated the supremacy of the Muslim clergy in schools. Other changes soon followed. By late 1925, a new dress code and "hat law" were enacted, while religious (Sufi) orders were abolished or closed down. A year later, a new penal code (patterned on the Italian model) was promulgated, while the passage of a new civil code (inspired by Switzerland) ended the application of the Islamic shari'a in Turkey.[3]

Among all the innovations, the religious changes were clearly the most profound—because they involved a rupture with several centuries of Ottoman practice. Mustafa Kemal himself was keenly aware of the radical character of his innovations. As usual in historical processes, his innovations were a response to a perceived challenge or provocation: in this case, the provocation contained in the collusion of political power and religion, the symbiosis of sultanate and caliphate (what I previously called the "politicization" of religious faith). During the planning stage of the abolition of the caliphate, Mustafa Kemal made a statement that clearly pinpointed the core of the issue: "The religion of Islam will be elevated [or purified] once it will cease to be a political instrument, as had been the case in the past."[4] Due to its radical nature, the abolition proved to be deeply controversial, both inside and outside of Turkey. In May 1926, a "Caliphate Conference" was held in Cairo and passed a resolution declaring the caliphate "a necessity in Islam." Similar conferences on the topic were convened later in Mecca and Jerusalem and adopted similar resolutions—but in each case without practical effect.[5] Intense controversy also surrounded the reform of national education because it sidelined or marginalized the traditional madrassa devoted to Qur'an recitation and memorization under the tutelage of clerics or *ulemas*. In lieu of religious instruction, the main emphasis in public education was to be placed on such "modern" and "secular" disciplines as science, chemistry, and engineering.

In large measure, Mustafa Kemal's turn to secularism was inspired by the model of the French Revolution and French republicanism, with their strong anticlerical bent. The choice of that model was not whimsical. As in the Turkish case, French secularism or "laïcism" was a response to a challenge or provocation: in the French instance, the legacy of the "Old Regime" with its linkage of "throne and altar," that is, the combination of political and clerical domination or autocracy. Many of the excesses of the French Revolution can be traced to the oppressiveness of the previous order (which does not reduce their character as "excesses"). Other features where Kemalism followed the French example were the emphasis on national unification and the celebration of "civilization" and civilizational "progress." The stress on national unity was evident in a number of areas: the governmental structure, the centralized educational system, the civil and penal codes, and even the prescription of uniform modes of dress. The commitment to civilizational progress was a steady and pervasive theme of the new republican order. As Mustafa Kemal stated in 1925: "In the face of knowledge, science, and the whole extent of radiant civilization, I cannot accept the presence in Turkey's civilized community of people primitive enough to seek material and spiritual benefits under the guidance of (religious) sheiks. The Turkish Republic cannot be a country of sheiks, dervishes, and their disciples. The best, the truest order is the order of civilization; to be a man it is enough to carry out the requirements of civilization."[6] It is not hard to hear in this speech echoes of the Enlightenment tradition and also of the preeminently French idea of a *mission civilisatrice*.

There is one aspect, however, where Kemalist initiatives and the French Revolution do not mesh: namely, regarding the agency of change. The French Revolution was carried forward by a mass movement, and especially by members of the lower classes (the sansculottes). By contrast, the Kemalist agenda was implemented by a social and political elite, mainly by military officers and some professional groups; to this extent, rather than being fomented by a grassroots mobilization, it had the character of a "top-down" revolution. As a result, Kemalism and the young Turkish Republic for quite some time were marked by a "democratic deficit"—a deficit underscored by the effective predominance of one-party rule (the Kemalist Republican People's Party) until World War II. The deficit was also manifest in a number of popular or tribal uprisings during the first decade of Kemalist rule. One such incident, starting in 1924, was the so-called Sheikh Said Rebellion, organized by a wealthy Kurdish tribal leader who was opposed to the abolition of the caliphate, the termination of religious orders or sects, and the adoption of Western-style criminal and legal codes. The government quickly struck back, declared the rebellion subversive or treasonable, and restored "public order" by military means. Two years later, a larger plot against the Kemalist leadership was uncovered in Izmir and led to sweeping investigations and the establishment of public tribunals for the purpose of trying, publicly exposing, and punishing the rebels. At least in the case of these show trials and purges, some echoes of the French Revolution can again be detected.[7]

Nearly a century has passed since the beginning of the Turkish Republic. Both politically and socially, the country is no longer the same as during the time of Mustafa Kemal, although his legacy certainly lives on. In many ways—one might say—the democratic deficit of the early republic has been removed or at least greatly attenuated. There is today in Turkey a functioning multiparty system; a vibrant civil society; and a rich, multifaceted intellectual life. Although still asserting occasionally its earlier heavy-handed authoritarianism, Kemalism today is only one political and ideological strand operating in a complex and competitive public sphere. Above all, the earlier Kemalist stress on Western-style secularism/laïcism has given way to a more balanced accommodation where popular cultural and religious traditions are given their due, thus honoring the democratic principle of the "free exercise" of religion—without making room for a politically oppressive Islamism. By cultivating this balanced accommodation, Turkey's public life today lives up—at least tendentially—to the idea of the "twin tolerations" postulated by comparative political scientist Alfred Stepan: namely, the need for "minimal boundaries of freedom of action that must somehow be crafted for political institutions vis-à-vis religious authorities, and for religious individuals and groups vis-à-vis political institutions." This favorable assessment is supported by comparativist Elizabeth Hurd when she writes: "The multiple forms of religious politics in contemporary Turkey offer concrete evidence of the multivocity, rather than univocity, of the Islamic tradition." Seen in this light, recent transformations in Turkish life testify "both to the inability of the Kemalists to monopolize definitions of and divisions between religion and politics, and to the diversity of Islamic tradition."[8]

The Islamic Republic

The multivocity or multidimensionality of Islam is clearly evident when one turns from Turkey to Iran. There is first of all the important difference between the orthodox Sunni tradition, maintained by the Ottoman Empire and its heir, and the more nonconformist and spiritualist character of Iranian Shiism. In the political arena, the difference surfaces in contrasting conceptions of rulership—respectively those of the "Just Sultan" (*sultan-i-a'del*) and of the "Hidden Imam" (*imam-i-qa'ib*)—with the contrast hinging on conflicting modes of legitimacy. In the words of comparativist Majid Tehranian: "The doctrine of the Just Sultan was developed by the medieval *ulema* to legitimate the authority of secular rulers (on the condition that they perform in accordance with the rules of the *shari'a*)." By contrast, the Shia conception was fashioned "to deny altogether the possibility of legitimate rule in the absence of the Hidden Iman—the Mahdi, the twelfth of [Caliph] Ali's direct descendants."[9]

Added to this contrast, there is another major cleavage having to do with the historical development of the two countries during the last century. While (as previously indicated) the Kemalist agenda in Turkey was in large measure a reaction to the perceived "politicization" of religion at the expense of secular modernization, the Iranian revolution guided by Ayatollah Khomeini rebelled precisely against the opposite trend: namely, the excessive "privatization," marginalization, or sidelining of Islam, caused by the modernist policies of the Pahlavi dynasty (Reza Pahlavi, 1925–41, and Muhammad Reza, 1941–79). The conflict between traditional religion and secular modernity was the central issue that overshadowed the entire dynasty but reached its dramatic climax during the later reign of Muhammad Reza. Angered by the resistance of traditional clerics, the Shah in 1963 enacted the so-called White Revolution, a set of reform policies that were Western inspired, business friendly, and anticlerical to the core. The following decade saw a protracted and steadily intensifying battle between the two camps—which finally ended with the demise of the dynasty in 1979.

In many ways, Ruhollah Khomeini and Mustafa Kemal were complete antipodes in terms of education, worldview, and practical politics. Instead of being educated in public schools with an emphasis on science and engineering, Khomeini from early on attended religious or clerical schools, where he delighted in the study of the Qur'an and of Persian and Arabic literature. Instead of enrolling at a military academy or "war college" as gateway to a military career, Ruholla received his advanced training in religious seminaries, first in Arak and then in Qom. During his years at the seminary, he concentrated mainly on the study of Islamic law (shari'a) and jurisprudence (*fiqh*), although he also developed an interest in philosophy (*irfan*) and poetry. After completing his studies, Ruholla served for several decades as a teacher at the seminaries of Najaf and Qom, where he lectured not only on the Qur'an but also on Islamic history, ethics, and politics. In 1963 he was named a *marja* (source of emulation) and Grand Ayatollah, a position that gave him great national visibility. As mentioned before, 1963 was also the year of the Shah's "White Revolution," with its agenda of anticlerical modernization. The conflict between the monarchy and the clergy—which had been simmering for some time—now erupted into the open. In a visit to Qom, the Shah denounced the *ulema* as "obscurantist and backward," while Khomeini boldly attacked the Shah as a tyrant and a "miserable, wretched man." Two days after his speech, Ruholla was arrested and placed under house arrest. A year later he was exiled.[10]

The years of exile were spent mostly in Najaf in Iraq and, to-

ward the end, for a few months in Paris. During that period, Khomeini slowly developed his own theory of Islamic government, while
also remaining in contact with religious opposition leaders in Iran.
In 1970, he delivered in Najaf a series of lectures that were subsequently published under the title *Hokumat-e Islami: Velayat-e faqih*
(Islamic government: Authority of the jurist). In large measure, the
ideas presented in that text anticipated the constitutional structure
adopted after the revolution. In comparison with earlier doctrines of
rulership, Khomeini's text introduced an important new principle of
legitimacy: the principle of "trusteeship," which holds that, during the
period of absence, the functions of the Hidden Imam can and should
be exercised by a group of leading jurists (*fuqaha*) who themselves
are guided by a Supreme Jurist. In the words of Tehranian: "In one
bold ideological sweep, Ayatollah Khomeini transformed the traditional Shi'a doctrine of legitimacy which subtly had made room for
the co-existence of temporal and spiritual authorities and a system of
checks and balances." Viewed against the historical background, the
doctrine of the "Trusteeship of Jurists" was a "radical departure" from
established conceptions and practices. Essentially, he adds, the new
doctrine proposed a "theocratic (or quasi-theocratic) state" by postu-
lating "a fusion of spiritual and temporal authority with Muslim jurists
seen as the legitimate heirs to the authority of God, the Prophet, and
the Immaculate Imams."[11]

Even during his exile, Khomeini's ideas circulated widely in
Iran—where they found a receptive audience due to the increasingly
repressive policies of the Shah. The groups opposing or challenging
the Shah were not all religious or clerical in character but included
secular nationalist and socialist movements; however, among them
Khomeini was clearly the most prominent and influential figure. During the last months of his exile, a steady stream of visitors came to
Paris seeking his advice and entreating him to return home. When,
bowing to intense pressure, the Shah finally left Iran in January 1979,
Khomeini a few weeks later flew back to Tehran, where he was trium-
phantly welcomed by several million people. Following his return, he
proceeded swiftly, but with circumspection. He immediately appointed an interim government to replace remnants of the old regime and
called for a national referendum to chart the future course of Iran.
Not unexpectedly, the referendum overwhelmingly endorsed the re-

placement of the Pahlavi regime by a new "Islamic Republic." The next step was to consolidate power by sidelining or outlawing competing revolutionary groups and by establishing an "Assembly of Experts" to draft a new constitution. The new constitutional document, adopted in November 1979, erected a governmental structure pretty much in line with Khomeini's earlier ideas. Basically, the structure provided for two tiers of rulership: a secular and a clerical tier, with the second superimposed on the first. While the secular tier comprises a parliament (*majlis*) and a president, the second and higher echelon includes a Council of Guardians or Religious Jurists (*fuqaha*), under the guidance of Khomeini as Supreme Jurist (*faqih*).

Despite the existence of a parliament and president, and despite its official name, post-revolutionary Iran is neither a "republic" nor a democracy in any accepted sense of these terms. This is due to the superimposition of the clerical layer—which approximates the regime closely to a theocracy. In his speeches and writings, Ayatollah Khomeini never made a secret of his disdain for democracy, especially liberal democracy. As he stated in his text *Islam and Revolution,* Islamic government "is not constitutional in the current sense, that is, governing by laws based on majority opinion. It is constitutional in the sense that the rulers are subject to a set of conditions . . . set forth in the Noble Qur'an and the Sunna of the Most Noble Messenger. . . . Islamic government may therefore be defined as the rule of divine law over men. No one has the right to legislate and no law must be executed except the law of the Divine Legislator."[12] The implementation of this theocratic Islamic conception took many forms. Soon after the revolution, Islamic law (shari'a) was introduced, and a dress code for men and women was established and rigorously enforced. Alcoholic beverages and most Western movies were banned, while the entire educational system at all levels was Islamized, including higher or university education. At the same time and as a corollary, Khomeini held no brief for democratic pluralism and competition. During his rule, oppositional groups or movements were severely restricted or banned and many of their leaders imprisoned and even executed—to the great dismay of those who had hoped for a more pluralistic outcome of the revolution.[13]

To understand the vehemence and pervasiveness of "Islamization" during Khomeini's rule one has to take into account again its character as a response: a response to the Shah's modernizing agenda, to Western political interference, and to the perceived ills of Western modernity as such. In the words of Mark Juergensmeyer: "The goal of the Islamic Revolution in Iran was not only to free Iranians politically from the Shah, but also to liberate them conceptually from Western ways of thinking." This view is seconded by intellectual historian Ali Mirsepassi when he states that "the hegemony of 'political Islam' was made possible through capturing the 'imaginary' of the Iranians in a way that presented itself as the only desirable answer to the country's dilemmas."[14] What one needs to note, however, is that the "Islamization" agenda was only one possible interpretation of Islam and of the political implications of Shi'a Islam in particular. As previously noted, Khomeini's conception of the "Trusteeship of Jurists" departed not only from the traditional Sunni version of political legitimacy but also—and more importantly—from the Shi'a idea of legitimate rule, a departure that was resented and criticized by many Iranian clerics from the very beginning. As political theorist Suzanne Maloney observes pointedly: "The basis for Khomeini's theory of Islamic governance—the guardianship of the religious jurist (*velayat-e faqih*)—rests on a novel and almost unprecedented re-interpretation of religious canons that was and continues to be contested by senior theologians." Above all, the imposition of direct clerical rule from "on high" on Iranian society was "neither a prominent Shi'a doctrine nor one which enjoyed widespread support among Iran's religious establishment."[15]

What these observations bring to the fore is the fact that theocratic rule in Iran is rejected not only by anticlerical secularists (or laïcists) but also by religious leaders and intellectuals devoted to a more tolerant and prodemocratic version of Islam. Prominent members of the latter group are Mohammad Khatami, the fifth president of Iran; Mehdi Karoubi, for several years chairman of the parliament; and Grand Ayatollah Hussein-Ali Montazeri, an early associate of Khomeini who later turned against him precisely on the issue of theocratic rule. Persisting as an undercurrent throughout Khomeini's tenure, this counter-interpretation of Iranian Islam steadily gained momentum after his death (1989) and finally erupted boldly twenty years later in the context of the presidential election of 2009. At that time, long-suppressed aspirations of broad segments of the population coalesced into a dynamic reformist movement that Mir-Hossein Mousavi, the reformist presidential candidate, dubbed the "Green Path of Hope." As one should note, the reform movement was neither clerical (in the reactionary sense) nor simply anticlerical (or laïcist); its members and supporters chose neither the path of Kemalism nor that of Khomeini-ism, neither radical modernism nor radical antimodernism. Rather, the goal was to fashion a genuinely democratic regime free of clerical autocracy, a regime making room for believers and nonbelievers in a multitextured civil society. In the words of Mousavi, the "Green Path of Hope" was formed "for the sake of people's rightful demands and for claiming their denied rights." These words are echoed by Ali Alizadeh in an essay titled "Why Are the Iranians Dreaming Again?" that stresses the rich texture of the movement: "Mousavi's people, the collective that appears at the rallies, include religious women covered in chador walking hand in hand with Westernized young women who are usually prosecuted for their appearance; war veterans in wheelchairs alongside young boys for whom the Iran-Iraq war is only an anecdote; and members of the working class who sacrifice their daily salary to participate in the rally next to the middle classes."[16]

Uprising in Egypt

Alizadeh's words can be transferred, without great difficulty, to the popular uprising that erupted less than two years later in Egypt. As in the case of the Iranian movement, the Egyptian uprising in January 2011 mobilized a broad cross-section of society (though with a preponderance of young people), transforming them from passive victims into autonomous agents of radical democratic change. Despite the similarity in terms of grassroots mobilization, there is one major difference that needs to be noted: while, in Iran, the Green Movement rebelled against clerical autocracy or absolutism, the uprising in Egypt was directed against an entrenched secular autocratic regime and despotism, moreover a regime that has tended to sideline or marginalize the expression of religious faith. At this point, historical context clearly needs to be taken into account. While for many liberal democrats in the West, religion often appears as an unwelcome intrusion into democratic politics, the situation is different in Muslim countries, where religion has often functioned as a barrier to autocratic political power. As political theorist Nader Hashemi correctly observes, citing concrete historical examples in support: "Significant segments of the Muslim world today believe that religion is not the natural ally of despotism, but a possible agent of stability, predictability, and limited government. In many cases, modern Arab societies associate secularism with postcolonial authoritarian regimes that repressed their people in the name of secular Arab nationalism." Given recent experiences in Northern Africa and the Near East, he adds, secularism for a generation of Arabs has been "linked to dictatorship, corruption, and nepotism."[17]

This does not mean, of course, that Muslim insurgents—and Arabs in particular—are eager to exchange secular despotism for religious autocracy. For most of them, the example of Khomeini's Iran is a stark reminder of the dangers associated with the clerical domination of politics (or the "politicization" of religion). Thus, as in post-Kemalist Turkey and with the Green Movement in Iran, Egyptian insurgents have been searching for a path between secularism/laïcism and clericalism—which is the path of a tolerant and pluralistic democracy. In the words of Italian professor Francesca Corrao: "To understand things better, one must bear in mind that in Tahrir Square, al Qaradawi [an insurgent] stressed the plurality of religions and respect for Muslims and Christians alike, and that bloggers showed a transnational solidarity that is the founding principle of Arab countries." This view is underscored by Moroccan journalist Zouhir Louassini, who pleaded: "What must we do to persuade Westerners that this is a *democratic* revolution? The posters carried by people were written in various languages because there is a desire to establish dialogue with others; one young woman even carried a poster with the words *Yes, we can.*"[18] The most telling comments on the uprising, however, come from the secretary general of the Arab League, Amr Moussa, who stated in an interview: "After January 25, we have a . . . different Egypt, one animated by a new vision based on two main goals: democracy and reform." With regard to the important question of the role of Islam, and in particular the Muslim Brotherhood, in the emerging Egyptian democracy, Amr Moussa added: "The Muslim Brotherhood is part and parcel of the Egyptian political scene. We cannot deny that. But at the same time, it is clear that this revolution, this uprising was not instigated by them, not led by the Muslim Brotherhood. The

Brotherhood was part of it. . . . I believe it is healthier to recognize this and to allow them to express themselves clearly and formally through a party or through whatever other mechanism. . . . This would put them very clearly in the theater [the public square] before you."[19]

What these comments intimate and, in fact, presuppose is the presence in Egypt of a vibrant "civil society" outside governmental control where people can express their different religious as well as secular/nonreligious views, without succumbing to the lure of either "privatization" or "politicization." It was the existence of such a budding civil sphere that enabled popular movements in Eastern Europe to shake off totalitarian oppression in so-called velvet revolutions. What seems to be happening—perhaps somewhat unexpectedly—in many Muslim societies is the formation of a new public space where grievances can be aired and aspirations be pursued and practically implemented. This formation certainly came as a surprise to many entrenched Middle Eastern rulers. In the words of journalist Mohammed Khan: "The catalyst of the political earthquake that we are witnessing was a massive popular uprising in Tunisia at the end of 2010." Emboldened by the overthrow of Ben Ali, the people in Egypt soon followed suit: "In just 18 days, Egyptian civil society—which we had been told by regional 'experts' either did not exist or was spineless—broke the shackles of oppression and overcame a dictator whose regime had become synonymous with abuse and corruption." As he adds, once the Pandora's box of civil society has been opened, its contagion cannot easily be contained or fenced in. As it happens, the "revolutionary bug" has now spread across the wider region. As a result, the people in Tunisia and Egypt seem to have written the opening pages of what can be called the "project for a new Arab century."[20]

As one should note, however, at least in Egypt the project of a new century was not carried forward with military means nor does it seem to aim at the enhancement of military, geopolitical power; rather, it is animated—at least in major part—by the yearning for the "good life," that is, for a pluralistic democratic society with freedom and justice for all. One of the remarkable aspects of the uprising in Egypt was the reliance of the insurgents (at least initially) on peaceful or nonviolent means—pretty much in line with the teachings of the Mahatma Gandhi and the "velvet revolutions" mentioned before. This aspect has been ably highlighted by philosopher Ramin Jahanbegloo, himself a committed Gandhian thinker and activist. "Nearly two years after the rise of the 'Green Movement' in Tehran," he observes, "now nonviolent uprisings against repressive regimes are spreading across the region from Tunisia to Yemen and, most importantly, Egypt." Despite geographic and cultural distances, he adds, these movements "exhibit a remarkable similarity to Gandhi's strategy for checking power and opposing violence in India decades ago"—a fact that gives hope "that nonviolent campaigns for democracy might be the essential paradigm of change" in the Middle East and the Maghreb. A crucial feature of this paradigm is that it injects ethical standards into contemporary politics, thus promoting and reinforcing "a universal ethic, as Gandhi had preached"—an ethic that "transcends religious and cultural particularities even as it is channeled through local grassroots movements."[21]

In their struggle for a viable, ethically informed democracy, the insurgents in Egypt join hands with members of the Iranian Green Movement and also with many fellow Muslims in post-Kemalist Turkey. In all three cases, the aim is not to banish religion from public life, but to save it from the lure of theocracy or clerical autocracy (the danger of "politicization") and also from the temptation of an otherworldly (and purely "privatized") retreat.[22] More positively stated, the aim is to promote the "good life" in this world (or in worldly society) free from injustice and oppression. The task is enormous, and it is prudent to enlist all available resources—including religious teachings—in this struggle. In the words of Nader Hashemi (previously mentioned), religion in Muslim societies has often served to promote social well-being and restrict autocratic governmental power. However, this resource may be too limited to curb the ferocious greed and power lust of some rulers. For this reason, it appears urgent and even imperative to retrieve and revitalize another resource that has been sidelined for too long in Muslim societies: the resource of philosophy and especially political or public philosophy.

As is well known, Muslim societies during the early centuries were vibrantly alive with philosophical, scientific, and artistic creativity and produced such great intellectual luminaries as al-Farabi, Ibn Sina (Avicenna), Ibn Rushd (Averroes), and Ibn Khaldun. Unfortunately, due partly to the Mongol invasions and partly to clerical obscurantism, this tradition later atrophied and (with some notable exceptions) was allowed to lie fallow. Here is a great challenge for Muslim insurgents and, in fact, for the entire Muslim world: to rekindle the legacy of the great Muslim philosophers and social-political thinkers and to connect it with the aspirations of contemporary democratic thought and practice. In this manner, the Muslim world or Muslim culture will be able to take its rightful place among freedom- and peace-loving people in the emerging cosmopolis or the ongoing "conversation of humankind."

12. Opening the Doors of Interpretation

In Memory of Nasr Abu Zayd
and Mohammed al-Jabri

> We need to construct on open democratic hermeneutic.
> —Nasr Abu Zayd, *Rethinking the Qur'an*

Interpretation is sometimes greatly underrated or undervalued; frequently it is seen as a mere method or subordinate tool of research. This view is seriously mistaken—as I shall try to show here mainly with regard to religious faith. As we know, the so-called Abrahamic religions—Judaism, Christianity, and Islam—are based in large measure on divine revelation, that is, on a message reaching human beings from "another shore." In the case of Islam, the Qur'an is even considered by most pious Muslims as the direct and unmediated "word" of God. Nor is this assumption restricted to the three cited world religions. In the case of Hinduism, the Vedic scriptures are called *shruti*, that is, a message transmitted to, and "heard" by, ancient sages and seers. Probably, a similar assumption also prevails in many other traditions of religious belief.

For agnostics or radical secularists, the notion of divine revelation or inspiration is devoid of sense, because for them all meaning is humanly constructed or fabricated. I do not share this agnostic view (most famously articulated by Ludwig Feuerbach) but rather take seriously the possibility of a divine message or revelation. The point I want to raise here, however, is that divine revelation—no matter how elevated or "transcendent"—cannot operate without, and in effect would misfire in the absence of, interpretation. Put differently: confronted with a divine message, human beings have to be able to see themselves as genuine addressees and hence to make sense of the message in their lives. Otherwise the message simply goes astray. This means that, in order for the divine message to make sense, human beings have to be able to relate it to their "framework of significance" (Charles Taylor), their "pre-understandings" (Gadamer), or their ongoing "language game" (Wittgenstein). In order to live, human beings have to understand—at least dimly—what is happening, and this understanding is provided by their concrete life context and customary vocabulary.

This does not mean, of course, that vocabularies and language games cannot be expanded, that frames of significance cannot be broadened or deepened. The very idea of "learning" depends on such expansion. However, where the frame of significance is stretched to the breaking point, beyond any form of intelligibility, the presumed message becomes gibberish and, in fact, a mode of external imposition or violence. In its genuine sense, divine revelation never moves to this breaking point or beyond the frame of possible human meaning. This point is powerfully illustrated by the words of Moses when he promulgated the divine commandments (Deuteronomy 30:11): "For this commandment which I command you this day is not too hard for you, nor is it far off. It is not in heaven, that you might say: 'Who will go up for us to heaven and bring it to us, that we may hear it and do it?' Neither is it beyond the sea, that you might say: 'Who will go over the sea for us and bring it to us, that we may hear it and do it?' But the word is very near you; it is in your mouth and in your heart, so that you can do it." The same point is also illustrated by the name "Israel," which Jacob received after wrestling with the angel of God (Genesis 32:28); for he could not have wrestled with God if God was utterly "transcendent" or unreachable. Being named Israel means that Jacob's life had been transformed through the human-divine encounter.

Now, it is important to note that in the divine-human encounter not only are human beings transformed (their understanding deepened and enlarged), but the meaning of the divine is also transformed: from a magical idol or shibboleth into a personally experienced God (or divine presence). This means that the divine has been powerfully reinterpreted and rethought. As a result, the interpreter is no longer a target of external (possibly clerical) control or manipulation, but he/she becomes a partner or participant in the transmission of the divine message. In the language of the Christian/Protestant Reformation, interpretation undercuts the exclusive privilege of a priestly elite, making room instead for the "universal priesthood" of believers. Differently put: religious faith is humanized and democratized, hence the strong opposition of both religious and political elites to the freedom of interpretation.

Seen against this background, interpretation is clearly not merely a subordinate tool. As shown in the development of Western (Latin) Christianity, interpretation—together with the translation of Scripture into vernacular idioms—has functioned as a powerful agency of religious, social, and political reform. As we also know, such reform has been stubbornly resisted by conservative or orthodox religious authorities. Nowhere is resistance more unyielding than in the case of Islam where—according to many observers—the "doors of *ijtihad*" have officially been closed for some seven hundred years. As it happens, the contemporary period—for a number of reasons—has witnessed and is witnessing determined efforts to pry open again these doors of *ijtihad* and thus to reestablish a more fruitful human-divine encounter. At this point, I want to draw attention chiefly to two leading Muslim protagonists who sadly passed away in 2010: Nasr Hamid Abu Zayd and Muhammed Abed al-Jabri. In a way, my comments are meant as a memorial tribute to these thinkers.

Nasr Hamid Abu Zayd

I was fortunate enough to be acquainted with both thinkers. In the case of Abu Zayd, our last meeting occurred in Italy about two months before his death. What struck me then again was his genuine friendliness and open-hearted disposition. During a leisurely stroll in Pisa, near the famous "leaning tower," he told me some episodes of his difficult life journey (with which I was only partially familiar). In a way, his life resembled the Pisa tower, being rooted or anchored in one place (his native Egypt) but leaning in a different direction (northern Europe). Yet, despite dislocations and disruptions, his personal disposition reflected a sense of equilibrium, balance, and serenity that I found touching and admirable. Abu Zayd was born in July 1943 in a small town not too far from Cairo. As a teenager he was once arrested and imprisoned for allegedly sympathizing with the Muslim Brotherhood; but this seems to have been just a youthful escapade (moreover, it was the time of secular nationalism). In secondary school he received some technical training that enabled him, after graduation, to work briefly for the National Communications Organization in Cairo. In 1968 he entered Cairo University, where he obtained his BA degree in Arabic studies (1972) and his MA in Islamic studies (1977). His master's thesis dealt with the role of exegesis in Islam (*ta'wil*). Following the completion of this thesis he went to America for a year (1978–79) in order to learn more about exegesis or interpretation.

This moment in Abu Zayd's life is important because it marks a crucial intellectual encounter. Its significance is vividly captured in an interview published on NEFAIS.net (a site designed for Islamic journalists). In the exchange, the interviewers remind Abu Zayd that, at that time, he was looking for an English equivalent for the term *ta'wil* and that Hassan Hanafi in Cairo had proposed to him the term *hermeneutics*. They ask him: "Did you then know about hermeneutics and about Hans-Georg Gadamer [the chief philosopher of hermeneutics]?" Abu Zayd: "Not at all; even the word 'hermeneutics' was unfamiliar to me."[1] Once in America, Abu Zayd launched into an intensive study of hermeneutics and, at this point, eagerly read Gadamer's *Truth and Method;* he also studied the works of Paul Ricoeur and Martin Heidegger—as well as Ibn Arabi. His inquiries led him to the strong conviction of the interrelatedness of religious, philosophical, and cultural traditions—a conviction, of course, fully shared by Gadamer and Ricoeur. As he eloquently states in that interview: "Arabic-Islamic philosophy cannot be understood in isolation from Greek, Indian, and Persian philosophy. It is impossible to separate them and to speak of a purely Islamic philosophy, insulated from external influences." Perhaps the central point Abu Zayd derived from his study of hermeneutics was the inevitable connection between the meaning of a text and the position or understanding capacity of the interpreter. Here is his crucial formulation:

> Is it possible to grasp the "objective" historical meaning of a text? Or is the process of textual understanding intrinsi-

cally connected with the role of the interpreter? This is the core question of hermeneutics. And it is precisely this question that—in different formulations—permeates the Arabic-Islamic tradition, ever since the beginning of Qur'anic interpretation and of *ta'wil*. Thus, the guiding question of the Mu'tazilites was: is it possible to understand the divine meaning of the Qur'an without having a preunderstanding of justice or the unity of God? If we approach the Qur'anic text starting from the presumption of its divine nature but without having an intelligible preunderstanding of divine truth, how can we know that this text is not a lie or falsehood??[2]

According to Abu Zayd, this question agitated not only the Mu'tazilites but also Ibn Rushd and—in a different way—Ibn Arabi. For the guiding question of Ibn Arabi was the question of God's "being" or existence. Thus, he asked: "Does God have an objective being that exists independently of us? Or is being the fruit of the interaction between the so-called divine and the human intelligence?" This question, Abu Zayd adds, is obviously a philosophical one and "brings us back to Heidegger and his understanding of 'being.'" Does the latter have independent, "objective" status outside the range of human understanding? This is also the question of Ibn Arabi, who asks about the relation between text and world, or text and being. For Ibn Arabi, "the Qur'an is the word of God written down in a book; but 'being' or existence is God's word more broadly, or His existential word." Hence, the theory of (textual) knowledge becomes for Ibn Arabi the theory of the understanding of being. "Is there not," Abu Zayd asks, "an affinity—not an identity but an affinity—between the question of Ibn Arabi and the question of being and its understanding in Heidegger's work, and also in that of Gadamer??"[3]

In the same context, Abu Zayd also raises the issue of cultural-religious "tradition" and its continuing significance today. Together with Gadamer, Abu Zayd treats tradition *not* as the "dead hand" of the past smothering all creative thought, but rather precisely as a recessed and never fully exhausted resource—a mode of our preunderstandings—whose significance needs to be constantly interpreted and reinterpreted in every generation anew. As he observes, a genuine tradition is that dimension of our inheritance that "reaches into the present and the future." This view collides with a mindless "tradition-alism," as well as with a Jacobin constructivism that claims to invent the present and future *ex nihilo* or *ab ovo*. Traditionalism claims that all the answers—objective and perennial answers—can be found in the past without further reflection, while constructivism pretends to be able to proceed without traditions or any preunderstandings. This conflict has played itself out in modern Western history (in the form of steadily intensifying "culture wars"); but it is not limited to the West. In Abu Zayd's words: "I believe that this conflict still pervades con-temporary Islamic thought. Here, a closer study of Gadamer's work can perhaps help to define the intellectual problems more adequately, and thereby to contribute to their resolution (or at least mitigation)."[4]

The discussed issues lead inevitably to the core question that I placed at the head of these pages: the relation between revelation and interpretation. Abu Zayd does not reject the notion of revelation, but he rejects its construal as a happening outside time and human under-standing. "I do not believe," he says firmly, "in the existence of texts outside of time—and I do it for religious reasons." Some Muslims and *ulema* consider the Qur'an as a transtemporal text, a text that exists in God's absolute and transcendent reason. Maybe so, but how can we have any access to this? In any case, lodged purely in God's transcen-dence, we cannot yet speak of "revelation," which means an unveiling and a communication. Now, it so happens that God chose to "reveal" his word "historically in the 7th century and in a specific language, namely, the Arabic, which had a prior history." Thus, the Qur'an was revealed in history, in a culture and language. "Ever since He sent us prophets and His word," Abu Zayd states, "God Almighty decided to be historical. This was God's decision, not mine. But if God decides to reveal Himself in history, how can I still claim that His revelation is not historical? Thus in the case of the Qur'an, I am dealing with a historical text, and *ta'wil* or the understanding of this text is also historically conditioned. . . . Now, if God has wanted to be (or reveal Himself) in history, how can I—a finite historical being—attempt to expel God from time??"[5] As one needs to add, as a historically con-tingent process, human interpretation can never be absolute or claim absolute correctness. Every text—including the Qur'an—is a fabric of multiple meanings, multiple discourses; hence interpretation is al-ways multiple (as Gadamer has taught), without being arbitrary or relativistic (because it remains oriented toward the genuine meaning or meanings of a text or a textual revelation).

Let me return to the life story with which I began. Following his stay in America, Abu Zayd returned to Cairo University, where he received his doctorate in 1981 with a thesis on Ibn Arabi. One year later he joined the faculty of the Department of Arabic Language and Literature, where he first served as an assistant professor and, after 1987, as an associate professor. From this time forward, Abu Zayd's life entered its limping or "leaning tower" phase. In 1992, he started proceedings that, under normal circumstances, would have led to his promotion to full professor. By that time, he had already published thirteen books, in Arabic and other languages, including *Imam Shafi'i and the Founding of Medieval Ideology* and *The Critique of Religious Discourse*. The Standing University Committee for Promotion was divided; but ultimately the voice of one prominent member prevailed: the voice that accused his work of containing "clear affronts to Islamic faith." In March 1993, the Cairo University Council confirmed the negative decision. But this was only the beginning of Abu Zayd's troubles. A year later, legal action was brought against him for heresy or apostasy, and still a year later, the Cairo Court of Appeals rendered a formal judgment against him. Being declared an apostate (*murtadd*), however, meant that he could no longer be legally married to a Muslim woman (in his case, the professor of French literature Dr. Ibtihal Younis); hence he was declared legally divorced. Although the Cairo University Council belatedly decided to reverse its earlier negative decision, for Abu Zayd this was too little and too late (especially since an Islamic Jihad organization threatened to kill him and his wife). In July 1995 the couple flew to Madrid and then proceeded from Spain to the Netherlands, where he was welcomed as a visiting professor at the University of Leiden.

The bad turn of events in Abu Zayd's life is shocking but not unintelligible. First of all, it occurred during a period of intense clerical and political repression in Egypt: a period when Dr. Ahmed Mansour was dismissed from Al-Azhar University and when Naguib Mahfouz was stabbed in the neck by a radical Islamist. In Abu Zayd's case, the reason was evident: his affirmation of *taw'il* and creative Qur'anic interpretation was a clear threat to religious and political autocracy. Here it is important to remember that Abu Zayd did not issue this threat as an agnostic or a radical secular opponent of religious faith. He *never* considered himself an apostate or heretic. As he explained tellingly and eloquently in another interview: "I am sure that I am a Muslim. My worst fear is that people in Europe may consider and treat me as a critic of Islam. I am not. I am not a new Salman Rushdie, and don't want to be welcomed and treated as such. I am a researcher, critical of old and modern Islamic thought. I treat the Qur'an as a *nass* (text) given by God to the Prophet Muhammad."[6] It is crucial here to note the difference. Abu Zayd's aim was not to debunk or destroy Islam but rather to understand and reinterpret it—which is a much more difficult endeavor.

Abu Zayd's life in exile was difficult—given his intense fondness of Egypt—but it was not without rewards in terms of public honors and scholarly acclaim. The decade he spent in Leiden (from 1995 to 2004) was marked by stellar academic achievements. During this time he published some of his most important books, such as *Text, Authority, and Truth, Discourse and Hermeneutics,* and *Thus Spoke Ibn Arabi* (all in Arabic). This was also the time when some of his texts began to appear in English, such as *Voice of an Exile: Reflections on Islam* (2004) and *Rethinking the Qur'an: Towards a Humanistic Hermeneutics* (2004). Among public honors, one should mention the Jordanian Writers Association Award for Democracy and Freedom (1998) and the Roosevelt Institute Medal for Freedom of Worship (2002). (Prior to this he had already received the Tunisian Order of Merit in 1993.) In 2004 he accepted appointment to the Ibn Rushd Chair of Humanism and Islam at the University of Utrecht. A year later he received the Ibn Rushd Prize for Freedom of Thought in Berlin. Around this time he also participated in a research project entitled "Jewish and Islamic Hermeneutics as Cultural Critique" at the Wissenschaftskolleg in Berlin. At the time of his death (due to a viral infection), Abu Zayd was involved as coeditor of a six-volume encyclopedia of the Qur'an and in a comprehensive project of Qur'anic interpretation (in both English and Arabic).

This is not the place to review in detail Abu Zayd's numerous writings. I limit myself to a few texts available in English. His most well-known book—one might call it his "signature text"—is *Rethinking the Qur'an: Towards a Humanistic Hermeneutics.* The book repeatedly and extensively pays tribute to insights culled from Gadamer's work.

The emphasis in the title on a "humanistic hermeneutics" has to do with his treatment of the Qur'an not as a distant, "perennial" essence enclosed in divine transcendence, but as a message addressed to human beings in their concrete life-worlds. Far from being a remote mantra, the Qur'an emerges here as a living phenomenon, as an address or discourse available to human understanding; in fact, it can be seen as a mode of "communication, dialogue, and debate" provoking argument, acceptance, or rejection. As a message or discourse, the Qur'an also issues a concrete social plea or exhortation: the plea for the pursuit of justice. Abu Zayd mentions an instance when even the Prophet Muhammad seemed to fall short of his own plea. This was the time when Muhammad was busy preaching to the rich people of Quraish, admonishing them to pay heed to justice. At this point, a poor blind man named Ibn Umm Maktum came to him asking for advice; but taken up by his own discourse, the Prophet pushed him aside—and the Qur'an itself strongly reprimands Muhammad for his negligence (Sura 80:1–10).[7]

Roughly contemporaneous with *Rethinking the Qur'an* is Abu Zayd's most autobiographical book: *Voice of an Exile: Reflections on Islam.* More than any other of Zayd's writings, the book introduces its readers into the lived experience and agonies of the Egyptian thinker. I can only lift up some salient passages. Repeatedly, Abu Zayd reflects on his central concern: the status of the Qur'an as divine *and* human or as divine message addressed to human beings. "Orthodox Islam," he observes at one point, "has always insisted that the Qur'an is God's eternal, uncreated speech," and "because it always existed, it was never created." The Mu'tazilites, however, looked at this issue differently. As they insisted, "there is a difference between God's essence—something eternal and beyond human understanding—and God's word which is created and accessible to reason." Here again, Abu Zayd favors the Mu'tazilites, saying: "I believe that in order to make sense of the Qur'an, we need to understand the text metaphorically rather than literally. I also believe that it is essential to interpret the text by taking into account the social-cultural context in which it was received."[8]

Perhaps the most revealing and forthright passage is found somewhere toward the middle of the book—a passage deserving to be quoted in full:

My basic argument about the Qur'an is that in order to make Islamic thought relevant, the human dimension of the Qur'an needs to be reconsidered. Placing the Qur'an firmly within history does not imply that the origins of the Qur'an are [purely] human. I believe the Qur'an to be a divine text revealed from God to the Prophet Muhammad through the mediation of the archangel Gabriel. That revelation, however, took place through the use of language—a language (Arabic) rooted in a historical context. The Qur'an addressed the Arabs living in the 7th century, taking into account the social reality of those particular people living on the Arabian Peninsula at that time. How else could they have understood the revelation??

As Abu Zayd adds forcefully: "I believe that one of the reasons we currently experience such stagnation in Islamic thought is that we overemphasize the divine dimension of the Qur'an at the expense of acknowledging its human characteristics."[9]

Reflecting his own lived experience, *Voice of an Exile* eloquently stresses again the Qur'an's plea for social justice and the removal of corruption and social oppression. In a chapter titled "The Nexus of Theory and Practice," we find these lines, which clearly demarcate the linkage of interpretation and action: "No matter what subject the Qur'an talks about . . . justice is at its core. . . . Qur'anic values are built on the concepts of freedom and justice—freedom of thought in order to bring about a just society." Unfortunately this plea for justice and freedom is too often silenced or ignored by religious and political authorities. In lieu of liberating practice we find "the stultifying practice of blindly following tradition, copying the past. . . . The tribal mentality is alive. The code is obedience." In view of this stultification, Abu Zayd sees the need to revive and deepen the legacy of the nineteenth-century Islamic reformers al-Afghani and Muhammad 'Abduh. "We have this legacy," he says. "I place myself within this legacy. My research in the field of Islamic Studies is all about trying to find a way of incorporating modernity and progress into Islamic thought." Taking up the legacy of 'Abduh, for Abu Zayd, means a duty to denounce injustice everywhere, including the injustice inflicted by autocratic rulers, but also the injustice suffered by Palestinians and people in Gaza. Basically struggling for justice involves the need to reform society as well as to reform religious thought: "Today we must not let ourselves be defined by a phony identity that manifests itself in terms of backwardness and resistance to progress, under the guise of defending Islam and our identity. Our aborted Renaissance looked to the future as it attempted to break free from outdated structures of thinking. . . . To carry on, we need an orderly way to talk about religion—a discourse."[10]

The task charted so eloquently in *Voice of an Exile* was carried forward in Abu Zayd's subsequent *Reformation of Islamic Thought* (2006). One paragraph must suffice here, taken from the last chapter of the book: "Without rethinking the Qur'an and without re-invoking its living status as a 'discourse' . . . democratic and open hermeneutics cannot be achieved. But why should hermeneutics be democratic and open? Because it is about the meaning of life. If we are serious about freeing religious thought from power manipulation, whether political, social, or religious, and want to empower the community of believers to formulate 'meaning,' we need to construct an open democratic hermeneutics."[11]

Mohammed Abed al-Jabri

In his commitment to a progressive and democratic reading of the Qur'an, Abu Zayd during his lifetime was ably seconded by the Moroccan philosopher Mohammed al-Jabri (who also passed in 2010). Here again I had the pleasure of a personal acquaintance. I met him for the first time in 2000, during a visit to the University of Rabat, where I had been invited to present a lecture. Having announced my visit beforehand, al-Jabri received me warmly and invited me for a meal. I found him to be a very stimulating and engaging thinker and, despite his spreading fame, a modest and unassuming human being. We talked mainly about his *Introduction à la critique de la raison Arabe,* whose English translation had appeared a few years before. I saw him again in 2006 on the occasion of the World Philosophy Day events organized by UNESCO in Rabat. At that time, as I recall, UNESCO awarded him the Ibn Sina Prize of Philosophy. Little did I know that I would be back four years later to commemorate him.

The life story of al-Jabri was less dramatic and less painful than that of Abu Zayd. With a few interruptions he was able to spend his mature life in his native Morocco (thus being spared the "leaning tower" trauma of the Egyptian). He was born in December 1935 in a small town near Oujda in southeastern Morocco. He began his college studies in 1958, spending one year at Damascus University in Syria and then continuing at the University of Rabat. After graduating in 1962, he served as a high school philosophy teacher and later as a school principal. In 1967 he began his graduate studies in philosophy and Islamic thought at the University of Mohammad V in Rabat, where he obtained his doctorate in 1970 with a dissertation on Ibn Khaldun. From this time forward, until his retirement in 2002, he held the position of professor of philosophy and Islamic thought at the same university. During his lifetime, he was showered with a great number of honors and awards, some of which he rejected. Thus, he turned down a huge monetary award from the former Iraqi president Saddam Hussein and another large sum from the Libyan leader Moammar Gadaffi. Among the prizes he accepted were a UNESCO Prize for Arab Culture in 1988, a Maghreb Award for Culture given by Tunisia in 1999, the Ibn Sina Medal from UNESCO at the World Philosophy Day of 2006, and the Ibn Rushd Prize for Freedom of Thought awarded in Berlin in 2008.

There are many similarities but also many dissimilarities between Abu Zayd and al-Jabri. By comparison, al-Jabri was more actively and directly engaged in political movements in his country and in the Arab world. During the 1960s, he was an active member of the "Union Nationale des Forces Populaires" (UNFP), which was a leftist wing of the nationalist Istiqlal Party. In July 1963 he was briefly jailed for his activities. Later, after the UNFP was banned, he served from 1975 to 1988 as a leading member of the Union Socialiste des Forces Populaires. In the course of his political activities, however, he became increasingly dissatisfied with prevailing ideological formulas—including socialism, Marxism, and liberalism. His dissatisfaction prompted him to turn with growing intensity to classical Islamic thought in the hope of finding resources for political and intellectual renewal in our time.

Another aspect of dissimilarity has to do with philosophical orientation and genealogy. As indicated before, Abu Zayd placed himself deliberately into a dual lineage or tradition: the lineage of classical Islamic philosophy (from the Mu'tazilites to Ibn Rushd) *and* the lineage of Sufism (with a focus on Ibn Arabi). This broad range of lineages was less, or not at all, congenial to al-Jabri. Honoring Ibn Rushd as his foremost philosophical mentor, al-Jabri tended to uphold the rational lucidity of "Western Islam" (*Maghreb*) as over against the mystical-illuminationist tendencies of "Eastern Islam" (*Mashreq*). Generally speaking, his work privileges *burhan* (deductive reasoning) and *bayan* (linguistic analysis) over *irfan* (mystical reading). Thus, it would be difficult to find in his writings references to Ibn Arabi or Rumi—and this despite the fact that he was a warm-hearted person and (as I discovered in conversation) quite able to cite Rumi or other Muslim poets without difficulty or hesitation.[12]

But I want to turn here to the commonality, not the dissimilarity, between the two thinkers. The central feature linking the two, in my view, was the effort to steer a course between or beyond religious obscurantism or fundamentalism, on the one hand, and secularist/laïcist dismissal of religious thought, on the other. As al-Jabri repeatedly observed, his aim was to overcome "the current polarization of Arab [or Islamic] thought": namely, between "an imported modernism" that entirely disregards Islamic traditions and (on the other side) an "Arab traditionalism or fundamentalism" that assures Arabs or Muslims of a spurious identity through nostalgic retrievals of the past.[13] Like Abu Zayd, al-Jabri held that religious revelation is addressed to human beings in their concrete historical situation and hence can be validly understood only by taking historical and social context into account. This does not mean that historical and social context is immune from critique or transformation; however, such transformation can only occur immanently, in full awareness of prevailing conditions. Together with Abu Zayd, al-Jabri affirmed that, given its contextuality, interpretation is always multiple and can never achieve absolute certainty or univocity. In addition to the role of context, this multiplicity is also due to the internal complexity and diversity of traditions, including religious traditions. Perhaps more than Abu Zayd, the Moroccan also ascribed the "conflict of interpretations" to the individual autonomy and freedom of individual interpreters (even when freedom is responsibly exercised). In the pursuit of his critical initiative, al-Jabri—again like Abu Zayd—placed himself in the company not only of early Arab philosophy (especially the Mu'tazilites and Ibn Rushd) but also in that of prominent Muslim reformers of the nineteenth century, whose work, in his view, urgently needs to be resumed and deepened today.

Al-Jabri's writings are sprawling and concentrate on a number of topics, such as culture, education, and politics; but his core concern was always the relation between Islam and the modern world. Among his early writings are: *La Pensée de Ibn Khaldun: La Assabia et l'Etat* (1971); *Pour une vision progressiste de nos difficultés intellectuelles et éducatives* (1977); and *Nous et notre passé* (1980). However, his central endeavor was the critical rethinking and renovation of Arab or Muslim intellectual life. This concern led him to his major project, *Critique de la raison Arabe,* which appeared in three volumes in Beirut starting in 1982 (and whose title clearly reflects Kantian affinities). The project was carried forward in three specific inquiries: "The Genesis of Arab Thought" (1984), "The Structure of the Arab Mind" (1986), and "The Arab Political Mind" (1990). As mentioned before, a part of his project appeared in 1999 in English as *Arab-Islamic Philosophy: A Contemporary Critique.* More recently, two new books appeared in English: *Democracy, Human Rights and Law in Islamic Thought* (2008) and *The Formation of Arab Reason: Text, Tradition and the Construction of Modernity in the Arab World* (2010).

It is impossible again to review the entire oeuvre. Let me just lift up some passages from *Arab-Islamic Philosophy* (the English translation of his introduction to *Critique de la raison Arabe*). The very title of the introduction discloses the basic aim of the study: "To Seek Our Modernity by Rethinking Our Tradition." The title immediately puts into question the customary disjunction between tradition and modernity. Moreover, by emphasizing *"our* modernity," the phrase challenges the Western Enlightenment pretense of representing *the* modernity, or the only possible kind of modernity. In al-Jabri's words (anticipating Taylor's notion of "multiple modernities"): "There is not *one* single absolute, universal and planetary modernity; rather, there are *numerous* modernities that differ from era to era and from place to place." What Europe or the West celebrates as "modernity" was a distinct historical stage born of the European Enlightenment, which cannot be replicated in other times and places. For people living outside Europe or the West, "European modernity" impinges from the outside, "pushing its adversary into withdrawal or confinement." This is why *"our"* aspiration toward modernity must necessarily "base itself on those components of the critical [or creative] mind present in Arab culture itself in order to trigger an internal dynamics of change." Thus, in the context of Arab-Islamic culture, modernity cannot mean "to refute tradition or break entirely with the past, but rather [an effort] to upgrade the manner in which we assume our relationship to tradition at the level of what we call 'contemporaneity,' which for us means catching up with the great strides that are being made worldwide."[14]

As in the case of Abu Zayd, the recognition of cultural-historical contexts does not mean a simple lapse into relativism, which would ignore the liberating demands of modern life. Nor does it warrant a glorification of the past in a fundamentalist vein. For al-Jabri, such glorification is a "medievalist" reaction with all its (antidemocratic) consequences: namely, "the persistence of the relation of ruler and ruled where the latter, reduced to the condition of a herd, lead their mental and social lives under the shepherd's tutelage." Unfortunately, such a reaction is all too widespread in the contemporary Arab-Islamic world, where we often find "a retreat to backward positions that would serve as ramparts and as defense mechanisms" of a stagnant and illusory identity. Against this retreat one needs to marshal a forward-looking approach that, without neglecting tradition, transforms the latter in the spirit of "rationality and democracy." Such an approach is able to rekindle the legacy of classical philosophy from al-Farabi to Ibn Rushd. For, al-Jabri comments: "Al-Farabi (like Ibn Rushd) was not an isolated man who was cut off from the world, . . . but a man who was concerned about the problems of the society in which he lived. He assumed the preoccupations of his contemporaries. . . . He was an optimist who believed in progress and in solving problems through reason, and it was this faith that motivated his dream of the 'virtuous city,' a city of reason, of harmony, of fraternity and of justice in which he invested all the sciences of his era."[15]

Some Comparisons

In their endeavor to interpret and critically rethink Islamic tradition(s), the Moroccan and Egyptian thinkers mentioned so far have not been alone. I have chosen them mainly for two reasons: my personal acquaintance with them and their instructive similarities and differences. A number of other prominent thinkers toiling in the same vineyard should at least briefly be mentioned. I limit myself here to two: the expatriate Algerian Muhammad Arkoun and the expatriate Iranian Abdolkarim Soroush. As it happens, the former also passed away in 2010. I was not so fortunate as to know Professor Arkoun personally; I only know him "secondhand," through reading his texts. He was born in 1928 in a Berber village in Algeria and later pursued his studies of philosophy and literature at the University of Algiers and the Sorbonne in Paris. Subsequently he taught at Lyon University (1969–72) and the Sorbonne (1972–92). Like Abu Zayd and al-Jabri he received many honors. In 1996 he was decorated as an officer of the French Legion d'Honneur, and in 2001 he was asked to deliver the prestigious Gifford Lectures in Edinburgh. He published numerous books, in Arabic, French, and English—some of which directly address the issue of the present essay. This is obviously true of his book *The Concept of Revelation: From the People of the Book to the Societies of the Book* (1988). Very close to the inquiries of the Egyptian and Moroccan thinkers are his texts *Pour une critique de la raison Islamique* (1984), *Arab Thought* (1988), and *Rethinking Islam: Common Questions, Uncommon Answers Today* (1994). Some of his Arabic texts deal explicitly with the problem of interpretation: *Al-Islam: Naqd wa ijtihad* (1990) and *Mina-l-ijtihad ilä naqd al-'aql al-islami* (1991).

In the present context I only want to quote one passage from his book *The Unthought in Contemporary Islamic Thought* (2002), reissued under the title *Islam: To Reform or to Subvert* (2006):

> The dialectic tension between the [sacred] Book and the [human] book is clearly manifest in the present tension between religion and politics, spiritual authority and political power, divine law and secular law, mythical truth and historical knowledge. . . . These concepts are often used to point out the contradictions, the polemical oppositions developed by their respective defenders. The opposition has reached the level of mutual exclusion through violence between fundamentalist defenders of the rule of God and the modern secular defenders of the rule of law, democratic values and human rights, presented respectively as the values of the "West" versus "Islam." What I have tried to suggest is the necessity to excavate new fields of research and critical thinking on these stakes not yet perceived, not considered because they are hiding in-

between the many concepts currently employed for ideological polarization.[16]

The second Islamic voice I want to lift up here is that of Aldolkarim Soroush, a well-known Iranian philosopher with whom I have maintained friendly relations over two decades. Soroush was born in 1945 in Tehran and grew up there. He first studied pharmacology at the University of Tehran; then, in the mid-1970s he went to the London School of Economics, where he studied analytical chemistry and the philosophy of science (the latter with Karl Popper). Shortly after the 1979 revolution he returned to Tehran, where he quickly emerged as a leading public intellectual. He first taught Islamic culture at Tehran's Teachers College and then moved on to the Academy of Philosophy and the Research Center for Humanities and Social Sciences in Tehran. He became an increasingly influential and controversial figure, mainly because he tested the insights of the philosophy of science (mainly Popper's stress on fallibility) against the reigning religious dogmatism. Some of his writings first became available in English through the publication of his *Reason, Freedom, and Democracy in Islam* (2000). Shortly afterward he was fired from his academic post and barred from any teaching and lecturing in Iran. Since that time he has served as a visiting professor at many places: Harvard, Yale, Princeton, Columbia, Georgetown, the Wissenschaftskolleg in Berlin, and the Free University in Amsterdam. In 2004 he was awarded the international Erasmus Prize in Rotterdam.

During the past decade, Soroush has devoted himself chiefly to the critical interpretation of Islam and the Qur'an. The core of his endeavor centers around the notion of the "expansion and contraction" of religious knowledge in history, an idea developed in a massive tome published in Farsi under the title *Bast-e Tajrubeh-e Nabavi*. An abridged version has appeared in English under the title *The Expansion of Prophetic Experience: Essays on Historicity, Contingency and Plurality in Religion* (2009). A basic tenet of this text is the distinction between the sacred "essence" and the historical-cultural "accidentals" of religion. I quote here a brief passage:

The accidentals [of religion] are those that could have been other than they are, unlike the essentials. . . . The goals of the Prophet *are* religious essentials. [But] in order to express and attain these intentions and to have them understood, the Prophet seeks the assistance of [accidentals, including] a particular language, particular concepts, and particular methods. All of this occurs in a particular time and place and for a particular people with particular physical and mental capacities. The purveyor of religion is faced with specific reactions and questions, and in response to them gives specific answers. . . . [Thus] these corpulent accidentals hide within them the precious essence of religiosity. In order to uncover this gem, we have no choice but to peel away those superficies.[17]

By way of conclusion I want to return to the broader political implications of interpretation. As mentioned repeatedly, every interpretation raises the issue of the relation between text and context and, in the case of religious faith, that between revelation and human understanding. It is in the interstices of this relation that human freedom emerges: the freedom of thought and of the free expression of thought. This opening or gap of human freedom inevitably contains within itself the promise of emancipation and democracy. The gap can only be covered over, or attempted to be closed, through autocracy and resort to forceful repression. To a greater or lesser extent, all the thinkers lifted up in these pages have suffered from the iron fist of repression. But the prospect of such repression was forecast by the leading European philosopher of interpretation: Gadamer. As he observed in his *Truth and Method*, interpretation cannot flourish in a society or regime dominated by autocratic power or a Hobbesian sovereign; as an exercise of free judgment, hermeneutics rather presupposes a dialogical give-and-take occurring in a transformative rethinking of tradition: "Where this is not the case—for instance, in an absolutist state where the will of the autocratic ruler is above the law [and above judgment]—interpretation cannot flourish, since the ruler(s) can abrogate the premises of interpretive judgment."[18] Hence, far from being just an innocuous method or tool, interpretation is the opening wedge for democracy seen as a regime of responsible freedom everywhere in the world.

Appendix A

Beyond Multiculturalism?

For Bhikhu Parekh

One of the delights of intellectual life is to pay tribute to teachers, mentors, and friends who have had a formative influence on one's own maturation. For me, Bhikhu Parekh has been such a mentor and longtime friend. We come from different backgrounds: I from a Continental European background modulated by North American experiences; he from an Indian background modulated by British experiences. But at one point our paths crossed—in ways that became decisive for my development. It happened in 1984. Bhikhu at that time was vice-chancellor at the University of Baroda and, in this capacity, organized a conference assembling a great number of political theorists from both India and the West. The meeting was a "eureka" event for me. I suddenly discovered, in a stark and dramatic way, my Eurocentric parochialism, evident in my utter ignorance of Indian culture and intellectual traditions. Thus, in organizing the meeting, Bhikhu opened a new world for me and set me on the path of cross-cultural and cosmopolitan inquiry. Both then and on later occasions, he also alerted me to the importance of Mahatma Gandhi for contemporary politics and political thinking. In this respect, too, my life was channeled in a new and fruitful direction.

In subsequent decades, I followed Parekh's writings and activities with a keen interest. I noticed that he was not only a theorist but managed to combine theory and practice. To give just some examples: he served as acting chair of the Commission for Racial Equality in the United Kingdom and as chair of the Commission on the Future of Multi-Ethnic Britain. Thus, when in 2000 his book *Rethinking Multi-*

culturalism: Cultural Diversity and Political Theory was published, I knew that it was not just another academic treatise on the topic, but a work sustained by vast erudition and concrete multicultural experiences. I wrote an extensive review of the book under the title "Multiculturalism and the Good Life" (which first appeared in 2003).[1] In my review, I highlighted a number of aspects that still seem to me salient today. One aspect has to do with the distinction between a purely empirical or descriptive and a normative or evaluative approach to the topic. While the former simply acknowledges the factual existence of cultural diversity without evaluative engagement, the second perspective involves (in Parekh's words) a "normative response" to such diversity, that is, the manner and character of the evaluative assessment of multiculturalism. Another, closely related aspect concerns the angle from which evaluative assessments are undertaken. Here Parekh adopted a sensible position between universalism and particularism (or relativism), by arguing that cultural diversity can be understood neither from an abstract "view from nowhere," treating all cultures as the same, nor from the angle of incommensurability and cultural self-enclosure. This insight led him in the direction of a "dialogical" (or hermeneutical) perspective, which stresses mutual ethical engagement and "the centrality of a dialogue between cultures and ethical norms, principles, and institutional structures."[2]

In recent times, the political climate in many Western countries has changed. The relative optimism and openness to cultural diversity that attended the demise of the Cold War has tended to give way to distrust, retrenchment, and "identity politics." Several factors account for this change. One prominent factor is September 11 and its pervasive impact on all aspects of social and political life. In lieu of the celebration of open borders, September 11 fomented fear of strangers (seen as potential enemies); seemingly endless "terror wars"; and the strengthening of the "national security state," manifest in steadily tightened surveillance and public control. Closely connected with this factor is the worsening of economic conditions, culminating in the financial meltdown of 2008—a worsening that triggered massive unemployment in many places, which in turn pitted domestic workers against immigrants and migrant workers. An additional factor in some countries was the renewed upsurge of organized religion—a process often producing interreligious and sectarian rivalries (in lieu of interfaith understanding). As a result of these and other factors, multiculturalism became increasingly suspect and a target of critique. What had earlier been heralded as promising horizons of democratic equality and cross-cultural symbiosis was tendentially cast in the somber colors of intergroup rivalry, enmity, and distrust.

Actually, at a closer look, some measure of critique had accompanied multiculturalism almost from the start. Already in 1989, at the end of the Cold War, one British writer (Fay Weldon) announced that the "attempt at multiculturalism" was destined to shipwreck—citing as evidence the Salman Rushdie affair and the hostility engendered by *The Satanic Verses*.[3] While initially a minority voice, critical sentiments mushroomed during the following decades, nurtured by some of the cited events as well as by the deepening problems of social integration posed by the massive influx of immigrants from formerly colonial countries into Britain and Continental Europe. After having simmered for some time under the surface of official pronouncements, disaffected voices by 2010–11 became a full-fledged chorus that governments could no longer ignore. By that time, prominent political leaders in Western countries took up the gauntlet and zeroed in on the presumed defects and "failure" of multiculturalism, deriving from its corrosive effects on national and social cohesion. Well-known and attracting much attention in this context were public speeches given by the British prime minister (David Cameron) and the German chancellor (Angela Merkel), in which both laid the blame for social disintegration and disharmony squarely at the doorstep of an earlier multiculturalist euphoria. Not to be outdone, some public intellectuals and political writers jumped into the fray—with some of them decrying the celebration of cultural multiplicity as a stepping stone to national suicide or "self-abolition."[4]

In light of this harsh and sometimes vitriolic rhetoric, recent attacks on multiculturalism are clearly deplorable and upsetting. They are also (and especially) upsetting given some of the underlying factors motivating the attacks: the upsurge of xenophobia and of nationalistic types of populism in many countries. Yet, seen from another angle, the impact of the controversy was not without redeeming qualities. Provoked by stinging critiques, defenders of multiculturalism were induced to rethink or reformulate their position—a rethinking prone to transform antagonism into a productive learning experience.

While not abandoning their basic agenda, many defenders came to see that the multicultural idea was not always well implemented or translated into a viable social practice. A major defect of a naive or shallow multiculturalism—it was found—was the neglect of the stubbornness of human self-interest, a stubbornness that can only be mitigated through sustained education and the fostering of cross-cultural practical engagement. Where this need is neglected, the coexistence of different cultural, ethnic, and religious groups can only lead to fragmentation, "ghettoization," and possibly conflict. This fact was clearly recognized by social theorist Tariq Modood—a strong champion of the multicultural agenda—when he wrote that "multiculturalism is incomplete and one-sided" without a continual effort at reintegration: "This is an aspect that has been understated [in the past] when the inattentive assumed that multiculturalism is all about emphasizing difference and separation" to the exclusion of community.[5]

The defects of a naive multiculturalism and the need for public reintegration have been stressed by Modood on repeated occasions, always with the aim of healing the wounds of intergroup nonrecognition or misrecognition. As he pointedly observed in an essay (2006): "When new groups enter a society, there has to be some education and refinement of . . . sensitivities in the light of changing circumstances and the specific vulnerabilities of new entrants."[6] Subsequently, Modood developed the distinct notion of "political" multiculturalism or of multiculturalism as a "civic idea" focused on shared citizenship and civic virtues. "Strong multicultural identities," he stated at that point, "are a good thing . . . but they need the complement of a framework of vibrant, dynamic, national narratives and the ceremonies and rituals which give expression to a shared public identity."[7] This emphasis on a common civic framework—always in the process of redefinition and renegotiation—is not unique to this author but can be found in numerous writings of roughly the same time. The titles of some texts are indicative of this outlook. Thus, Per Mouritsen and Knud Jørgensen published a collection titled *Constituting Communities: Political Solutions to Cultural Conflicts*, while Anne Phillips authored *Multiculturalism without [Shared] Culture*. To be sure, the "civic" orientation was not universally endorsed—a fact evident in the title of an edited volume called *An Ambiguous Rescue: Multiculturalism and Citizenship; Responses to Tariq Modood*.[8]

Concerns about deficiencies of multiculturalism have prompted numerous writers to resort not only to a rethinking but to a rephrasing of the agenda, involving the substitution of "interculturalism" for the older term. Modood—who ultimately rejects the new term—has reflected on the advantages and disadvantages of the innovation. In an essay coauthored with fellow theorist Nasar Meer, he has outlined four main areas in which, according to its supporters, interculturalism differs from, and is superior to, the notion of multiculturalism (in its traditional usage). The first and major area has to do with the greater emphasis placed by the new term on cultural interaction, dialogue, and mutual engagement, as contrasted with the mere coexistence and juxtaposition of multiple unrelated groups. The second aspect, closely related to the first, involves a different conception of pluralism, in the sense that a more integrated or "integral" pluralism is preferred to an atomistic plurality of ghettoes. In the words of one of its defenders, an implication of interculturalism is that "culture is acting in a multidirectional [or cross-fertilizing] manner." The third feature, following from the second, is the greater accent on holistic integration, that is, the concern with social cohesion and harmony. To cite again one supporter: "While multiculturalism boils down to celebrating difference, interculturalism is about understanding each other's cultures, sharing them and finding common ground on which people can become more integrated." The final aspect has to do with a certain moral or ethical orientation of interculturalism that enables it to expose and criticize oppressive or demeaning cultural practices. As one supporter has noted, devoid of ethical standards, multiculturalism "may end up giving public recognition to groups which endorse fundamentally illiberal and even irrational goals."[9]

As it seems to me, the intervention of "interculturalism" was salutary and welcome to the extent that it exposed certain shortcomings of a simplistic multiculturalism. But of course, not all formulations of that perspective have been shortsighted or simplistic; some of them—most prominently the formulation of Bhikhu Parekh—have explicitly acknowledged the need for interaction, mutual learning, and engagement, and thus also the ethical quality of multiculturality properly conceived. As we read in Parekh's famous text, cultures cannot be encapsulated against each other; for: "However rich it may be, no culture embodies all that is valuable in human life and develops the full range of human possibilities. Different cultures thus correct and complement each other, expanding each other's horizon of thought."[10] Thus, once the remonstrations of interculturalism are duly noted and incorporated, the older vocabulary may still be usable as a "polyse-mic" concept. This dual aspect is properly endorsed by Meer and Modood in their reflections on terminology. One the one hand, they note, older formulations have often tended to ignore "how central notions of dialogue and communication are to multiculturalism." On the other hand, however, they find it possible to rescue the term, stat-ing: "While advocates of interculturalism wish to emphasize its posi-tive qualities in terms of encouraging communication, recognizing dynamic identities, promoting unity, and challenging illiberality, each of these qualities already feature in (and are on occasion foundational to) multiculturalism too."[11]

Enriched by intercultural insights and emendations, multicultur-alism—in my view—continues to be a valuable perspective today, by serving as an antidote to xenophobia and populist identity politics. In addition, the perspective also addresses long-standing dilemmas besetting Western liberalism and liberal democracy, especially the dilemmas resulting from a rigid public-private bifurcation and the banishment of cultural as well as religious commitments into the netherworld of idiosyncratic beliefs. This banishment had been de-nounced already by Parekh when he wrote, with specific reference to the American "wall of separation": "Part of the reason why religion arouses strong passions in the United States has perhaps to do with the fact that it is not taught in schools as an academic subject. Reli-gious citizens pick up their religion from sectarian churches, and the non-religious, having never been systematically exposed to it, find it alienating and frightening." This observation is corroborated and re-inforced in some of Charles Taylor's writings, especially his comment that public discussion about cultural and religious issues is "essential to a healthy society under diversity" and "both a sign and support of real mutual respect among people of different fundamental commit-ments." By contrast, "the kind of pale 'ecumenicism' where each feels constrained [or inhibited] from speaking about the other's views is ac-tually a way of preserving, under the mothballs of respectful silence, all the old misconceptions, prejudices, and contempt."[12]

Provided it does not shrink into shallow relativism, multiculturalism has always supported the need for cross-cultural and interfaith discussion and hence opposed the chimera of public "neutrality"—all the while keeping its distance from cultural or religious autocracy or domination. In recent times, this balanced multicultural outlook has been ably reaffirmed by a number of writers, always with an edge against both antiseptic indifference *and* monological dogmatism or oppression. Thus, Canadian philosopher Sonia Sikka picks up the Parekh-Taylor line by arguing that "the principled exclusion of religious views from public debate, as a result of the commitment to neutrality, ironically gives an unwarranted power and legitimacy to religious positions that cannot withstand critical scrutiny, with negative consequences for both religion and politics." As Sikka acknowledges, a pale or relativistic multiculturalism has sometimes converged with a neutralizing liberalism by purging the public sphere of vigorous cross-cultural and interfaith discussion. What she proposes as a remedy for this collusion is, first of all, a "lifting of the gag order" on religious and cultural speech on the level of civil society and, second, the inclusion of education about religious and cultural traditions in all publicly funded schools and colleges. As she writes, the treatment of religious and cultural commitments as a matter of either private belief or self-enclosed identity "may serve, in practice, to undermine the better possibilities in this regard, while encouraging the worse."[13]

To reiterate a point: the deprivatization of religious and cultural attachments does not sanction their "politicization" in the sense of their imposition through governmental fiat (which would run afoul of constitutional "antiestablishment" provisions in many countries). As Sikka prudently observes: "It does not follow from my argument that substantive debate about religious views should occur on *all* public levels; there are good reasons for preserving liberal and multicultural constraints within *governmental* institutions."[14] Wedged between private belief and state authority, multiculturalism properly conceived thus occupies a place in civil society that Hannah Arendt has called the "public realm" (and others the "public sphere"). In his 2000 text, Parekh made the bold proposal for the creation of a "public forum" where issues arising from religious, cultural, and ethnic differences would be discussed and negotiated. In Parekh's words, the common good in a multicultural society is "generated not by transcending cultural and other particularities, but through their interplay in the cut and thrust of dialogue"—where dialogue is not restricted to the cognitive level but descends into the depths of emotions, suffering, and hope. Such an engagement forms the heart of "dialogical democracy" (which, on the global level, finds a parallel in "dialogical cosmopolitanism"). Crucial in this engagement, Parekh concludes, is the cultivation of sympathy and trust: "a deepening of mutual understanding between different groups, sensitizing each to the concerns and anxieties of others" which performs a "vital community-building role."[15]

Appendix B

Cosmopolitan Confucianism?
Chinese Traditions and Dialogue

I greatly appreciate this opportunity to participate in this second "Nishan Forum on World Civilizations," a forum that seeks to underscore and strengthen the idea of the "harmony of cultures with diversity."[1] This is indeed an important idea and one that has been dear to my heart for some time. I greatly welcomed the motto of a "dialogue among civilizations" launched by the president of Iran, Mohammad Khatami, at the end of last century, a motto picked up by the United Nations General Assembly when it decided to designate 2001 as the "Year of Dialogue among Civilizations." A year later, in 2002, I published a book titled *Dialogue among Civilizations: Some Exemplary Voices*. About the same time, I joined a global nongovernmental organization that is called "World Public Forum—Dialogue of Civilizations." I have been active in that organization since that time and presently serve as its executive cochair.

I am very happy to see that the idea of civilizational dialogue has also found a home in China, more particularly in the Nishan Forum, whose inaugural meeting in 2011 coincided with the tenth anniversary of the UN "Year of Dialogue." I am even more happy noting the location of the Nishan Forum near the birthplace of Confucius. No better place could have been found for a forum on world civilizations, because Confucius, in my mind, embodies perfectly what it means to be civilized. Here I have to confess to you my long-standing fascination with, and attraction to, the sage of Qufu. It is now roughly two decades ago, in 1991, that I first visited China. The occasion was an international conference held at the University of Nanjing on the topic "Traditional Chinese Thought and Culture and the Twenty-First Century." The central focus of the conference was the relevance and viability of indigenous Chinese traditions in the face of the relentless modernization and Westernization of the globe. Among Chinese traditions, Confucianism clearly occupied the limelight of attention. The University of Nanjing was kind enough to provide me with a guide who, after the conference, took me to Qufu and also the sacred mountain of Taishan. So, my roots in the Confucian tradition are deep (although I am not, and do not claim to be, a professional Sinologist).

The issue I want to address today is the relation between world civilizations, and especially the dialogue among civilizations, and Confucianism. The issue needs to be explored on two levels. First, I want to profile more clearly the meaning of a dialogue among civilizations; and for this purpose I need to differentiate such dialogue from other possible—and historically recorded—relations between cultures or civilizations. Next, I want to examine how Confucianism fits into these relations among cultures and what role it can play there. Finally, I ask: Is Confucianism a suitable partner in the dialogue among civilizations today?

Relations between Civilizations

Relations between cultures—we know well—are not always friendly, welcoming, or dialogical. A main example of abstention from dialogue is the limit case of deliberate nonrelation, that is, the avoidance of cultural contact. For a variety of motivations—which may range from fearful apprehension to haughty arrogance—a culture may choose to shun outside contacts and to concentrate entirely on the cultivation of indigenous legacies or traditions. In common parlance, this practice of avoidance is called "isolationism." Avoided outsiders are not necessarily demeaned (although there is a strong tendency to do so); they may also be considered simply irrelevant or insignificant. They are in any case not recognized as equal members of the human family. Epithets designating outsiders may range from the neutral expression "foreigners" to such clearly pejorative labels as "infidels," "savages," or "barbarians."

There are advantages and disadvantages associated with isolationism. From the perspective of the avoiding culture, a main advantage is the exclusion of harmful or destructive influences, especially influences seen as debilitating for indigenous ways of life. Such protectionism is particularly important (and even sensible) in the case of weak or fledging societies in danger of being overrun by external products and practices. The disadvantage of isolationist policies is the danger of cultural stagnation or ossification, of the progressive routinization of social conduct, stifling all impulses of innovation or cultural reform. Isolationism of this kind was practiced to a large extent during the Qing dynasty in China—and the price to be paid was scientific and economic stagnation (rendering China vulnerable to unequal treaties and other forms of external control). For different reasons, isolationism—the avoidance of "foreign entanglements"—was practiced by the United States during much of the nineteenth century, but with less grievous results. In large measure, the internal dynamism of a young and expanding nation provided a sheet anchor against stagnation—although tendencies toward dogmatic fixation were evident in "Know Nothing" movements (directed against immigrants) and other modes of self-enclosure.

Another type of nonrelation or (better) defective relation between cultures or civilizations is unilateralism, that is, the one-sided imposition of ideas and practices by one culture on another. Sometimes, the imposition or transference may be only partial and occurs less through strategic design than through cultural contagion or osmosis.[2] Thus, what is often referred to as "Westernization" is in many ways a nearly subliminal process of the dissemination of cultural symbols, signals, and preferences. When this dissemination is backed up by military and administrative power (as it frequently is), we speak of "imperialism" and/or "colonialism"; a widely used code word for the latter today is cultural-political "hegemony."[3] The pursuit of imperial or hegemonic policies is a constant temptation of big nations and large civilizations—although it can also surface among smaller or medium-size countries striving for bigness or greatness (such as a "Greater Germany," a "Greater Serbia," or a "Greater This or That"). The perceived benefit of such policies is the acquisition of geopolitical power, of landmasses and resources. The drawback is the endemic defect of unilateralism, that is, the atrophy of the ability to learn (from others) and hence the danger of autistic self-enclosure (which approximates imperialism to isolationism).

As history teaches, imperialism/colonialism has been a steady companion or by-product of Western civilization, from the Macedonian and Roman empires in antiquity to the British and French empires in modern times. To a lesser extent, imperialist ventures can also be found outside the Western orbit, for example, in Islamic culture and some East Asian countries (mainly Japan). Curiously, although certainly a big or large civilization, China has historically not been drawn to political or military imperialism (although its cultural contagion has certainly affected much of Asia). One can speculate about the different proclivities toward imperialism. As cultural historians tell us, China has traditionally found a certain fullness or wholeness in the Middle Kingdom, which mitigated the impulse for expansion. By contrast, Western civilization was always marked by a sense of lack or haunting disorder, which fueled the desire to impose political order on the world, both at home and abroad.[4]

Irrespective of the correctness or incorrectness of this speculation, one conclusion can be drawn: namely, that wholeness or completeness cannot be found through unilateralism, that is, the top-down imposition of order from one civilization on others. This leads me to what I consider the most promising or beneficial mode of the encounter between cultures or civilizations: the mode of "dialogue among (or between) civilizations." In this mode, cultures do not spurn or shun each other; nor do they seek to foist one way of life on other cultures (in an exercise of cultural and/or political imperialism). Rather cultures here are willing to undergo a learning experience promoted through dialogue, mutual testing, and constructively critical interrogation. Under the auspices of interrogation, wholeness or completeness cannot be presupposed or unilaterally fabricated. Instead, wholeness here is an ongoing process and only tentatively anticipated in the cut and thrust of mutual engagement. To this extent, wholeness cannot be summed up in a static formula but is a dynamically moving feast accomplished through imaginative and creative renewal.[5]

Creative encounters of this kind are relatively infrequent in history; but they are not without precedents. Thus, in the early centuries (CE), sustained learning processes took place between Christian theologians and Greco-Roman intellectual and cultural traditions. A few centuries later, these processes extended into a triadic conversation among Christian, Islamic, and Greco-Roman strands of thought.

Almost a millennium earlier, one may recall, fruitful cultural exchanges were carried on in the Far East, among Buddhist, Daoist, and Confucian traditions or ways of life. Whatever the frequency of such exchanges may have been in the past, our contemporary age of rapid globalization renders dialogical engagement not only more possible but also a near-mandatory obligation—unless we want to descend into unilateral domination or the "clash of civilizations."

Confucianism and World Civilizations

If the ideal types of cultural encounter are as I have sketched them above, what are the implications for Confucianism and contemporary practitioners of the Confucian tradition? What are the lessons that especially Chinese Confucianists can draw from my discussion? As it seems to me, practitioners have sometimes wavered between the sketched options, and this may have something to do with their preferred definition of Confucianism. The Taiwanese scholar Liu Shuxian distinguishes among three versions or strands of Confucianism: a spiritual or philosophical version, a public or "politicized" version, and a popular or grassroots set of beliefs. Already before him, the mainland philosopher Liang Shuming had differentiated a "spiritual" or philosophical Confucianism from a public or "institutional" type—a distinction particularly useful for present purposes. Clearly, if the accent is placed on the public or institutional variant, then Confucianism is basically an indigenous perspective of little significance for the outside world. Confucian teachings, from this angle, are mainly an appendix of imperial rule and a constitutive element of Chinese, especially Han, identity. In the words of Liu Shuxian: public or politicized Confucianism served "as the official ideology of the dynasties."[6]

In contemporary China, politicized Confucianism is by no means defunct (although it is clearly overshadowed by neoliberal and socialist ideas). In fact, in the eyes of some prominent thinkers, the Confucian legacy is an ideal instrument for the political regeneration of China—and a bulwark against corrupting Western influences. A good example is the mainland thinker Jiang Qing. A defender of traditional cultural values, Jiang is mainly troubled by the onslaught of modernization, Westernization, and globalization—tendencies that in their combination threaten to undermine "Chineseness" or the fabric of

Chinese identity. As an antithesis to these dangers, he considers it crucial today to emphasize the political or public dimension of Confucianism—a dimension that, in his view, was first developed by the Gongyang scholarship of the Han dynasty. Only by recuperating this public strand—which does not involve a neglect of ethics—will it be possible to ward off the corrosive effects of modernity and Western liberal democracy, which are ultimately rooted in selfishness. As he writes: "In the guise of modernity, men become animals full of desire. . . . My understanding of tradition as opposed to modernity is that human desire must somehow be restricted by heavenly law." On the political level, selfishness converts liberal democracy into a form of Social Darwinism that "will ultimately destroy the human race." By contrast, "Confucianism puts its ultimate wager of human salvation on the reemergence of a sage king."[7]

By using the language of salvation, it is clear that Jiang also attributes to Confucianism a distinctly religious quality—a fact evident in his statement: "The restoration of Confucian religion can restore China's historical and cultural destiny, or Chineseness."[8] This aspect is even further underscored by the sociologist and social theorist Kang Xiaoguang, who combines a political or politicized version of Confucianism with the latter's elevation to the role of a public or civil religion. Together with Jiang, Kang is opposed to Western modernity and liberal democracy; his central commitment is to Chinese nationalism or cultural recovery—which, in his view, requires sustained efforts to "re-Confucianize" China. Fashioned as a civic religion, Confucianism for Kang can provide substantive legitimacy for the Chinese government, a legitimacy lost or badly tarnished in recent times. More specifically, it can supply justification for (what he calls) "benevolent government" or benevolent authoritarianism wielded by eminent Confucian scholars. Thus, the project of re-Confucianizing China is not just an academic or purely scholarly endeavor (as assumed by some so-called New Confucians). In Kang's words, the project involves two simultaneous agendas: "to Confucianize the Chinese Communist Party and to Confucianize Chinese society. When Confucianism replaces Marxism-Leninism as state ideology and Confucian scholars replace the communist cadres, the process of creating a benevolent government is complete."[9]

As it seems, at least in the case of Kang Xiaoguang, the project of Confucianization is not entirely limited to the two agendas but includes a third, more ambitious goal: the missionary aim to transform the entire world in the image of the Chinese tradition. In line with older Chinese conceptions of cosmic unity or harmony, Kang also envisages a kind of "idealistic" globalization leading ultimately to global unity under Confucian auspices. As one can see, the cultivation of indigenous traditions here shades over into cosmopolitical outreach; in terms of my earlier sketch, isolationism acquires overtones of imperial hegemony. I do not know how much appeal this nationalist agenda enjoys in China today; my sense is that it is rather limited. Most of the Confucian scholars (or practitioners of New Confucianism) with whom I am familiar do not support it but rather favor a more balanced, dialogical approach that combines cultivation of indigenous traditions with an openness to the winds of change coming from Western modernity, critical rationality, and liberal democracy. An outstanding example of this perspective is the famous manifesto of 1958 titled "Manifesto for a Reappraisal of Sinology and a Reconstruction of Chinese Culture" signed by four leading Confucian scholars in East Asia: Tang Junyi, Zhang Junmai, Mou Zongsan, and Xu Fuguan.

The Manifesto clearly had a dual aim, captured in the two terms "reappraisal" and "reconstruction." On the one hand, the authors criticized the tendency of some Western Sinologists to look down on traditional Chinese culture from the citadel of modern Western rationality and, thus, to adopt the haughty stance of "Orientalists." On the other hand, the Manifesto encouraged Confucian scholars to be receptive to Western trends and perspectives (critically evaluated) and thereby to become able to reinterpret and reconstruct in new ways traditional teachings. Receptivity in the Manifesto also extended clearly to the political domain, where the authors envisaged a reconciliation—coupled with mutual correction—of Confucian meritocracy with central aspects of modern democracy. In general terms, the document urged philosophers and scholars everywhere—in both the West and the East—to reflect seriously on the teachings of all cultures and to keep or retain what is best.[10] This spirit of cosmopolitan learning was exemplified and continued in the works of the authors, especially those of Tang Junyi and Mou Zongsan. Although they did not study abroad, both were fully versed in both Chinese and Western philosophy and were masters in pursuing genuinely comparative or cosmopolitan investigations. Tang's *The Spiritual Values of Chinese Culture* offers an innovative "reconstruction" of Chinese philosophical traditions enriched by insights culled from both Plato and Hegel. On the other hand, Mou Zongsan is renowned for his probing juxtaposition of Buddhist and Confucian teachings and also his innovative reinterpretation of Confucianism with the help of Kantian or quasi-transcendental arguments.[11]

China and Relationism

As it seems to me, the Manifesto of 1958 charted a viable and promising course for Confucian thought and practice in our globalizing century. The document did not counsel Confucian self-enclosure in the service of an exclusivist Chinese identity. Nor did it endorse hegemonic expansionism, the missionary dissemination of Confucian teachings in the absence of reciprocal learning processes. In avoiding both of these temptations, the document (I believe) was true to the guiding spirit of the sage of Qufu and his heirs. If there is something like a Confucian ontology or metaphysics, then it is not an ontology of rigid self-identity nor of arrogant triumphalism, but one of continuous learning in close relationship with all peoples and all things in the world. In this respect, I follow the insight of philosopher Zhao Tingyang when he pinpoints as the central feature of Chinese culture the theme of "relationism" (which is equally far removed from relativism and absolutism). As he observes at one point: "Chinese philosophy engages itself so much in the problems of relations that its metaphysics or ontology of co-existence could also be identified as *relationology*." On this point, he concurs with the New Confucian philosopher Du Weiming when he observers that the self or selfhood—to the extent that it is recognized in the *Analects*—is not an isolated atom but a "relational self" or a "center of relationships" that ultimately embrace the world in a "fiduciary community."[12]

To be sure, the centrality of relationships in Confucian thought is not a novel discovery. As a matter of fact, the core of Confucian teachings is often summed up in the idea of five basic relationships (*wu-lun*): those of husband and wife, father and son (or parent and child), older sibling and younger sibling, ruler and minister, and friend and friend. What needs to be noted here is that these relationships are not simply empirical-sociological constellations but ethical bonds involving distinct obligations and responsibilities. Clearly, such bonding relations are not peculiarly Chinese or limited to a given historical or geographical context but can be found in all societies everywhere and at all times. What is distinctive about Confucianism is that ethical bonds are not stipulated in a top-down fashion as abstract norms but are derived from concrete contextual encounters—whose meaning can be generalized (not in the mode of logical deduction but) through analogical transference. Moreover, not all the mentioned relations are tied to intimate family contexts (which may be culturally highly specific). Some of them are of a broader and potentially public character. This is especially true of the relations between ruler and ministers and between friends and friends—which present little or no obstacles to cultural transference.

What additionally needs to be recognized is that Confucian teachings are not exhausted by the five relationships. Equally and perhaps even more important is the underlying spirit or basic ethical inspiration undergirding these teachings: an inspiration manifest in a set of cardinal virtues ranging from *jen* (humaneness, benevolence) and *li* (appropriate conduct) to *yi* (righteousness or justice) and *zhi* (wisdom). Pride of place among these virtues is usually accorded to *jen*. In the words of the eminent historian of Chinese philosophy Wing-tsit Chan, *jen* should be seen as a general virtue "which is basic, universal, and the source of all specific virtues."[13] Its preeminence is equal to the Golden Rule. In the words of the *Analects* (6:28): "You want to establish yourself, then seek to establish others. . . . From what is near to you to seize the analogy [that is, to take the neighbor or other as yourself]—this is the way of *jen*." Yet, as Du Weiming emphasizes, *jen* is not simply an abstract maxim but always functions in human relationships that are concrete and diversified and shaped, at least in part, by particular customs, ceremonies, or rituals. This is why he treats this virtue as a "living metaphor," that is, a metaphor for an ethical and properly humanized way of life. Its practice, he adds, involves a "continuous process of symbolic exchange through the sharing of communally cherished values with other selves."[14]

What the virtue of *jen* implies is a broad openness to others (a willingness to "establish" others), which is opposed to self-enclosure or the celebration of narrow self-identity. In our age of relentless globalization, this openness has to be extended in a cosmopolitan direction: not only to Western modernity but also to Indian culture, Islamic culture, and the cultures of Africa, Latin America, and Southeast Asia. No doubt, this process involves not only outreach and a steady adjustment to new experiences but also a simultaneous deepening of self-understanding, including a deeper cultivation of the Confucian tradition. No one has described this dialectical or dialogical process better than Du Weiming in his reflections on the two-pronged trajectory of New Confucianism in our time. As he points out, Confucian thought and practice today needs to be grasped as a twofold process: "a continuous deepening of one's subjectivity [or self-awareness] and an uninterrupted broadening of one's sensitivity [or sensibility]." The two sides of the process are intimately entwined or interdependent. In order to fully plumb its self-understanding, the Confucian self must overcome and decenter itself without erasing its willingness to learn; it must struggle "to eliminate selfish or egoistic desires" while at the same time extending its hospitality and receptivity to broadening horizons of the world.[15] As it seems to me, these comments agree quite well with the opening lines of the *Analects* (1:1), where Confucius tells us: "To learn and at proper times to repeat what one has learned, is that not after all a pleasure? That friends should come to visit one from afar, is this not after all delightful?"

Appendix C

The Complexity of Difference

Comments on Zhang Longxi

I have been asked to comment on an essay by the distinguished Chinese cultural historian and theorist Zhang Longxi titled "The Complexity of Difference."[1] Professor Longxi is the director of the Centre for Cross-Cultural Studies at the City University of Hong Kong and also chief editor of a beautiful journal called *Ex/Change*. A few years ago, he accepted for publication in this journal an essay of mine on Leibniz and the "natural theology of the Chinese."[2] The present assignment is difficult for several reasons. First of all, there is the difficulty and complexity of the issues raised in Longxi's essay. Basically, these issues revolve around a problem or conundrum that is central to philosophy in both West and East: the conundrum of the relation between universalism and particularism, between sameness and difference, between the "one" and the "many." Of late, especially under the impact of the process of globalization, the problem has gained new intellectual as well as social-political significance. Given the fact that the problem has been treated with great profundity by such eminent Western thinkers as Aristotle and Hegel—and in the East by Shankaracharya and Wang Yangming—my role as a commentator is bound to be daunting. As it happens, this difficulty is compounded by another, nearly opposite complication: the fact that, over long stretches of his text, I find myself in complete agreement with Longxi's argument. In my view, his paper admirably captures and elucidates what he calls "the complexity of difference" and succeeds in making this complexity more accessible and transparent.

In light of this situation, my observations are going to have the

213

character more of amplifications or addenda than of corrections and contestations. Initially, however, it may be opportune to stress important points of convergence. As Zhang Longxi rightly remarks, the proper path to follow in personal and cultural relations is the middle path between the extremes of absolute sameness and radical "otherness" or alterity. Unfortunately, under the influence of Thomas Kuhn and some "post-modern" writers, undue emphasis has been placed on such notions as "incompatibility" and "incommensurability"—terms that tend to undermine mutuality and relationality. From here, there is a sliding slope leading into relativism and (what Lindsay Waters has called) "resurgent tribalism." This sliding slope has been recognized and criticized by well-known analytical philosophers like Hilary Putnam and Donald Davidson,[3] but before them by leading representatives of hermeneutical philosophy like Gadamer and Paul Ricoeur—and as I see it, Longxi himself stands firmly in this hermeneutical tradition. Even before these thinkers, however, the basic incoherence of the "incommensurability" thesis had been pinpointed by Hegel when he asserted that any statement of "difference" already presupposes a standpoint transcending and linking the different elements. The point is well recaptured by Zhang Longxi in this admirable passage: "If things are really incommensurate, then, no one can even make a claim that they are incommensurate, because to make such a claim presupposes that one knows both sides of the dichotomy and knows them to be truly incommensurate. . . . By pointing out this logical difficulty, we can effectively dislodge the incommensurability argument."[4]

Longxi's point is supported by numerous writers on cross-cultural studies, including the renowned China expert Benjamin Schwartz, who wrote that "China is not a mass of self-enclosed atomic facts but vast regions and networks of human experiences," adding: "Despite the indeterminacy of translation and the real problems of 'culture-boundedness,' it is possible to grasp the concerns which lie behind the discourse of other cultures. Difference is ever present but it is not ultimately inaccessible."[5] Schwartz's primary focus on Chinese culture prompts me at this point to put an addendum to Longxi's paper that, I believe, would not be uncongenial to him: the observation that the conundrum of sameness and otherness, of universalism and particularism, has surfaced also as a major issue in recent Chinese philosophy. I am referring to the debate between such thinkers as Guo Qiyong and Liu Qingping, a debate gathered together in a volume titled (in translation) *Debates on Confucian Ethics,* published in Wuhan in 2004. A major issue in this debate is the ethical status or legitimacy of "filial piety." Coming from a universalist perspective (partly influenced by Kant), Liu Qingping has denounced filial piety as a violation of general norms and a source of possible moral corruption. On the other hand, adopting a more socially contextual or particularistic stance, Guo Qiyong has sought to recuperate the ethical significance of the practice as a stepping stone to the development of broader civic virtues. In the words of Liu Qingping, his intervention is meant to "creatively transform traditional Confucianism from a particularistic doctrine into a universalistic idea." For Guo Qiyong, on the other hand, ethics involves a process of maturation, where "the beginning of love for one's parents is followed by love for other people which is followed by things." For, "if one does not love one's own parents, brothers, and sisters, we cannot imagine that the person will love the parents, brothers, sisters of others, finally forming one body with Heaven, Earth, and the myriad things."[6]

With some hesitation (befitting someone who is not a Sinologist), I entered this debate not long ago. In an essay titled "On Love with Distinction: A Chinese Debate," I have taken a position that avoids both an abstract universalism neglectful of relevant differences and a radical particularism that might slide into relativism and incommensurability. In defending this position I basically followed or rather anticipated Zhang Longxi's pursuit of a middle path that respects the "complexity of difference." For the purposes of my essay, I reached out for support in a number of directions. First of all, I invoked some time-honored Western philosophical teachings, especially Aristotle's emphasis on the steady and ongoing cultivation of virtues and on the importance of finding the "mean" or midpoint (*mesotes*) in one's endeavors. In addition and with equal relish, I relied on famous Chinese teachings, such as the works of Wang Yangming and the famous "doctrine of the mean" (*chung-yung*), about which Du Weiming has written that it is not "a categorical imperative in the Kantian sense," but rather "a standard of inspiration" or "an experienced ideal." To round out my arsenal of supporting thinkers, I also turned to the writings of Martin Heidegger and especially his dual accent on both human finitude and the potentially infinite "care for Being"—where the latter striving never completely cancels our finitely situated or rooted condition.[7]

At this juncture, and by way of conclusion, I want to point to a further "complexity" besetting the universalism/particularism conundrum. In some situations, I believe, it may not be possible or ethically legitimate to maintain a balanced midpoint of perspectives. For practical-political reasons, it may sometimes be necessary to accentuate one (more limited) position over another. Thus, on the level of basic citizen rights, one sometimes needs to support a universalist stance, in order to ward off practices of discrimination; on other occasions, for example, regarding religious practices (like wearing the veil), one may wish to support particular differences. Likewise, in regard to women's equal rights (to employment and compensation), one may wish to ignore the difference of gender; in other respects (for instance, regarding maternity leave) one may want to respect precisely this same difference. In all such cases, weighing the "pros" and "cons" requires the exercise of prudent judgment—which again presupposes the diligent cultivation of civic virtues. In my view, this cultivation is an urgent need in our globalizing age when the simple-minded pursuit of either universalism or particularism can spell political disaster. On this point again, Zhang Longxi's essay contains a brilliant passage that deserves to be lifted up and widely applauded: "Against the false universalism of the colonialist or imperialist times, when European concepts and standards were used as universal measurements to judge non-European cultures and found them lacking, the emphasis in our time on cultural difference and the internal validity of value systems makes a lot of sense morally, politically, and philosophically. To deny the possibility of cross-cultural understanding and knowledge, to insist on the incommensurability of the East and the West, however, only leads to the other extreme of the isolation of cultures and the danger of clash of civilizations."[8] It is against the latter danger that philosophical hermeneutics provides a powerful antidote. For this reason, hermeneutics can with good reason be invoked as a major resource in the needed "dialogue among civilizations" in our time.

Appendix D

Dialogue in Practice

Conversation with Members of a "Youth Forum"[1]

Q: We would like first of all to thank you very much for being with us today. For us, young people, it is a unique possibility to learn from you in an informal way. And we would like not only to learn from you but hopefully have an informal discussion. During the Youth Forum a lot of people with very different backgrounds met, and we were working together for a few days. The questions we want to raise deal with democracy and religion, and we notice that the relationship between Islam and democracy is very complex. So we would like to ask: What do you think, how complex is the relationship between Islam and democracy in reality?

A: First of all I'm greatly concerned about democracy. In 2010 I published a book called *The Promise of Democracy*. What is that promise? In my view, the promise of democracy is that people can rule themselves. It so happens that 2009 was the year in which we celebrated a book written by Gandhi one hundred years ago: it was titled *Indian Self-Rule*. What is the point of Indian self-rule? It means that Indian people are not ruled by others, not dominated, not exploited; and this means that they have to rule themselves; Gandhi called this *swaraj*. The promise of democracy is this kind of *swaraj*, that I'm not ruled by others, nor do I rule others, but we all are able to rule ourselves. This means that we are able to control our selfish impulses and be responsible for our actions. What I advocate in my own book is this ethical conception of democracy where people do not only pursue selfish interests, their own desires or impulses, but pursue the Common Good, what the Greeks called "the good life," the life of goodness. Not the life of leisure, not *la dolce vita,* but rather a life devoted to goodness, to the pursuit of the Common Good, which is beyond our individual self-interests.

My book was published in 2010, but I wrote it earlier (2009), just at the time when the world was suffering from the effects of excessive corporate selfishness, from the collapse of financial markets, the collapse of neoliberal capitalism as we knew it. So capitalism was seriously questioned at that time because the capitalist system is based on the profit motive, my profit, corporate profit, not a common profit. This crisis of Western markets demonstrated that we have to formulate a new conception of democracy. Not democracy that is built purely on private greed, but a democracy devoted to ethical standards, of justice and good life. This was basically also Gandhi's argument. In *Hind Swaraj,* he said: "It is not just sufficient to drive away the British and to replace British governors by Indian governors. It is not sufficient that we are now dominated by native elites. What we need is really that we are able to govern ourselves." This is a very important notion of government, of democracy as a regime, and we all have to learn about this.

Frequently democracy is identified with liberalism or neoliberalism. Frequently democracy is said to mean economic or laissez-faire liberalism. But we have seen in the financial fiasco that this cannot be correct. This identification of democracy and economic liberalism needs to be revised or overcome. We have to find ethical standards to curb the relentless pursuit of self-interest. Where do we find these ethical resources? Well, we find them to some extent in the great cultural traditions. Gandhi found them in the great tradition of Indian culture, which is spelled out in the teachings of the Upanishads, the Bhagavad Gita. Gandhi always had a copy of the Bhagavad Gita with him in his pocket and read verses of it in the evening. The Bhagavad Gita is like a bible for Indians. Of course, in Asia we also have other cultural traditions, such as Confucianism, Daoism, and Buddhism. Confucianism teaches that we only find ourselves in relationships with others. We are not isolated individuals; we cannot pursue only our individual in-

terests. There are famous relationships: fathers/mothers, parents/
children, friends and friends, younger child to older child, and of
course people to each other; all these relationships involve ethical responsibilities. Such responsibilities we cannot avoid. Similar
things could be said about Daoism and Buddhism.

In the West we have other ethical traditions. We have, of course,
the great Greek tradition, especially the tradition of Plato and Aristotle. But we also have a biblical tradition: we have the Jewish
tradition and the Christian tradition. But we have also—and this
leads me to the point of your question—the Islamic tradition,
which is a great resource of religious, spiritual, and ethical inspiration. So, Islam also can contribute to the building of an ethical
society. Now the issue we have to face when we talk about religious
resources is that, in the past, religious leaders were frequently also
government leaders, political elites. In Christianity the pope and
the cardinals were frequently associated with kings, with rulers.
But that is also true in the Orthodox tradition, where the Orthodox
hierarchy frequently was in close connection with tsarist regimes.
Now we are asking how religion, especially Islam, is compatible
with democracy. Our question is not how Islam is compatible with
monarchy, just as we are not asking how Christianity is compatible
with monarchy. We are asking: How is it compatible with democracy? And, as I have said, democracy means self-rule. So it means
that we cannot be ruled by either political elites or religious elites.
This means ultimately that, in a democracy, individuals have to be
their own religious leaders, that people can no longer rely on external authorities but have to rely on their own resources.

The problem of compatibility arises only if religion or clerical
elites insist on exercising political rule and seek to dominate people. Unfortunately, this happens and has happened often. We have
had this problem in Christianity, and it took a long time for Christian churches to accommodate themselves to democracy. Contrary
to some extreme agnostics or secularists, this does not mean that
religion becomes irrelevant in democracy; actually it becomes
more relevant, because every individual has to be his or her own
religious leader. Long ago, Martin Luther expressed this in the
idea of the "universal priesthood of believers." Democracy does
not negate faith but grants to everybody the "freedom of faith."

This idea was again exemplified by Gandhi; he was very faithful as a Hindu, but he also was a democrat, so for him no religious elite could govern India. The people have to govern India. What does this mean for churches and religious leaders? It means that they can exercise the role of teachers, of counselors, of spiritual advisors in society. Democracy does not abolish churches or religious leaders. This is a mistaken notion of an extreme secularism or laïcism that says "we do away with all churches." That was also the great mistake of communism. It was a mistake because people have a longing for the spiritual, a longing for something more than the things of this world. So, what I am saying is that religions can help people to govern themselves; they can provide resources on how to practice democracy ethically.

Some time ago I wrote an article titled "For a Religion of Service," not a religion of domination. This motto also applies to Islam, especially some Islamists who try to establish what is called "theocracy," where God is said to rule but actually the clergy rules. This is very dangerous. To an extent, such an attempt has been made in Iran, in the Islamic republic of Iran, where you find a partial theocracy. Iran has two levels of government: One level is popularly elected and thus democratic. There is a parliament (*majlis*), and there is a president who is also popularly elected. But above and beyond this democratic structure there is a higher elite, a "guardian council" that is composed mainly of ayatollahs, priests. And these ayatollahs can nullify what the democratic structure has done. So, there are actually two governments. They are bound to collide, because they are opposite to each other. I have made a proposal and submitted it to many Iranian friends. I told them: "Look at England. Everybody says England is a democracy. But England has two chambers: a lower chamber and an upper chamber which is called the House of Lords. And in the House of Lords you find the archbishop of Canterbury. Clergy are in the House of Lords by right. Others are elected or appointed to the House of Lords. So I proposed: Why don't you transform what is called the Council of Guardians into a House of Lords? Then you can collaborate, cooperate between the two chambers." I understand, the ayatollahs are not very keen. But in my view it is the only solution. If you want to avoid chaos, revolution, or civil war, it is really the only option. Such a solution would preserve democracy but at the same time preserve the religious resources that democracy needs. So there is a possibility of an Islamic democracy.

The fact that Islamic democracy is possible is demonstrated in Turkey, where most Muslims are also democrats. Malaysia also has a majority of Muslims and a democracy. The same is true of Indonesia. So, the thesis that Islam is incompatible with democracy is simply false. Of course Muslims have a problem because they have among them many fanatics. But all religions have fanatics. We have to safeguard the true message. The true message of every religion is to promote life, not only life but the "good life." But fanatics promote death or terror, which means the killing of people. No religion tolerates killing of innocent people. And that is true not only for Jews but for Christians and Muslims. So, those who resort to killing really violate their own religion.

But there are counter-examples, and a particularly good example is again Gandhi. He was a religious person, I mean not outwardly but inwardly religious. But one of his main principles was nonviolence, what he called *ahimsa*. He devoted all his life to the struggle for democracy without violence. So that is true religion. I believe that Gandhi can always be a model, a mentor to inspire us. Gandhi was an inspiration for Nelson Mandela in South Africa and also for Martin Luther King in America. King struggled for the rights of black people without violence. And many leaders in East European countries, like Vaclav Havel, also were inspired by nonviolence. That is what we mean by "velvet revolution." So at the end, all of it comes together. I started out with *swaraj*, with democracy, then turned to the relation of democracy and religion, then democracy and Islam, and finally I came back to Gandhi.

Q: With your permission we would like to ask two additional questions. What do you think about democracy in the Western countries today? Is democracy not being replaced by ochlocracy, plutocracy, and demagoguery? They forget democracy in the meaning presented by Aristotle and Jefferson. Today democracy means just the power of big numbers, but not of the most competent or upright people. And the second question: Don't you think that religion is often a tool in the hands of the state? Religion is just a means to control the masses by the rulers?

A: Thank you very much. I cannot speak about all governments in the West. But I know very well the situation in United States, because I have lived there for fifty years. So, I know that we do not really have a democracy in the United States. We have only the outward forms of democracy. We have elections. And what happens in elections? Money wins. The candidate who has more money wins, because TV costs money, newspapers cost money. So we have what Plato called plutocracy—the richest rule. Unfortunately many of our media are controlled by financial and corporate elites: the TV stations and major newspapers are owned by billionaires and corporations. How can the ordinary citizen compete against corporate money? So the situation is bad. But there are efforts to correct it. The election of Barack Obama in 2008 was, I think, a demonstration that if the people wake up and organize themselves at the grassroots, they finally make a difference. So much on the first question.

The other question: religion unfortunately can be used as an instrument of domination and manipulation. This is true. Because people have this longing, this search for religious guidance, they can easily be taken advantage of. There are always religious charlatans who exploit people. So, you have to be very careful with religion and especially when religion is in politics. You have always to ask yourself: What do they want to do? What is behind this? What kind of strategy do they follow? In Latin: *Cui bono*? Who benefits?

Q: Thank you for your answers. I have another question, directly related to Islam. Don't you think that the cause why Islam is often opposed to democracy nowadays is because some countries insist that Islam and democracy are incompatible and they enforce this separation for their own political concerns?

A: Thank you. Yes, my concern is to bring Islam and democracy closer together. But there are people who want to separate them as much as possible. These people are both in the West and in Islam. There are people in the West who believe that a nondemocratic Islam is helpful to their own purposes, their own politics. For instance, Saudi Arabia is not a democracy; they do not even have a constitution. And yet Saudi Arabia is a friend of the West. Why? Because the Saudis are useful, they provide recourses. Maybe a democratic revolution would finish that. On the other hand, there is of course a very extreme movement within Islam that claims that democracy is a form of heresy, of infidelity. They argue that democracy makes the horrible mistake of replacing the authority of God with the authority of people.

But this is a mistake on the part of radical Muslims, because their claim implies that God is totally outside of human beings. And so if people want to rule themselves they necessarily have to deny God. But that doesn't follow because God and humans are not opposites. So, yes, on both sides there are enemies of democracy.

Q: I want to ask you about principles of life. I know that Mahatma Gandhi had used sacred scriptures to discover the principles of life. Referring to the New Testament, he said that if all people would follow the teachings of Jesus Christ, there would be no wars. And my question: Is it enough to use the New Testament, the Bible or Qu'ran, and other sacred scriptures, or do we not also need religious leaders for that?

A: I think obviously we need not only scriptures; these are just books. You have to learn how to read these books. And that is why religious leaders are important. They can teach us how to read. I mentioned before Martin Luther King. He was a religious leader and a political leader. He was a preacher in his church, and he interpreted scripture. It is not a matter of doing away with religious leaders. It is to give to religious leaders the proper role, the role of giving advice, the role of teachers, but not of governors. Ultimately, in a democracy, all people have to be able to read and interpret.

Q: Thank you very much for sharing with us that democracy and Islam are not just theoretically compatible, but you gave us some great examples like Turkey, Malaysia, and Indonesia, and you told us also the reasons.

A: Could I just ask you one thing in return? I am now rather old. I have to place my hope into the young people. You are the future. But you have to follow the right path, what Muslims call *zirat al-mustaqim*. This is the path of righteous people, and it is in the first surah of the Qu'ran. So this is my hope: that you will find that right path. Many of the teachings of the last century have proven to be insufficient: liberalism, socialism, communism. So your task is to find a new way, where people can live together in solidarity but also in freedom. I can be free even though I am committed to you; I can be free in our connection. To find the way is to link my freedom with responsibility, social responsibility. This path is called the Good Life.

Q: Mr. Dallmayr, what do you think is the role of the state in educating the youth?

A: The education of the youth is the most important task of any generation, because youth is our future. And the task of education rests with the family, the schools, society, and lastly the state. Public education, offered by the state, is important because it brings together children and young people from all walks of life. If we give them good instruction, if we give them a good example, then they can follow the right path.

Q: What should these examples consist of?

A: The examples should be to show what it means to be a good and responsible person. A father should be good father, a mother should be a good mother to her children, young people should be respectful of the parents, friends should be good friends, and people in politics should pursue just policies. This would give good examples.

Q: What do you think is the difference between the education of the older generation and that of the new generation? What are the changes in the educational process then and now?

A: I think the educational system has opened up. A hundred years or even fifty years ago, education was more restricted. It followed a traditional curriculum and was limited to a regional or national tradition. But today we have a process of globalization, so people interact across the entire globe. So we suddenly have to learn about different cultures, different teachings, different traditions. This is what we call "multiculturalism." And this has entered into the schools, into the curriculum. If properly handled, it can be very fruitful.

Q: A last question: Your view on the young people today? Are there negative features in the young people that you would criticize?

A: The thing that worries me about young people is sometimes the abuse of freedom. But I do not really blame the young people for it; I blame the older generation for giving a bad example to the young people. If the parents are alcoholics, how can you prevent the child from becoming alcoholic? If the parents use drugs, how can you keep the child from becoming a drug addict? So this is the negative side. But the positive side is that young people are very open to new experiences and very eager to learn about many things in the world. Of course, they have the Internet; they have email, Facebook, so they can communicate with the whole world. And there is a great desire to expand horizons and to learn many new things. The older generation was sort of born into certain ideologies that were very limiting, like capitalist liberalism or state socialism. The young generation has the opportunity to find a new way, and hopefully a better way.

Thank you.

Notes

Preface

1. Johan Gottfried Herder, "Letters for the Advancement of Humanity," in *Werke in zehn Bänden* (Frankfurt: Deutscher Klassiker Verlag, 1994), 7: 363. The Canadian-Indian philosopher Sonia Sikka offers these comments: "Thus, *Besonnenheit*, the capacity that allows human beings to relate to themselves so as to be able to say 'I,' arises as a self-reflexive moment within nature. Through it, human beings are granted a unique form of awareness, as well as a capacity for self-regulation. . . . When accompanied by an added awareness that the nature working within them is the same as the nature working within all things, they also take on the character of the sacred." See Sikka, *Herder on Humanity and Cultural Difference: Enlightened Relativism* (Cambridge: Cambridge University Press, 2011), 64.

Introduction

1. See Fred Dallmayr, "Postsecular Faith: Toward a Religion of Service," in *Integral Pluralism: Beyond Culture Wars* (Lexington: University Press of Kentucky, 2010), 67–83.

2. See Hans-Georg Gadamer, "The Universality of the Hermeneutical Problem," in *Philosophical Hermeneutics*, trans. and ed. David E. Linge (Berkeley: University of California Press, 1976), 1–20.

3. Albert Camus, *The Myth of Sisyphus, and Other Essays*, trans. Justin O'Brien (New York: Vintage Books, 1955), 91. Compare also Maurice Merleau-Ponty, "Man, The Hero," in *Sense and Non-Sense*, trans. Hubert L. Dreyfus and Patricia A. Dreyfus (Evanston: Northwestern University Press, 1964), 182–87.

1. Being in the World

1. See Martin Heidegger, *Sein und Zeit*, 11th ed. (Tübingen: Niemeyer, 1967), 21, 24–25; Heidegger, *Being and Time*, trans. John Macquarrie and Edward Robinson (New York: Harper and Row, 1962), 43, 45–46. (In the above and subsequent citations, the translation has been slightly altered for the sake of clarity.)

2. Heidegger, *Sein und Zeit*, 53–54; Heidegger, *Being and Time*, 78–80.

3. Heidegger, *Sein und Zeit*, 55–57, 59; Heidegger, *Being and Time*, 81–84, 86.

4. Heidegger, *Sein und Zeit*, 86; Heidegger, *Being and Time*, 118–19. On the notion of "frame of significance," see also Charles Taylor, *The Ethics of Authenticity* (Cambridge: Harvard University Press, 1962), 37–40; see also his "Engaged Agency and Background in Heidegger," in *The Cambridge Companion to Heidegger*, ed. Charles B. Guignon (Cambridge: Cambridge University Press, 1933), 317–36.

5. Heidegger, *Sein und Zeit*, 193; Heidegger, *Being and Time*, 237. With particular reference to solicitude and its relation to freedom, Heidegger at another point distinguishes between two types of interhuman care: one that takes over the other's freedom through managerial control and another that helps and allows the other properly to be free. See *Sein und Zeit*, 122; *Being and Time*, 158–59. At a later point, he elaborates on the distinction between "authentic" and "inauthentic" existence, emphasizing that "authenticity" (*Eigentlichkeit*) does not mean an individual freedom removed from relationships and modes of care, but a more genuine manner of shouldering the task of care. See *Sein und Zeit*, 298; *Being and Time*, 343–44. The latter point is well expressed by Charles Taylor when he writes: "Authenticity is not the enemy of demands that emanate from beyond the self; it supposes such demands." See *Ethics of Authenticity*, 41.

6. Martin Heidegger, "Letter on Humanism," in *Martin Heidegger: Basic Writings*, ed. David F. Krell (New York: Harper and Row, 1977), 224–25.

7. Heidegger, "Letter on Humanism," 228–29. As Heidegger adds (229): "With the existential determination of what being 'human' means, nothing is decided regarding the 'existence of God' or the 'non-existence of God,' no more than about the possibility or impossibility of gods."

8. Heidegger, *Sein und Zeit*, 326, 364–66; Heidegger, *Being and Time*, 373–74, 415–18. The "immanent-transcendent" status is discussed in a section titled "The Temporal Problem of the Transcendence of the World" (415).

9. Heidegger, *Sein und Zeit*, 2–4, 365; Heidegger, *Being and Time*, 22–24, 417.

10. Martin Heidegger, *Zur Bestimmung der Philosophie*, in *Gesamtausgabe*, vols. 56–57 (Frankfurt: Klostermann, 1987), 73. The text has been translated by Ted Sadler as *Towards a Definition of Philosophy* (London: Continuum, 2002). See also Richard Polt, *"Ereignis,"* in *A Companion to Heidegger*, ed. Hubert L. Dreyfus and Mark A. Wrathall (Malden, MA: Blackwell Publishing, 2005), 376–77. Regarding "die Sprache spricht" see Charles Taylor, "Heidegger on Language," in Dreyfus and Wrathall, *Companion to Heidegger*, 451–52; on "das Ding dingt" see James C. Edward, "The Thinging of the Thing," in Dreyfus and Wrathall, *Companion to Heidegger*, 456–57.

11. For the 1951 essay see Martin Heidegger, "Bauen Wohnen Denken," in *Vorträge und Aufsätze*, part 2 (Pfullingen: Neske, 1954), 19–36; see

also "Das Ding" (1950), in the same volume, 37–59. For a translation of the former see Krell, *Martin Heidegger: Basic Writings*, 319–39; for a translation of the latter see Heidegger, *Poetry, Language, Thought*, trans. Albert Hofstadter (New York: Harper and Row, 1971), 163–86. On *Ereignis* and the *Geviert* see Polt, "Ereignis," 375–91; see also Richard Capobianco, *Engaging Heidegger* (Toronto: University of Toronto Press, 2010).

12. See in this respect my chapter "Democratic Action and Experience: Dewey's 'Holistic' Pragmatism," in *The Promise of Democracy: Political Agency and Transformation* (Albany: State University of New York Press, 2010), 43–65. On the relation between Heidegger and pragmatism compare, e.g., Mark Okrent, *Heidegger's Pragmatism: Understanding, Being, and the Critique of Metaphysics* (Ithaca: Cornell University Press, 1988); Richard Rorty, "Heidegger, Contingency, and Pragmatism," in Dreyfus and Wrathall, *Companion to Heidegger*, 511–32; and Charles B. Gurgnon, "On Saving Heidegger from Rorty," *Philosophy and Phenomenological Research* 46 (1986): 401–17.

13. See Alfred North Whitehead, *Process and Reality* (New York: Macmillan, 1929). On the relation between Heidegger and Whitehead compare, e.g., Ron L. Cooper, *Heidegger and Whitehead: A Phenomenological Examination into the Intelligibility of Experience* (Athens: Ohio University Press, 1993); Calvin O. Schrag, "Whitehead and Heidegger: Process Philosophy and Existential Philosophy," *Dialectica* 49 (1959): 42–46; Raymond J. Devetterre, "Whitehead's Metaphysics and Heidegger's Critique," *Crosscurrents* 30 (1980): 309–22; Adam Scarfe, "Heidegger with Whitehead on Temporality and Transcendence," *Existentia* 13 (2003): 53–64.

14. See John B. Cobb Jr. and David Ray Griffin, *Process Theology: An Introductory Exposition* (Philadelphia: Westminster Press, 1976), 52–53. Compare also Nicholas Rescher, *Process Metaphysics: An Introduction to Process Philosophy* (Albany: State University of New York Press, 1996); Ilya Prigogine, *From Being to Becoming* (San Francisco: Freeman and Co., 1980); Charles Hartshorne, *Omnipotence and Other Theological Mistakes* (Albany: State University of New York Press, 1984); Charles Hartshorne, *Creative Synthesis and Philosophic Method* (Chicago: Open Court, 1970); Griffin, *Reenchantment without Supernaturalism: A Process Philosophy of Religion* (Ithaca: Cornell University Press, 2001); and Cobb, *Process Theology as Political Theology* (Philadelphia: Westminster Press, 1982).

15. William E. Connolly, *A World of Becoming* (Durham: Duke University Press, 2011), 15–16, 173. Although relying on a number of thinkers, the study seems to be especially indebted to Whitehead. The latter, he writes (168), "seeks to bring art and science into close communication. I find myself drawn to him on these points, sharing his aspiration to reform our conceptual armory to bring it into contact with recent developments in science and to incorporate into science, political thought, and everyday life alike more appreciation of a world of becoming."

16. Connolly, *World of Becoming*, 128–30, 135, 138. As he adds, in a graphic depiction of our present-day malaise (138): "In this (nearly) global machine, dissonant forces, drawing upon competitive practices of sovereignty, resentments tied to uneven exchange, speculative practices beyond the reach of those affected, and a regional division of dominant religious institutions become condensed into a global resonance machine of cross-regional antagonism." At another place, I have portrayed the collusion among three types of inequality: economic wealth, political-military power, and technical knowledge. See my "Globalization and Inequality: A Plea for Cosmopolitan Justice," in *Dialogue among Civilizations: Some Exemplary Voices* (New York: Palgrave/Macmillan, 2002), 67–84.

17. Connolly, *World of Becoming*, 143, 147. At this point, Connolly adds a criticism of a frequent fascination among "Leftist" movements with political power and violence (147): "Pure negativity on the Left does not sustain either critique or militancy for long, but rather, it tends eventually to lapse into resignation or to slide toward the authoritarian practices of the Right that already express with glee the moods of negativity, hubris, and existential revenge. We have witnessed numerous examples of such disappointing transitions in the last several decades, when a negative or authoritarian mood is retained while the creed in which it was set is changed."

18. See *The Way of Life, According to Lao Tzu*, trans. Witter Bynner (New York: Perigee Books, 1972), chap. 29, p. 58.

2. Cosmopolitanism

1. See Heinrich Heine, *Sämtliche Schriften*, ed. K. Briegleb (Munich: dtv, 1997), 3: 379, 710; and Ulrich Beck, *Cosmopolitan Vision*, trans. Ciaran Cronin (Cambridge, UK: Polity Press, 2006), 1, 79. Regarding the history of cosmopolitanism, compare Derek Hester, *World Citizenship and Government: Cosmopolitan Ideas in the History of Western Political Thought* (New York: St. Martin's Press, 1996), and S. Thielking, *Weltbürgertum* (Munich: Fink, 2000).

2. Seyla Benhabib, *Another Cosmopolitanism*, ed. Robert Post (New York: Oxford University Press, 2006), 17. Benhabib proceeds to distinguish among several possible meanings. For an instructive discussion of different meanings see Stan van Hooft, *Cosmopolitanism: A Philosophy for Global Ethics* (Montreal: McGill-Queens University Press, 2009), 4–9.

3. See Benhabib, *Another Cosmopolitanism*, 20. Van Hooft defines cosmopolitanism as a "virtue"; see *Cosmopolitanism*, 8.

4. David Held, *Cosmopolitanism: Ideals and Realities* (Cambridge, UK: Polity Press, 2010), ix–x, 5. See also his *Cosmopolitanism: A Defense* (Cambridge, UK: Polity Press, 2003), and *Global Covenant: The Social Democratic Alternative to the Washington Consensus* (Cambridge, UK: Polity Press, 2004).

5. Beck, *Cosmopolitan Vision*, 9.

6. Held, *Cosmopolitanism: Ideals and Realities*, 5–7. Compare also Richard Falk, *Predatory Globalization: A Critique* (Cambridge, UK: Polity Press, 1999); Saskia Sassen, *Globalization and Its Discontents* (New York: New Press, 1998); and Charles S. Morris, *Money, Greed, and Risk* (New York: Times Business, 1999).

7. Beck, *Cosmopolitan Vision*, 80. See also S. Lash and J. Urry, *Global Culture Industry: The Mediation of Things* (Cambridge, UK: Polity Press, 2005); and Arjun Appadurai, "Disjuncture and Difference in the Global Cultural Economy," *Public Culture* 2 (1990): 1–19.

8. Beck, *Cosmopolitan Vision*, 10, 41. Compare also Stanley Fish, "Boutique Multiculturalism," *Critical Inquiry* 23 (1997): 378–96.

9. Zygmunt Bauman, *Globalization: The Human Consequences* (Cambridge, UK: Polity Press, 1998), 2, 13–14, 17. See also Paul Virilio, *The Lost Dimension* (New York: Semiotext, 1991), 13. The similarities between the electronically created cyber-dimension "beyond" space and time and a certain Christian transcendentalism is noted by Margaret Wertheim, who writes: "While early Christians promulgated heaven as a realm in which the human soul would be freed from all the frailties and failings of the flesh, so today's champions of cyberspace hail it as a place where the self will be freed from the limitations of physical embodiment." See Wertheim, "The Pearly Gates of Cyberspace," in *Architecture of Fear*, ed. Nan Elin (New York: Princeton Architecture Press, 1997), 296.

10. Bauman, *Globalization*, 2–3, 18.

11. See Immanuel Kant, "Perpetual Peace: A Philosophical Sketch," in *Kant's Political Writings*, ed. Hans Reiss, trans. H. B. Nisbet (Cambridge: Cambridge University Press, 1970), 98–99nn105–6. As Kant adds: "The stranger cannot claim the *right of a guest* to be entertained . . . He may only claim a *right of subsistence*, for all men are entitled to present themselves in the society of others by virtue of their right to the communal possession of the earth's surface." As one should note, the German *Recht*, like the Latin *ius*, can mean both "law" and "right." By *republicanism*, Kant at that point (101) means a regime "whereby the executive power is separated from the legislative power," while democracy is seen as a totalizing regime that is "necessarily a despotism."

12. John Rawls, *The Law of Peoples* (Cambridge: Harvard University Press, 1999), 3 n1, 17, 36–37. Regarding the distinction from Kant's "transcendental idealism," Rawls states (86–87): "We are giving content to an idea of practical reason and three of its component parts: reasonableness, decency, and rationality. The criteria for these three normative ideas are not [transcendentally] deduced, but enumerated and characterized in each case." Another distinctive feature is the interpretation of "law" (*ius*) in terms of "human rights" (48). Compare also Rawls, *A Theory of Justice* (Cambridge: Harvard University Press, 1971).

13. See Charles R. Beitz, *Political Theory and International Relations* (Princeton: Princeton University Press, 1979); Beitz, ed., *International Ethics* (Princeton: Princeton University Press, 1985); Henry Shue, ed., *Nuclear Deterrence and Moral Restraint* (Cambridge: Cambridge University Press, 1989); Shue and David Rodin, eds., *Preemption: Military Action and Moral Justification* (New York: Oxford University Press, 2007); Thomas W. Pogge, *Realizing Rawls* (Ithaca: Cornell University Press, 1989); Pogge, *World Poverty and Human Rights: Cosmopolitan Responsibilities and Reforms* (Cambridge, UK: Polity Press, 2002); and Pogge, *John Rawls: His Life and Theory of Justice* (New York: Oxford University Press, 2007). Following Pogge, the Rawlsian legacy has been pursued by numerous other scholars. See especially Gillian Brook, *Global Justice: A Cosmopolitan Account* (Cambridge: Cambridge University Press, 2009); Darcel Moellendorf, *Cosmopolitan Justice* (Boulder: Westview Press, 2002); Richard Vernon, *Cosmopolitan Regard: Political Membership and Global Justice* (Cambridge: Cambridge University Press, 2010); and Patrick Hayden, *John Rawls: Towards a Just World Order* (Cardiff: University of Wales Press, 2002). In Hayden's case, however, the Rawlsian legacy is curiously criss-crossed by borrowings from multiculturalism and radical empiricism; compare his *Multiplicity and Becoming: The Pluralist Empiricism of Gilles Deleuze* (New York: Peter Lang, 1998).

14. Compare, e.g., Jürgen Habermas, *Europe: The Faltering Project*, trans. Ciaran Cronin (Cambridge, UK: Polity Press, 2009); and Habermas, *Time of Transitions*, ed. and trans. Ciaran Cronin and Max Pensky (Cambridge, UK: Polity Press, 2006).

15. See Benhabib, *Another Cosmopolitanism*, 1, 4, 16. In her comments on "networks" and globalization, Benhabib sets herself in opposition to Michael Hardt and Antonio Negri, *Empire* (Cambridge: Harvard University Press, 2000); and Thomas Friedman, *The Lexus and the Olive Tree: Understanding Globalization* (New York: Farrar, Straus, Giroux, 1999). The accent on "individual" rights and liberties is even more pronounced in (so-called) liberal cosmopolitanism, as defended chiefly by Will Kymlicka; see his "Liberal Nationalism and Cosmopolitan Justice," in Benhabib, *Another Cosmopolitanism*, 128–44, and his *Politics in the Vernacular: Nationalism, Multiculturalism, and Citizenship* (New York: Oxford University Press, 2001).

16. Benhabib, *Another Cosmopolitanism*, 18–20, 23–24. One should also recall in this context Habermas's famous text *Between Facts and Norms: Contributions to a Discourse Theory of Law and Democracy*, trans. William Rehg (Cambridge: MIT Press, 1996).

17. David Held, "Democracy and the New International Order," in *Cosmopolitan Democracy: An Agenda for a New World Order*, ed. Daniele Archibugi and Held (Cambridge, UK: Polity Press, 1995), 96–97, 99–100, 108, 112. The deeper theoretical premises of his approach are spelled out

in his *Cosmopolitanism: Ideas and Realities*, where he enumerates eight normative principles of global order (69): "(1) equal worth and dignity; (2) active agency; (3) personal responsibility and accountability; (4) consent; (5) collective decision-making about public matters through voting procedures; (6) inclusiveness and subsidiarity; (7) avoidance of serious harm; and (8) sustainability."

18. Held, "Democracy and the New International Order," 116; Held, *Cosmopolitanism*, 16. In the latter text, "fundamental metaprinciples" bear in fact the "justificatory burden" and serve as the "organizing notions of ethical discourse." As he adds, however, somewhat surprisingly (19): "Contrary to popular criticism, cosmopolitanism is the triumph of difference and local affiliations."

19. Benhabib, *Another Cosmopolitanism*, 19–20, 60, 70–71. Compare also Seyla Benhabib, *The Claims of Culture: Equality and Diversity in the Global Era* (Princeton: Princeton University Press, 2002); and Benhabib, *The Rights of Others: Aliens, Residents and Citizens* (Cambridge: Cambridge University Press, 2004).

20. See John Dewey, "How We Think" in *John Dewey: The Middle Works, 1899–1924*, vol. 6, ed. Jo Ann Boydston (Carbondale: Southern Illinois University Press, 1978), 190–91, and "The Need for a Recovery of Democracy," in *John Dewey: The Middle Works*, vol. 10, ed. Jo Ann Boydston (Carbondale: Southern Illinois University Press, 1980), 41–42. See also Dewey, "My Pedagogic Creed," in *John Dewey, The Early Works, 1882–1898*, vol. 5, ed. Jo Ann Boydston (Carbondale: Southern Illinois University Press, 1972), 84–86; and Dewey, "Democracy and Education," in *John Dewey: The Middle Works, 1899–1924*, vol. 9, ed. Jo Ann Boydston (Carbondale: Southern Illinois University Press, 1980), 93. Compare also James Scott Johnston, *Inquiry and Education: John Dewey and the Quest for Democracy* (Albany: State University of New York Press, 2006); and my "Democratic Action and Experience," 43–65.

21. See Hans-Georg Gadamer, *Truth and Method*, 2nd rev. ed., trans. Joel Weinsheimer and Donald G. Marshall (New York: Crossroad, 1989), 295, 307–9, 329, 367–70. See also his *Hermeneutics, Religion, and Ethics*, trans. Joel Weinsheimer (New Haven: Yale University Press, 1999); and his essays "Hermeneutics as Practical Philosophy" and "What Is Practice [*Praxis*]? The Conditions of Social Reason," both in *Reason in the Age of Science*, trans. Frederick G. Lawrence (Cambridge: MIT Press, 1981), 69–87, 93–102. As articulated by Alasdair MacIntyre, neo-Aristotelianism involves an emphasis on ethical virtues shaped in "practices," performed in particular settings, and recounted in "narratives." See MacIntyre, *After Virtue: A Study in Moral Theory*, 3rd ed. (Notre Dame: University of Notre Dame Press, 2008); Paul Blackledge and Kelvin Knight, eds., *Virtue and Politics* (Notre Dame: University of Notre Dame Press, 2011). Compare also Elizabeth An-

scombe, *Human Life, Action, and Ethics* (Charlottesville, VA: Imprint Academic, 2005); Elijah Millgram, *Ethics Done Right: Practical Reasoning as a Foundation of Moral Theory* (Cambridge: Cambridge University Press, 2005); and Stephen M. Gardiner, ed., *Virtue Ethics, Old and New* (Ithaca: Cornell University Press, 2005).

22. See in this respect my *Dialogue among Civilizations*, especially its opening chapter "Dialogue among Civilizations: A Hermeneutical Perspective" (17–30). See also Michális S. Michael and Fabio Petito, eds., *Civilizational Dialogue and World Order* (New York: Palgrave Macmillan, 2009); and Majid Tehranian and David W. Chappel, eds., *Dialogue of Civilizations: A New Peace Agenda for a New Millennium* (New York: Tauris, 2002).

23. As indicated before, the need for "hospitality" was initially emphasized by Kant in his "Perpetual Peace"; more recently it was underscored by Jacques Derrida in his *On Cosmopolitanism and Forgiveness*, trans. Mark Dooley and Michael Hughes (London and New York: Routledge, 2001); the French original was titled *Cosmopolites de tous les pays, encore un effort!* (Paris: Editions Galilée, 1997).

24. Regarding *perichoresis* see Raimon Panikkar, *The Rhythm of Being: The Gifford Lectures* (Maryknoll, NY: Orbis Books, 2010), 42, 59, 174, 276. Regarding Leibnizian "monads" see Hans Heinz Holz, *Leibniz* (Stuttgart: Kohlhammer Verlag, 1958), 49–50. Regarding Spinoza see *The Book of God*, ed. and intro. Dagobert D. Runes (New York: Philosophical Library, 1958), 107–8. From a Buddhist perspective a similar thought has been expressed by the Dalai Lama in his book *The Universe in a Single Atom: How Science and Spirituality Can Save Our World* (New York: Random House, 2005). Compare also my *Small Wonder: Global Power and Its Discontents* (Lanham, MD: Rowman and Littlefield 2005).

25. See *Songs of Kabir: From the Adi Granth*, ed. and trans. Nirmal Dass (Albany: State University of New York Press, 1991), 63; Muhammad Hedayetullah, *Kabir; The Apostle of Hindu-Muslim Unity* (Delhi: Motilal Banarsidass, 1977), 190–92. See also Mencius 4A11, as cited by Bryan W. van Norden, "Mencius," in *Readings in Classical Chinese Philosophy*, ed. Philip J. Ivanhoe and van Norden, 2nd ed. (Indianapolis: Hacket Publishing Company, 2005), 138.

3. After Babel

1. The meanings of the Latin terms are, in sequence, "man" the toolmaker, the speaker, the inquirer, and the symbolizer. On the latter term compare, e.g., Edward H. Henderson, "Homo Symbolicus: A Definition of Man," *Man and World* 4 (1971): 131–50.

2. Plato, *The Republic*, Book 2, 369C–375A; see Eric H. Warmington and Philip G. Rouse, eds., *Great Dialogues of Plato* (New York: New American Library, 1956), 165–71.

3. In Aristotle's words: "A pilot will judge a rudder better than a ship builder; in the same way, the diner—not the cook—will be the best judge of a feast" (*Politics*, 1282a8). See also his statements: "The end and purpose of a *polis* is the good life (*eu zen*), and the institutions of social life are means to that end" (*Politics*, 1280b32); "We may therefore lay down that all associations aim at some good; and we may also hold that the particular association which is the most sovereign and includes all the rest, will pursue this aim above all and will thus be directed toward the highest of all goods" (*Politics*, 1252a). The first point, regarding the uniformity or homogeneity of Plato's imagined city, was also noted by Aristotle, who, in his critical comments, goes so far as to say that "a city which becomes more and more unitary eventually ceases to be a *polis* at all" (*Politics*, 1261a). Compare *The Politics of Aristotle*, trans. Ernest Barker (Oxford: Clarendon Press, 1946), 1, 40, 120, 126; and my *In Search of the Good Life: Some Exemplary Voices* (Lexington: University Press of Kentucky, 2007).

4. Economic Policy Institute, "The State of Working in America," as reported by Harold Meyerson in "In the Taxing Debate, Find Out Where the Money Is," *South Bend Tribune*, Apr. 22, 2011. Relying on data from the US Commerce Department, Meyerson also points to the increasing tendency of "outsourcing" labor: "U.S. multinationals eliminated the positions of 2.9 million American employees during the past decade, while adding 2.4 million in other lands." Compare in this context also Larry M. Bartels, *Unequal Democracy: The Political Economy of the New Gilded Age* (Princeton: Princeton University Press, 2008); and Jacob S. Hacker et al., eds., *Remaking America: Democracy and Public Policy in an Age of Inequality* (New York: Russell Sage Foundation, 2007).

5. Aristotle, *Politics*, 1295a24, 1295b29; Barker, *Politics of Aristotle*, 180, 182.

6. See United Nations, *Human Development Report 1999* (Oxford: Oxford University Press, 1999); World Bank, *World Development Report 2000* (Oxford: Oxford University Press, 2000). See also Falk, *Predatory Globalization;* and my "Globalization and Inequality," 67–84.

7. See "Summary and Overview," http://hdr.undp.org/en/reports/global/hdr2010 (accessed June 14, 2011). For additional literature on the grim effects of unregulated financial capitalism see, e.g., Richard D. Wolff, *Capitalism Hits the Fan: The Global Economic Meltdown and What to Do about It* (Northampton, MA: Olive Branch Press, 2011); and Angus Sibley, *The "Poisoned Spring" of Economic Libertarianism* (Washington, DC: Pax Romana, 2011). For some remedies see Gar Alperovitz, *America beyond Capitalism: Reclaiming Our Wealth, Our Liberty, and Our Democracy* (Hoboken, NJ: Wiley, 2005); and Herman E. Daley and John B. Cob Jr., *For the Common Good: Redirecting the Economy toward Community, the Environment, and a Sustainable Future*, 2nd ed. (Boston: Beacon Press, 1994).

8. United Nations, *Human Development Report 1999.* The report in this context pays tribute to Karl Polanyi's "brilliant exposition more than sixty years ago of the myth of the self-regulating market—the idea that markets could exist in a political and institutional vacuum. Generally, markets are very bad at ensuring the provision of public goods, such as security, stability, health, and education. . . . Without complementary societal and state action, markets can be weak on environmental sustainability, creating the conditions for environmental degradation, even for such disasters as mud flows in Java and oil spills in the Gulf of Mexico." Compare Karl Polanyi, *The Great Transformation: The Political and Economic Origins of Our Time* (1944; reprint, Boston: Beacon Press, 1957).

9. Jonathan Sacks, *The Dignity of Difference: How to Avoid the Clash of Civilizations* (London and New York: Continuum, 2002), 113–16. Referring to various editions of the UN's *Human Development Report* and other available data, Sacks states (29): "By the end of the millennium, the top fifth of the world's population had 86% of the world's GDP while the bottom fifth had just 1%. The assets of the world's three richest billionaires were more than the combined wealth of the 600 million inhabitants of the least developed countries." These and similar findings support his complaint that global capitalism represents a system of "immense power" whose effects in terms of maldistribution constitute "a scar on the face of humanity" (15, 28). Compare also my "The Dignity of Difference: A Salute to Jonathan Sacks," in *Small Wonder,* 209–17.

10. Sacks, *Dignity of Difference,* 32, 78. Compare also MacIntyre, *After Virtue.*

11. See Sacks, *Dignity of Difference,* 136, 140–41; Martha Nussbaum, *Not for Profit: Why Democracy Needs the Humanities* (Princeton: Princeton University Press, 2010), 44–46. Compare also Nussbaum, *Cultivating Humanity: A Classical Defense of Reform in Liberal Education* (Cambridge: Harvard University Press, 1997); and my *In Search of the Good Life.*

12. Sacks, *Dignity of Difference,* 17–18, 21.

13. Aristotle, *Politics,* 1274b32; Barker, *Politics of Aristotle,* 93.

14. Iris Marion Young, "Polity and Group Difference: A Critique of the Ideal of Universal Citizenship," in *Theorizing Citizenship,* ed. Ronald Beiner (Albany: State University of New York Press, 1995), 175–76, 181–84. Compare also her *Justice and the Politics of Difference* (Princeton: Princeton University Press, 1990).

15. Charles Taylor, "Why Democracy Needs Patriotism," in Martha Nussbaum, *For Love of Country?* ed. Joshua Cohen (Boston: Beacon Press, 1996), 121.

16. See Richard Falk, "An Emergent Matrix of Citizenship: Complex, Uneven, and Fluid," in *Global Citizenship: A Critical Introduction,* ed. Nigel Dower and John Williams (New York: Routledge, 2002),

27–28; see also Christian van den Anker, "Global Justice, Global Institutions and Global Citizenship," in Dower and Williams, *Global Citizenship*, 167–68.

17. Richard Falk, "The World Order between Inter-State Law and the Law of Humanity: The Role of Civil Society Institutions," in *Cosmopolitan Democracy: An Agenda for a New World Order*, ed. Daniele Archibugi and David Held (Cambridge, UK: Polity Press, 1995), 163–79.

18. David Held, "Democracy and the New International Order," in Archibugi and Held, *Cosmopolitan Democracy*, 111, 116. See also Held, *Cosmopolitanism: Ideals and Realities*.

19. Kant, "Perpetual Peace," 93–130.

20. In Sacks's words: "We are not in sight of a global contract whereby nation-states agree to sacrifice part of their sovereignty to create a form of world governance. There is, however, an alternative, namely a global *covenant*. Covenants are more foundational than contracts. . . . Covenants are beginnings, acts of moral engagement. . . . There is at least a starting point for a global covenant in which the nations of the world collectively express their commitment not only to human rights but also to human responsibilities, and not merely a political, but also an economic, environmental, moral and cultural conception of the common good, constructed on the twin foundations of shared humanity and respect for diversity." See *Dignity of Difference*, 205–6.

4. Humanizing Humanity

1. This essay was presented as a keynote lecture at the "First World Humanities Forum," held by UNESCO in Busan, Korea, Nov. 24–26, 2011.

2. *Constitution of the United Nations Educational, Scientific and Cultural Organization*, "Preamble," http://portal.unesco.org (accessed June 14, 2011).

3. Compare, e.g., Michael Bailey and Des Freedman, *The Assault on Universities: A Manifesto of Resistance* (New York: Palgrave Macmillan, 2011); Ellen Schrecker, *The Lost Soul of Higher Education: Corporatization, the Assault on Academic Freedom, and the End of the American University* (New York: New Press, 2010); Jennifer Washburn, *University, Inc.: The Corporate Corruption of American Higher Education* (New York: Basic Books, 2005); and Noam Chomsky, "Public Education under Massive Corporate Assault," Aug. 5, 2011, http://www.readersupportednews.org/off-site-opinion-section/7.

4. Nussbaum, *Not for Profit*.

5. Even without a close attachment to the Aristotelian legacy, political theorist Hannah Arendt in her writings stipulated a tripartition of human endeavors: labor, work, and action—where the second corresponds to technical know-how and the third to Aristotle's practical branch. See, e.g., Arendt, *The*

Human Condition: A Study of the Central Dilemmas Facing Modern Man (Chicago: University of Chicago Press, 1958), 9.

6. For some background see Robert Flint, *Philosophy as Scientia Scientiarum and a History of Classifications of the Sciences* (Edinburgh and London: Blackwood, 1904); see also my "Political Science and the Two Cultures," in *Beyond Dogma and Despair: Toward a Critical Phenomenology of Politics* (Notre Dame: University of Notre Dame Press, 1981), 21–42.

7. Compare, e.g., Henry M. Wriston, *The Nature of a Liberal College* (Appleton, WI: Lawrence University Press, 1937); and Brand Blanshard, *The Uses of a Liberal Education, and Other Talks to Students* (La Salle, IL: Open Court, 1973).

8. On the Baconian *Organon* and his "classification" of knowledge see, e.g., Henry E. Bliss, *The Organization of Knowledge and the System of the Sciences* (New York: Holt, 1929), 316–20.

9. See Giambattista Vico, *On the Study Methods of Our Time (De Nostri Temporis Studiorum Ratione)*, trans. Elio Gianturco, intro. Donald P. Verene (Ithaca: Cornell University Press, 1990).

10. See Johann Gottfried Herder, *Auch eine Philosophie der Geschichte zur Bildung der Menschheit*, with an epilogue by Hans-Georg Gadamer (Frankfurt-Main: Suhrkamp, 1967). Compare Sikka, *Herder on Humanity.* As one should note, the *Humanität* invoked here is not an anthropocentrism, but a humanism open to the transhuman. See in this respect my "Who Are We Now? For an 'Other' Humanism," in *Promise of Democracy*, 135–54; see also Heidegger, "Letter on Humanism," 193–242.

11. For a more detailed account of these schemes see my "Political Science and the Two Cultures," 30–36.

12. In terms of the republic of knowledge, the "practical turn" can be found, e.g., in Martin Heidegger's emphasis on the central category of "care" (*Sorge*) and its differentiation into care about things, care for others, and self-care. See Heidegger, *Being and Time*, par. 41–42, pp. 235–44. The scheme can be compared with Max Scheler's pointed distinction among instrumental *Leistungswissen*, metaphysical *Erlösungswissen*, and humanistic *Bildungswissen;* see his *Die Wissensformen und die Gesellschaft* (Leipzig: Neue Geist Verlag, 1926). A similar practical shift, but along more neo-Kantian lines, can be found in Jürgen Habermas, *Knowledge and Human Interests*, trans. Jeremy J. Shapiro (Boston: Beacon Press, 1971). Compare also Bernard Crick, *In Defence of Politics* (Baltimore: Penguin Books, 1964); and Wilhelm Hennis, *Politik und praktische Philosophie* (Neuwied and Berlin: Luchterhand, 1963).

13. See Gadamer, *Truth and Method*, 356–57.

14. Gadamer, *Truth and Method*, 9–11. (In the above and subsequent citations, the translation has been slightly altered for the sake of clarity.)

15. Gadamer, *Truth and Method*, 14, 18.

16. Gadamer, *Truth and Method*, 31–32.

17. Gadamer, *Truth and Method*, 19–21. As Gadamer adds (21): "According to Vico, what gives to human striving its direction is not the abstract universality of reason but the concrete universality represented by the community of a group, a people, a nation, and ultimately of humanity at large. Hence, developing this communal sense is of decisive importance for human life."

18. Gadamer, *Truth and Method*, 24–25. See also Thomas Reid, *The Philosophical Works*, ed. William Hamilton, 8th ed. (Hildeshein: Georg Olms, 1967), 2: 774. Unsurprisingly, Alasdair MacIntyre in his *After Virtue* devotes close attention to the teachings of the Scottish "enlightenment" (37–39, 272). Compare also Louis Schneider, ed., *The Scottish Moralists on Human Nature and Society* (Chicago: University of Chicago Press, 1967).

19. Nussbaum, *Not for Profit*, 2.

20. Nussbaum, *Not for Profit*, 2, 15, 24. Among pioneering defenders of the humanities during the last two centuries, Nussbaum (18, 57–68) mentions especially the philosophers Rousseau and John Dewey and the educators Friedrich Frobel in Germany, Johann Pestalozzi in Switzerland, Bronson Alcott in the United States, and Maria Montessori in Italy. The most prominent Indian educator celebrated throughout the book is the poet Rabindranath Tagore. One probably would have to add Rudolf Steiner to her list.

21. Nussbaum, *Not for Profit*, 79–80, 86, 91. One aspect strongly emphasized by Nussbaum is multilingual training, the demand that "all students should learn at least one foreign language" (90). Compare in this context also Peter Kemp, *Citizen of the World: The Cosmopolitan Ideal for the Twenty-First Century*, trans. Russell L. Dees (New York: Humanities Books, 2011).

22. Nussbaum, *Not for Profit*, 143. For a similar perspective see also Nussbaum, *Cultivating Humanity*; and Elise Boulding, *Building a Global Civic Culture: Education for an Interdependent World* (Syracuse: Syracuse University Press, 1990).

23. *Constitution* (UNESCO), "Preamble."

5. Ethics and International Politics

1. This response was presented at a symposium organized by the School of International Relations at St. Andrew University in Scotland, July 1–3, 2010. For the texts of the papers to which I respond, see *Journal of International Political Theory* 7 (2011): 221–51.

2. Still on the issue of dialogue Shapcott comments that, despite some disagreements, I am "quite happy to extend good will towards the Habermasian shore"—a statement I find accurate and perceptive. I do not consider Habermasian critical theory "wrong," just somewhat limiting; in the same way I find Kant and Rawls not wrong but limiting. I am also pleased by his comment that I have "also been successful in demonstrating the contribu-

tions of Heidegger and post-structuralism to the thinking about universalism" or cosmopolitanism.

3. See my "Comparative Political Theory: What Is It Good For?" in *Western Political Thought in Dialogue with Asia,* ed. Takashi Shogimen and Cary J. Nederman (Lanham, MD: Lexington Books, 2008), 13–24.

4. See Fred Dallmayr, *Beyond Orientalism: Essays on Cross-Cultural Encounter* (New York: State University of New York Press, 1996), esp. 1–37; Dallmayr and Ganesh Devi, eds., *Between Tradition and Modernity: India in Search of Identity* (Delhi: Sage Publications India, 1998); Dallmayr and Zhao Tingyang, eds., *Contemporary Chinese Political Thought: Debates and Perspectives* (Lexington: University Press of Kentucky, 2012).

5. See Fred Dallmayr, *Peace Talks—Who Will Listen?* (Notre Dame: University of Notre Dame Press, 2004); Dallmayr, *In Search of the Good Life;* Dallmayr, *Promise of Democracy.*

6. See, e.g., Fred Dallmayr and Thomas McCarthy, eds., *Understanding and Social Inquiry* (Notre Dame: University of Notre Dame Press, 1977).

7. See my *Between Freiburg and Frankfurt: Toward a Critical Ontology* (Boston: MIT Press, 1991), published in the UK as *Life-World, Modernity and Critique: Paths between Heidegger and the Frankfurt School* (Cambridge, UK: Polity Press, 1991).

8. See Fred Dallmayr, *Border Crossings: Toward a Comparative Political Theory* (Lanham, MD: Lexington Books, 1999); Dallmayr and Devi, *Between Tradition and Modernity;* Dallmayr, *Alternative Visions: Paths in the Global Village* (Lanham, MD: Rowman and Littlefield, 1998); Dallmayr, *Achieving Our World: Toward a Global and Plural Democracy* (Lanham, MD: Rowman and Littlefield, 2001); and Dallmayr, *Dialogue among Civilizations.* Perhaps one needs to add here a fourth leg concerned mainly with ethical-political questions, reflected in these texts: Dallmayr, *In Search of the Good Life;* Dallmayr, *Promise of Democracy;* and Dallmayr, *Integral Pluralism.*

9. Beardsworth speaks of my "exemplary ambivalence toward political liberalism," noting that—despite my critique of neoliberalism—I do not "berate liberalism [or modernity] per se, unlike more radical forms of postmodernism." This is very correct. Basically I side with John Dewey's view that liberty is not a transcendental attribute but an ongoing task achieved in social-political interaction.

10. In this context, Beardsworth adds some comments on the Gandhian policy of "nonviolence" (*ahimsa*) that I find questionable (and also not directly pertinent). In my view, Gandhi did not espouse an absolute nonviolence, but simply the greatest possible nonviolence under the circumstances (most Gandhi scholars would agree). His policy likely would face great difficulty in totalitarian regimes; but so would Beardsworth's notion of a politics of "lesser violence."

11. See, e.g., Gadamer, *Hermeneutics, Religion, and Ethics.* On Heideggerian ethics compare Lawrence J. Hatab, *Ethics and Finitude: Heideggerian Contributions to Moral Philosophy* (Lanham, MD: Rowman and Littlefield, 2000); and my "Heidegger on Ethics and Justice," in *The Other Heidegger* (Ithaca: Cornell University Press, 1993), 106–31.

6. Befriending the Stranger

1. See Bernhard Waldenfels, *Order in the Twilight*, trans. David J. Parent (Athens: Ohio University Press, 1996); Waldenfels, *In den Netzen der Lebenswelt* (Frankfurt: Suhrkamp, 1985); and Waldenfels, *Der Stachel des Fremden* (Frankfurt: Suhrkamp, 1990). Compare also my "Border Crossings: Bernhard Waldenfels on Dialogue," in *Achieving Our World*, 129–46.

2. See Thomas Hobbes, *Leviathan*, intro. A. D. Lindsay (London: Dent and Sons, 1953), chaps. 13, 17–18, 21, 26; and Hobbes, *De Cive; or, The Citizen*, ed. Sterling P. Lamprecht (New York: Appleton-Century-Crofts, 1949), chaps. 1, 5–6, 13.

3. See Carl Schmitt, *The Concept of the Political*, trans. George Schwab (Chicago: University of Chicago Press, 2007), 25–26; Schmitt, *Political Theology: Four Chapters on the Concept of Sovereignty*, trans. George Schwab (Cambridge: MIT Press, 1985), 5. Compare also Gabriella Slomp, *Carl Schmitt and the Politics of Hostility, Violence and Terror* (New York: Palgrave MacMillan, 2009); and my chapters "The Concept of the Political: Politics between War and Peace" and "The Secular and the Sacred: Whither Political Theology?" in *Integral Pluralism*, 23–44, 45–66.

4. Joseph Lieberman, "Democrats and America's Enemies," *Wall Street Journal*, May 22, 2008. Compare in this context Tom Engelhardt, *The United States of Fear* (Chicago: Haymarket Books, 2011); and Engelhardt, *The American Way of War: How Bush's War Became Obama's* (Chicago: Haymarket Books, 2010).

5. Albena Azmanova, "Against the Politics of Fear: On Deliberation, Inclusion, and the Political Economy of Trust," *Philosophy and Social Criticism* 37 (2011): 401–12. Compare also her "Capitalism Reorganized: Social Justice after Neo-Liberalism," *Constellations* 17 (May 2010): 309–406; and her *The Scandal of Reason: A Critical Theory of Political Judgment* (New York: Columbia University Press, 2012).

6. See my *Peace Talks—Who Will Listen?* esp. chaps. 1 and 2.

7. See Bryan S. Turner, "National Identities and Cosmopolitan Virtues: Citizenship in a Global Age," in *Beyond Nationalism? Sovereignty and Citizenship*, ed. Fred Dallmayr and José M. Rosales (Lanham, MD: Lexington Books, 2001), 202–3.

8. Richard Falk, *The Great Terror War* (New York: Olive Branch Press, 2003), 6–8. As he adds (39): "Megaterrorism is a unique challenge, differing from earlier expressions of global terrorism, by magnitude, scope and ideol-

ogy, representing a serious effort to transform world order as a whole, and not merely change the power structure of one or more sovereign states."

9. Falk, *Great Terror War,* 9–10, 29.

10. Falk, *Great Terror War,* 31, 179.

11. Richard Falk, *The Declining World Order: America's Imperial Geopolitics* (New York and London: Routledge, 2004), 221.

12. See Joseph S. Nye, *The Paradox of American Power* (New York: Oxford University Press, 2003); Nye, *Soft Power: The Means to Success in World Politics* (New York: Public Affairs, 2004); and Andrew Linklater, *Boundaries in Question: New Directions in International Relations* (New York: St. Martin's Press, 1995). Compare also Paul Gilbert, *New Terror, New Wars* (Washington, DC: Georgetown University Press, 2003); Anthony F. Lang Jr. and Amanda R. Beattie, eds., *War, Terror and Terrorism* (New York: Routledge, 2008); Andrew Schopp and Matthew B. Hill, eds., *The War on Terror and American Popular Culture: September 11 and Beyond* (Madison, NJ: Fairleigh Dickinson University Press, 2009); James F. Hodge and Gideon Rose, eds., *Understanding the War on Terror* (New York: Council on Foreign Relations, 2005); Allen Douglas, ed., *Comparative Philosophy and Religion in Times of Terror* (Lanham, MD: Lexington Books, 2006); and James A. Piazza and James I. Walsh, eds., "Symposium: Torture and the War on Terror," *PS: Political Science and Politics* 43 (July 2010): 407–50.

13. Chandra Muzaffar, *Global Ethic or Global Hegemony?* (London: Asean Academic Press, 2005), 15–16, 165–66. Among other things, Muzaffar is well known as president of the international nongovernmental organization "Just World Trust."

14. See Chandra Muzaffar, *Rights, Religion, and Reform: Enhancing Human Dignity through Spiritual and Moral Transformation* (London and New York: Routledge Curzon, 2002), 105; see also Falk, *Great Terror War,* 180.

15. Schmitt, *Concept of the Political,* 28–29. The precepts of Abrahamic religions can readily be extended to the Hindu-Jain opposition to violence (*ahimsa*) and the Buddhist stress on compassion (*karuna*).

16. Compare, e.g., Dalai Lama and Fabien Ouaki, *Imagine All the People* (Boston: Wisdom Publications, 1999); Dalai Lama, "The Nobel Peace Prize Lecture," in *The Dalai Lama: A Policy of Kindness,* ed. Sidney Piburn (Ithaca: Snow Lion, 1990); Daisaku Ikeda, *New Horizons of a Global Civilization* (Tokyo: Soka Gakkai, 1997); Bishop Desmond Tutu, *God Has a Dream: A Vision of Hope for Our Time* (New York: Doubleday, 2004).

17. Stanley Hauerwas, "Christian Nonviolence," in *Strike Terror No More: Theology, Ethics, and the New War,* ed. Jon L. Berquist (St. Louis: Chalice Press, 2002), 246–47.

18. See John B. Cobb Jr., "A War against Terrorism," in Berquist, *Strike Terror No More,* 7–9; Walter Wink, "We Must Find a Better Way," in Berquist, *Strike Terror No More,* 335.

19. See John Milbank, "Sovereignty, Empire, Capital, and Terror," in Berquist, *Strike Terror No More*, 75; Max L. Stackhouse, "Theologies of War: Comparative Perspectives," in Berquist, *Strike Terror No More*, 209–10.

20. See *The Spirit of Laws of Montesquieu*, ed. and intro. David W. Carrithers (Berkeley: University of California Press, 1977), 107, 117–24, 132–33.

21. John Dewey, "The Ethics of Democracy," in *John Dewey: The Early Works, 1882–1898*, vol. 1, ed. George F. Axtelle et al. (Carbondale: Southern Illinois University, 1969), 240. Compare also my "Democratic Action and Experience," 43–65.

22. John Dewey, "Creative Democracy—The Task before Us" (1939), in *John Dewey*, vol. 14, *The Later Works, 1925–1953*, ed. Jo Ann Boydston (Carbondale: Southern Illinois University, 1988), 228.

7. The Body Politic

1. This essay was presented at the Peace BAR Festival, held at Kyung Hee University in Seoul, Korea, Oct. 31–Nov. 1, 2011.

2. See in this connection my discussion of Spinoza's work, especially Spinoza's distinction between *natura naturans* and *natura naturata*, in *Return to Nature? An Ecological Counterhistory* (Lexington: University Press of Kentucky, 2011), 11–32.

3. Ernst H. Kantorowicz, *The King's Two Bodies: A Study in Mediaeval Political Theology* (Princeton: Princeton University Press, 1957).

4. Hobbes, *De Cive*, 21–22. (In the above and subsequent citations, the Hobbesian idiom has been somewhat simplified.)

5. Hobbes, *De Cive*, 21 n22, 24.

6. Hobbes, *Leviathan*, chap. 6, p. 23, chap. 11, p. 49, chap. 13, pp. 64–66, chap. 14, p. 67. (In the above and subsequent citations, the Hobbesian idiom has been somewhat simplified.)

7. Hobbes, *Leviathan*, p. 1, chap. 17, p. 89.

8. Hobbes, *Leviathan*, chap. 17, pp. 89–90. Compare Schmitt, *Political Theology*, 5, 36–37. See also my "The Secular and the Sacred: Whither Political Theology?" in *Integral Pluralism*, 45–66.

9. In a somewhat different sense, the ambivalent status of human beings between *naturans* and *naturata* is also manifest in the two sayings "homo homini Deus" and "homo homini lupus," both of which Hobbes endorses in his dedicatory letter preceding *De Cive*: "To speak impartially, both sayings are very true: that man to man is a kind of God, and that man to man is an errant wolf. The first is true if we compare citizens amongst themselves, and the second if we compare cities. In the one, there is some analogy of similitude with the Deity, to wit: justice and charity, the twin sisters of peace. But in the other, good men must defend themselves by taking to them for a sanctuary the two daughters of war: deceit and violence—that is in plain terms a mere brutal rapacity." See *De Cive*, 1–2.

10. John Locke, *Two Treatises of Civil Government*, intro. W. S. Carpenter (London: Dent and Sons, 1953), Book 2, chap. 2, par. 1, p. 118, and par. 7, p. 120, and chap. 3, par. 19, p. 126. The bracketing of Hobbesian war is rendered even more curious by Locke's admission that the individual execution of natural law may lead to violent death: "Man being born . . . with a title to perfect freedom and an uncontrolled enjoyment of all the rights and privileges of the law of nature, equally with any other man or number of men in the world, has by nature a power not only to preserve his property—that is, his life, liberty, and estate—against the injuries and attempts of other men, but to judge of and punish the breaches of that law in others, as he is persuaded the offense deserves, even with death itself, in crimes where the heinousness of the fact in his opinion requires it." See chap. 7, par. 87, pp. 158–59.

11. Locke, *Two Treatises of Civil Government*, Book 2, chap. 2, par. 13, p. 123, and par. 15, p. 124, and chap. 7, par. 89, p. 160.

12. Locke, *Two Treatises of Civil Government*, Book 2, chap. 5, par. 26, p. 130, and par. 30, p. 131, chap. 7, par. 89, p. 160, and chap. 8, par. 95, p. 164.

13. See Jean-Jacques Rousseau, *The Social Contract and Discourse on the Origin of Inequality*, ed. and intro. Lester G. Crooker (New York: Pocket Books, 1967), Book 1, chap. 1, p. 7, and chap. 6, pp. 17–18. In Rousseau's words (chap. 6, p. 19): "This public person which is thus formed by the union of all individual members formerly took the name of *city* [*civitas*] and now takes that of *republic* or *body politic* which is called by its members *state* when it is passive, *sovereign* when it is active, *power* when it is compared to similar bodies." The distinction between active and passive (*naturans* and *naturata*) is also carried over into the role of members: "With regard to the associates, they take collectively the name of *people*, and are called individually *citizens* as participating in the sovereign power, and *subjects* as subjected to the laws of the state." Regarding the "general will" as sovereign compare this statement (Book 4, chap. 1, p. 109): "So long as a number of men in combination are considered a single body, they have but one will, which relates to the common preservation and to the general well-being."

14. See Jeremy Bentham, "Anarchical Fallacies: A Critical Examination of the Declaration of Rights," in *The Works of Jeremy Bentham* (Edinburgh: W. Tait, 1839), 2: 500–501.

15. Guido de Ruggiero, "Positivism," in *Encyclopaedia of the Social Sciences* (New York: Macmillan, 1932), 6: 54.

16. Auguste Comte, *A General View of Positivism*, trans. J. H. Bridges (New York: R. Speller, 1957), 49. See also his *System of Positive Polity*, 4 vols. (London: Longman, Green and Co., 1875–77); and his *The Catechism of Positive Religion*, trans. Richard Congreve (London: Chapman, 1858).

17. See Herbert Spencer, *First Principles* (New York: A. L. Burt, 1880), 407; see also his *Social Statics* (New York: Appleton, 1892). In the domain of

politics, Spencer's "laissez-faire" liberalism was expressed chiefly in his *Man Versus the State* (Caldwell, ID: Caxton, 1940), a text that became something like a gospel of liberal antistatism favoring the private accumulation of profit.

18. An important precursor in this sense was Claude Adrien Helvétius (1715–1771), whom Bentham himself credited with first having stated the principle "the greatest happiness of the greatest number." In the words of Helvétius: "The springs of action in man are corporeal pains and pleasures. Pleasure and pain are, and always will be, the only principles of action in man. . . . Corporeal pleasure and pain are [also] the real and only spring of all government." See his *De l'Homme* (1773), translated by W. Hooper as *A Treatise on Man* (New York: B. Franklin, 1969), 1: 3.

19. See Jeremy Bentham, *An Introduction to the Principles of Morals and Legislation* (Oxford: Clarendon Press, 1876), 3, 17–19, 102; see also his *Theory of Legislation* (Boston: Weeks-Jordan, 1840), 1: 65.

20. John Protevi, *Political Physics: Deleuze, Derrida and the Body Politic* (London and New York: Athlone Press, 2001), 1–2, 4.

21. Protevi, *Political Physics*, 2–3, 5, 7–10.

22. On some of those counter-trends see my *Return to Nature?*

23. On the connection of politics and friendship see, e.g., John von Heyking and Richard Avramenko, eds., *Friendship and Politics: Essays in Political Thought* (Notre Dame: University of Notre Dame Press, 2008); Jacques Derrida, *Politics of Friendship*, trans. George Collins (New York: Verso, 1997); and my "Distancing the Other: Jacques Derrida on Friendship," in *Achieving Our World*, 147–70.

24. On Montesquieu see my chapter "Montesquieu's *Persian Letters*," in *In Search of the Good Life*, 95–115; on Spinoza see my "Nature and Divine Substance: Spinoza," in *Return to Nature?* 11–32.

25. Maurice Merleau-Ponty, *The Visible and the Invisible, followed by Working Notes*, ed. Claude Lefort, trans. Alphonso Lingis (Evanston: Northwestern University Press, 1968), 259, 263. Compare also my "Nature and Life-World: Merleau-Ponty," in *Return to Nature?* 97–116; and James R. Mensch, *Embodiments: From the Body to the Body Politic* (Evanston: Northwestern University Press, 2009).

26. Frank Schalow, *The Incarnality of Being: The Earth, Animals, and the Body in Heidegger's Thought* (Albany: State University of New York Press, 2006). As he writes (136, 143): "The political body [for Heidegger] is not simply any aggregate of individuals, since there would be no distinguishing trademark of its practice versus other forms of rule. At the same time, the materiality of the body is more than a metaphor of the mode of organization that draws [individual] people into community. . . . If there is any democratic element to the Heideggerian *polis*, then it lies in the admission of 'multivocity,' in the playing out of the exchange of many voices which, at best, implies sanctifying maximum participation among all members of society." Compare

also my *Other Heidegger;* and my "Conversation across Borders: *E Pluribus Unum?*" in *Dialogue among Civilizations,* 31–47.

27. On Gandhi compare Anthony J. Parel, *Gandhi's Philosophy and the Quest for Harmony* (Cambridge: Cambridge University Press, 2006); Douglas Allen, *Mahatma Gandhi* (London: Reaktion Books, 2012); and my "*Satyagraha:* Gandhi's Truth Revisited," in *Alternative Visions,* 105–21. Generally on social-political healing see Erwin A. Jaffe, *Healing the Body Politic: Rediscovering Political Power* (Westport, CT: Praeger Publishing, 1993). The book uses "power" in the sense of Hannah Arendt as shared "empowerment." For another text inspired by Arendt see Elisabeth Young-Bruehl, *Mind and the Body Politic* (New York: Routledge, 1989).

8. A Secular Age?

1. Concerning the "crisis of modernity" compare, e.g., Oswald Spengler, *The Decline of the West* (1918; reprint, New York: Knopf, 1939); René Guénon, *La crise du monde moderne* (1928), translated by M. Pallis and R. Nicholson as *The Crisis of the Modern World* (London: Luzac, 1962); Romano Guardini, *Das Ende der Neuzeit* (1950), translated by Frederick D. Wilhelmsen as *The End of the Modern World* (New York: Sheed and Ward, 1956); and Leo Strauss, "The Crisis of Our Time," in *The Predicament of Modern Politics,* ed. Harold J. Spaeth (Detroit: University of Detroit Press, 1964), 41–54. Compare in this context the chapter "Global Modernization: Toward Different Modernities," in my *Dialogue among Civilizations,* 85–104.

2. In one of his previous writings, Taylor distinguishes between the "boosters" and the "knockers" of modernity. See his *Ethics of Authenticity,* 11, 22–23.

3. Charles Taylor, *A Secular Age* (Cambridge: Harvard University Press, 2007), 2–3.

4. Taylor, *Secular Age,* 8–10. The comment on existentialism obviously is tailored to the writings of Albert Camus. Regarding deep ecology, the judgment is modified a few pages later (19), where we read that "there are attempts to reconstruct a non-exclusive humanism on a non-religious basis, which one sees in various forms of deep ecology."

5. Taylor, *Secular Age,* 13–16.

6. Taylor, *Secular Age,* 16, 19–20.

7. Taylor, *Secular Age,* 539–42. In another succinct formulation he states (566): "Modern science, along with the many other facets described—the buffered identity, with its disciplines, modern individualism, with its reliance on instrumental reason and action in secular time—make up the immanent frame. . . . Science, modern individualism, instrumental reason, secular time, all seem proofs of the truth of immanence."

8. Taylor, *Secular Age,* 543, 547–49, 555–56. Taylor's discussion of the

different "frames" or "worlds" is often quite ambiguous—to the point of jeopardizing the distinction itself. Thus, with regard to naturalism we read at one point (548): "Belonging to the earth, the sense of our dark genesis, can also be part of Christian faith, but only when it has broken with certain features of the immanent frame, especially the distinction nature/supernature."

9. See Charles Taylor, *A Catholic Modernity?* ed. James L. Heft, S.M. (New York: Oxford University Press, 1999), 16–19. Compare also his *Sources of the Self: The Making of the Modern Identity* (Cambridge: Harvard University Press, 1989); and his *Ethics of Authenticity.*

10. At one point, Taylor complains that we have moved "from an era in which religious life was more 'embodied,' where the presence of the sacred could be enacted in ritual . . . into one which is more 'in the mind.'" As a corollary of this move, "official Christianity has gone through what we can call an 'excarnation,' a transfer of embodied, 'enfleshed' forms of religious life, to those which are more 'in the head.'" See *Secular Age,* 554.

11. Taylor, *Secular Age,* 19. In his stress on verticality, Taylor seems to have been influenced by a certain "transcendentalist" strand in French postmodernism, manifest especially in the writings of the later Jacques Derrida (under the influence of Emmanuel Levinas and his notion of the radically "Other"). For a different, more "open" conception of humanism compare, e.g., Jacques Maritain, *Integral Humanism: Temporal and Spiritual Problems of a New Christendom,* trans. Joseph W. Evans (Notre Dame: University of Notre Dame Press, 1973); and Heidegger, "Letter on Humanism," 189–242.

12. Raimon Panikkar, *Worship and Secular Man* (Maryknoll, NY: Orbis Books, 1973), 1–2, 10–13. Compare also the chapter "Rethinking Secularism—With Raimon Panikkar," in my *Dialogue among Civilizations,* 185–200.

13. Panikkar, *Rhythm of Being,* xxvi–xxx, xxxii.

14. Panikkar, *Rhythm of Being,* 3–4. As he adds somberly (4): "Today's powers, though more anonymous and more diffused, are quite as cruel and terrible as the worst monsters of history. What good is a merely intellectual denunciation in countries where we can say anything we like because it is bound to remain ineffectual. . . . There is little risk in denouncing provided we do not move a finger."

15. Panikkar, *Rhythm of Being,* 4–5. In this context, Panikkar offers some very instructive asides (5): "Now the foremost way to communicate life is to live it; but this life is neither an exclusively public domain, nor merely private property. Neither withdrawing from the world nor submerging ourselves in it is the responsible human attitude."

16. Panikkar, *Rhythm of Being,* 6–7, 17, 23–24. As he adds (24): one must "constantly be on guard against one of the most insidious dangers that bedevils such endeavors: the totalitarian temptation. My attempt is holistic, not global; I am not offering a system."

17. Panikkar, *Rhythm of Being,* 22, 32–33. As the text adds a bit lat-

er (51): "Being is not a thing. There is nothing 'outside' Being. Hence, the Rhythm of Being can only express the rhythm that Being itself *is*." For Heidegger's formulations see his "Letter on Humanism," esp. 235–36; and his *What Is Called Thinking?* trans. Fred D. Wieck and J. Gleen Gray (New York: Harper and Row, 1968). A better translation of the latter title would be "What Calls for Thinking?"

18. Panikkar, *Rhythm of Being*, 34–35.

19. Panikkar, *Rhythm of Being*, 10, 36, 38–39, 42. Somewhat later (52) the text adds: "Rhythm is a *meta-transcendental* quality—that is, a property that belongs to every being as Being. Rhythm adds nothing to Being, but only expresses a property of Being qua Being. If truth is considered a transcendental because it expresses Being as intelligible, that is, in relation to the intellect, rhythm belongs to Being considered not in relation to the intelligence or the will, but in relation to its totality [or Whole]." This view is said to be also in accord with "the *advaitic* vision of the Rhythm of Being."

20. Panikkar, *Rhythm of Being*, 110, 128, 133–35. In an intriguing aside he adds (135): "The hypothesis I would advance is that Western, mainly Christian and later Muslim monotheism, is a blend of biblical monotheism and the Hellenic mind represented mainly by Plotinus. . . . Neither Plato nor Aristotle . . . was a strict monotheist." For a critique of (imperial-style) political theology see my chapter "The Secular and the Sacred: Whither Political Theology?" in *Integral Pluralism*, 45–66.

21. Panikkar, *Rhythm of Being*, 171–72, 174, 179, 216, 230.

22. Panikkar, *Rhythm of Being*, 350–51, 359. As he asks dramatically (358): "Who or what will put a halt to the lethal course of technocracy? More concretely: who will control armaments, polluting industries, cancerous consumerism, and the like? Who will put an end to the unbridled tyranny of money?"

23. Panikkar, *Rhythm of Being*, 270–71; Taylor, *Secular Age*, 15–17, 19.

24. Taylor, *Secular Age*, 17–18. In the same context, Taylor makes some references to Buddhism—which, likewise, remain ambivalent and deeply contestable.

25. Dallmayr, *Small Wonder*, 4. See also Arundhati Roy, *The God of Small Things* (New York: Random House, 1997).

26. This is a free translation of Hölderlin's lines: "Wo aber Gefahr ist, wächst das Rettende auch." See Friedrich Hölderlin, "Patmos," in *Poems and Fragments*, trans. Michael Hamburger (Ann Arbor: University of Michigan Press, 1966), 462–63. Compare in this context Maurice Merleau-Ponty, *Visible and the Invisible*; also Merleau-Ponty, "Cézanne's Doubt," in *Sense and Non-Sense*, 9–25.

9. Post-Secularity and (Global) Politics

1. Gilles Kepel, *The Revenge of God*, trans. Alan Braley (University Park: Pennsylvania State University Press, 1994).

2. This is the development leading from *Theory of Justice* to *Political Liberalism* (New York: Columbia University Press, 1993).

3. Jürgen Habermas, "An Awareness of What Is Missing," in Habermas et al., *An Awareness of What Is Missing: Faith and Reason in a Post-Secular Age*, trans. Ciaran Cronin (Cambridge, UK: Polity Press, 2008). See also Habermas, *Between Naturalism and Religion: Philosophical Essays*, trans. Ciaran Cronin (Cambridge, UK: Polity Press, 2008).

4. Habermas, "Awareness of What Is Missing," 20–21.

5. Habermas, "Awareness of What Is Missing," 16–17, 22. With this statement, Habermas basically accepts the positivist stage theory (first formulated by Auguste Comte) that history moves from religion to metaphysics and then to (post-metaphysical) science.

6. Jürgen Habermas, "'The Political': The Rational Meaning of a Questionable Inheritance of Political Theology," in *The Power of Religion in the Public Sphere*, ed. Eduardo Mendieta and Jonathan Vanantwerpen (New York: Columbia University Press, 2011), 25–26. The conference was held in New York City's Cooper Union in Oct. 2009.

7. On Tertullian see *De praescriptione haereticorum* (Freiburg: Mohr, 1892), esp. chap. 7. The conflict between Athens and Jerusalem was also a central theme in the work of Leo Strauss; see on this point my "Leo Strauss Peregrinus," *Social Research* 61 (1994): 877–906.

8. Gianni Vattimo, *After Christianity*, trans. Luca D'Isanto (New York: Columbia University Press, 2002), 38–39. Compare in this context also Kitaro Nishida's comment: "Just as there is no world without God, there is no God without the world. . . . And as Eckhart said, one sees the true God where even God has been lost": *An Inquiry into the Good*, trans. Masao Abe and Christopher Ives (New Haven: Yale University Press, 1990), 168–69. For background see Emmanuel Levinas, *Of God Who Comes to Mind*, trans. Bettina Bergo (Stanford: Stanford University Press, 1998); Jacques Derrida, *The Gift of Death*, trans. David Wills (Chicago: University of Chicago Press, 1995); Jean-Luc Marion, *Reduction et donation* (Paris: Presses Universitaires de France, 1989); and Dominque Janicaud, "The Theological Turn of French Phenomenology," trans. Bernard G. Prusak, in Jaincaud et al., *Phenomenology and the "Theological Turn"* (New York: Fordham University Press, 2000), 16–103.

9. See Gadamer, "Universality of the Hermeneutical Problem," 1–20. In his *Knowledge and Human Interests*, Habermas tries to limit hermeneutical understanding to the humanities, while exempting natural science and psychoanalytic self-knowledge from such understanding—a procedure that ignores "post-empiricist" trends in science as well as the issue of depth hermeneutics. See in this respect my "Borders or Horizons? An Older Debate Revisited," in *Small Wonder*, 176–98; and my "Life-World and Critique," in *Between Freiburg and Frankfurt*, 13–24.

10. Charles Taylor, "Why We Need a Radical Redefinition of Secularism" in Mendieta and Vanantwerpen, *Power of Religion in the Public Sphere*, 49–50, 52–53. Giving some concrete examples, Taylor adds (54): "The two most widespread this-worldly philosophies in our contemporary world, utilitarianism and Kantianism, in their different versions, all have points at which they fail to convince honest and unconfused people." Extending this point to the relation between himself and Habermas, he states: "He finds this secure [secular] foundation in a 'discourse ethics,' which I unfortunately find quite unconvincing." What Taylor fails to notice is that his rejection of the "epistemic break" also puts pressure on his own ontological or metaphysical break between transcendence and immanence (which I critiqued in the previous chapter).

11. See in this context my "Postsecular Faith," 80–81.

12. The above passages can be read as a subtle commentary on the (much later) doctrine of *sola gratia*.

13. Habermas, "Awareness of What Is Missing," 19. For a somewhat more helpful text see Hauke Brunkhorst, *Solidarity: From Civic Friendships to a Global Legal Community*, trans. Jeffrey Flynn (Cambridge: MIT Press, 2005).

14. Taylor, "Why We Need a Radical Redefinition," 46, 56.

15. Aristotle, *Nicomachean Ethics*, trans. Terence Irwin (Indianapolis: Hackett, 1985), 14–15 (1097a35–1097b15), 34–35 (1103a31–1103b1). See also Chandra Muzaffar, *Rights, Religion and Reform: Enhancing Human Dignity through Spiritual and Moral Transformation* (London and New York: Routledge Curzon, 2002), 104; and my "Religion and the World: The Quest for Justice and Peace," in *Integral Pluralism*, 85–101.

16. In the gospel of John (4:23–24), Jesus simply says: "But the hour is coming and now is, when the true worshipper will worship the father in spirit and truth, for such the father seeks to worship him. God is spirit, and those who worship him must worship in spirit and truth." For the statement of Armstrong see http://www.ted.com/speakers/karen_armstrong.html (accessed Apr. 11, 2012). Her words are distantly echoed by Gadamer when he writes: "Just as health is not known in the same way as a wound or disease, so the holy is perhaps more a way of being than of being believed." See his "Reflections on the Relation of Religion and Science," in *Hermeneutics, Religion, and Ethics*, 127.

17. See in this context Paulo Freire, *Pedagogy of the Heart*, trans. Donaldo Macedo and Alexandre Oliveira (New York: Continuum, 1997); see also my "Polis and Cosmopolis," in *Margins of Political Discourse* (Albany: State University of New York Press, 1989), 1–21; and my *Promise of Democracy*.

10. Political Self-Rule

1. This essay was first presented at an international Gandhi conference held in New Delhi, India, in Aug. 2009. (I draw in this essay on some of my own earlier writings on Gandhi.)

2. Edward Said, *Culture and Imperialism* (New York: Knopf, 1993), 282, 291, 319, 323. Compare also Anthony Smith, *The Geopolitics of Information: How Western Culture Dominates the World* (New York: Oxford University Press, 1980).

3. M. K. Gandhi, *Hind Swaraj and Other Writings*, ed. Anthony Parel (Cambridge: Cambridge University Press, 1997), 26–28. Originally composed in Gujarati, the text was translated into English by Gandhi himself.

4. Gandhi, *Hind Swaraj*, 30–33, 35–37.

5. Gandhi, *Hind Swaraj*, 42–43, 67. As he adds (73): "The *swaraj* that I wish to picture before you and me is such that, after we have once realized it, we will endeavor to the end of our life-time to persuade others to do likewise. But such *swaraj* has to be experienced by each one for himself."

6. Gandhi, *Hind Swaraj*, lii–liii. In the words of Bhikhu Parekh: "For Gandhi, *swaraj* referred to a state of affairs in which individuals were morally in control of themselves and ran their lives in such a way that they needed no external coercion. . . . For Gandhi, *swaraj* thus presupposed self-discipline, self-restraint, a sense of mutual responsibility, the disposition neither to dominate nor be dominated by others, and a sense of *dharma*." See his *Gandhi* (Oxford: Oxford University Press, 1997), 75–76.

7. Gandhi, *Hind Swaraj*, p. 29.

8. Ramashray Roy, *Self and Society: A Study in Gandhian Thought* (New Delhi: Sage Publications India, 1984), 78.

9. Gandhi, *Hind Swaraj*, 73, 188–89.

10. See in this context Isaiah Berlin, *Four Essays on Liberty* (London: Oxford University Press, 1977).

11. R. Roy, *Self and Society*, 63, 189–90. The possibility of a transformative freedom was actually acknowledged by Isaiah Berlin; but he confined this mode narrowly to mystical or ascetic lifestyles—a confinement aptly criticized by Roy (186–87).

12. Ronald J. Terchek, "Gandhi and Democratic Theory," in *Political Thought in Modern India*, ed. Thomas Pantham and Kenneth L. Deutsch (New Delhi: Sage Publications, 1986), 308. The citation is from M. K. Gandhi, ed., *Non-Violence in Peace and War* (Ahmedabad: Navajivan, 1948), 1: 269.

13. Terchek, "Gandhi and Democratic Theory," 309, 312. See also Ronald Duncan, *Selected Writings of Mahatma Gandhi* (Boston: Beacon Press, 1951), 78–79.

14. Thomas Pantham, "Beyond Liberal Democracy: Thinking with Mahatma Gandhi," in Pantham and Deutsch, *Political Thought in Modern India*, 334, 337–39. The citations are from Mahatma Gandhi, *Democracy: Real and Deceptive*, comp. R. K. Prabhu (Ahmedabad: Navajivan, 1961), 32; *Harijan*, May 8, 1937; and *Harijan*, Mar. 31, 1946.

15. Michael J. Sandel, *Public Philosophy: Essays on Morality and Poli-*

tics (Cambridge: Harvard University Press, 2005), 9–11, 27, 33. Compare also Sandel, *Justice: What's the Right Thing to Do?* (New York: Farrar, Straus and Giroux, 2009); and James Tully, *Public Philosophy in a New Key,* vol. 1. *Democracy and Civic Freedom* (Cambridge: Cambridge University Press, 2008).

16. Arendt, *Human Condition,* 230–31. In her eloquent language: "One of the most persistent trends in modern philosophy since Descartes and perhaps its most original contribution to philosophy has been an exclusive concern with the self, as distinguished from the soul or person or man in general, an attempt to reduce all experiences, with the world as well as with other human beings, to experiences between man and himself. . . . World alienation, and not self-alienation as Marx thought, has been the hallmark of the modern age."

17. Hannah Arendt, "What Is Freedom?" in *Between Past and Future: Six Exercises in Political Thought* (Cleveland: World Publishing Co., 1963), 148–49, 153.

18. See Charles Taylor, "What's Wrong with Negative Liberty?" in *The Idea of Freedom: Essays in Honor of Isaiah Berlin,* ed. Alan Ryan (Oxford: Oxford University Press, 1979), 193; and his *Ethics of Authenticity,* 68, 74, 77–78.

19. John Dewey, "Democracy Is Radical" (1937), in *John Dewey: The Later Works: 1925–1953,* vol. 11, ed. Jo Ann Boydston (Carbondale: Southern Illinois University Press, 1980), 298; and "Reconstruction in Philosophy" (1920), in *John Dewey: The Middle Works: 1899–1924,* vol. 12, ed. Jo Ann Boydston (Carbondale: Southern Illinois University Press, 1981), 186.

20. John Dewey, "Creative Democracy—The Task Before Us" (1939), in *John Dewey: The Later Works, 1925–1953,* vol. 14, p. 228.

11. Radical Changes in the Muslim World

1. Regarding the three types of reaction compare, e.g., Robert J. Holton, *Globalization and the Nation State* (London: Macmillan, 1998), which distinguishes among "homogenization" (cooptation), "polarization" (rejection), and "hybridization"; Jung In Kang, "Beyond Eurocentrism: Re-examining Cultural Discourse Strategies to Overcome Eurocentrism in the Context of Polycentric Multiculturalism," *Korean Political Science Review* 38 (2004): 183–200, which distinguishes among "assimilation," "reversal," and "syncretism"; also my "Introduction," in *Comparative Political Theory: An Introduction* (New York: Palgrave Macmillan, 2010), 27–28, which distinguishes among "assimilation," "rejectionism," and "reformism." Regarding the treatment of revolution as a near-apocalyptic "event," compare Alain Badiou, *Infinite Thought: Truth and the Return to Philosophy* (New York: Continuum, 2003), 48–50; Jacques Rancière, *La mésentente* (Paris: Galileé, 1995), 139; and Nick Hewlett, *Badiou, Balibar, Rancière: Rethinking Eman-*

cipation (London: Continuum, 2007). See also Arnold Toynbee, *A Study of History*, 2 vols. (New York: Dell, 1965).

2. Regarding the modes of relation between politics and religion, especially the "defective" modes of "privatization" and "politicization," see my "Postsecular Faith" and "Religion and the World."

3. See, e.g., Erik J. Zürcher, *Turkey: A Modern History* (New York: I. B. Tauris, 1983); Patrick B. Kinross, *Atatürk: The Birth of a Nation* (London: Phoenix, 2001); Andrew Mango, *Atatürk: The Biography of the Founder of Modern Turkey* (Woodstock, NJ: Overlook Press, 2002); and Stanford J. Shaw, *History of the Ottoman Empire and Modern Turkey* (Cambridge: Cambridge University Press, 1976).

4. Mango, *Atatürk*, 404.

5. Debates about the issue spread far and wide and even reached India, where it inspired the so-called Khilafat movement, whose adherents (comprising both Muslims and Hindus) perceived the abolition as a Western or neocolonial plot. In the words of Stephan Hay, "the movement attempted to unite Indian Muslims against what was regarded as an attack by the British on the Caliph (Khalifa) of the Ottoman Empire. With the Muslim journalist, Abul Kalam Azad, they worked with M. K. Gandhi in an unsuccessful attempt to bring about unity between Muslims and Hindus." See *Sources of Indian Tradition*, vol. 2, *Modern India and Pakistan*, ed. Stephen Hay, 2nd ed. (New York: Columbia University Press, 1988), 175.

6. Mango, *Atatürk*, 367.

7. Compare, e.g., Touraj Atabaki and Erik J. Zürcher, eds., *Men of Order: Authoritarian Modernization under Atatürk and Reza Shah* (New York: I. B. Tauris, 2004); and Zürcher, *Political Opposition in the Early Turkish Republic: The Progressive Republican Party, 1924–1925* (Leiden: Brill, 1991).

8. See Alfred Stepan, "Religion, Democracy, and the Twin Tolerations," in *World Religions and Democracy*, ed. Larry Diamond, Marc F. Platter, and Philip J. Costopoulos (Baltimore: Johns Hopkins University Press, 2005), 3; and Elizabeth Shakman Hurd, *The Politics of Secularism in International Relations* (Princeton: Princeton University Press, 2008), 72.

9. Majid Tehranian, "Khomeini's Doctrine of Legitimacy," in *Comparative Political Philosophy*, ed. Anthony J. Parel and Ronald C. Keith, 2nd ed. (Lanham, MD: Lexington Press, 2003), 231–32.

10. Tehranian describes the conflict in these terms: "The *ulema* and the monarchy were polarized as symbols of two diametrically opposed visions of the future of Iran. . . . The Islamic vision stemmed from an impulse to return to the purity and sacred justice of pristine Islam. The secular vision attempted to revitalize the pre-Islamic memories of Iranian nationalism in order to capture the power and glory of Iran's imperial past. . . . To the *ulema*, who were not necessarily a monolithic and homogeneous group, it seemed

as though the entire trend of Iranian society was going against their sense of truth, goodness and justice." See "Khomeini's Doctrine of Legitimacy," 224, 226.

11. Tehranian, "Khomeini's Doctrine of Legitimacy," 230, 232.

12. Ruholla Khomeini, *Islam and Revolution*, trans. Hamid Algar (Berkeley: Mizan Press, 1981), 55–56.

13. In the words of Ali Mirsepassi: "In retrospect it is astounding that the many left-wing groups and organizations ignored the obvious fact that post-revolutionary Iranian society was being transformed into an Islamic-totalitarian state and made no effort to form a broad secular-radical united front to oppose this trend." See his *Intellectual Discourse and the Politics of Modernization: Negotiating Modernity in Iran* (Cambridge: Cambridge University Press, 2000), 168.

14. Mirsepassi, *Intellectual Discourse*, 94; Mark Juergensmeyer, *The New Cold War? Religious Nationalism Confronts the Secular State* (Berkeley: University of California Press, 1993), 19. A somewhat more nuanced opinion is offered by Elizabeth Hurd, who notes the different possible shadings of the terms *religious* and *secular:* "The Iranian Revolution, then, was not simply a 'religious' backlash against 'secular' modernity as it is often portrayed. It was a challenge to and an attempt to reconfigure the fundamental categories through which the religious and the secular are conceived and practiced." See Hurd, *Politics of Secularism*, 77.

15. Suzanne Maloney, "Identity and Change in Iran's Foreign Policy," in *Identity and Foreign Policy in the Middle East*, ed. Shibley Telhami and Michael Barnett (Ithaca: Cornell University Press, 2002), 98. The last sentence is a citation from John Esposito, *The Islamic Threat: Myth or Reality?* 3rd ed. (New York: Oxford University Press, 1999), 116.

16. Ali Alizadeh, "Why Are the Iranians Dreaming Again?" in *The People Reloaded: The Green Movement and the Struggle for Iran's Future*, ed. Nader Hashemi and Danny Postel (Brooklyn: Melville House, 2010), 6; see also "Mousavi Issues First Statements on 'Green Path of Hope,'" http://www.ilna.ir/fullStory.aspx?ID=71239 (accessed Feb. 12, 2012). In many ways, the movement draws its inspiration from an earlier reformist intellectual, Ali Shariati (1933–1977), who also tried to steer a path beyond clericalism and anticlericalism, as well as beyond liberalism and socialism. In the words of John Esposito, the conflict of Iranian aspirations was nowhere clearer "than in the juxtaposition of Ayatollah Khomeini and Dr. Ali Shariati." While Khomeini "embodied clerical authority and power," Shariati and other Islamic modernists "represented a far more non-clerical, innovative, creative reformist approach." See his *Islamic Threat*, 115.

17. Nader Hashemi, "The New Mideast Will Still Mix Mosque and State," *Wall Street Journal*, Mar. 11, 2011, http://online.wsj.com.

18. For the above citation, see Maria Elena Viggiano, "Islamic Revolu-

tions? No, Uprising of the Young," in *2011: Reset Dialogue on Civilizations*, http://www.resetdoc.org/story/00000021512 (accessed Feb. 12, 2012).

19. See "Arab League Secretary General Amre Moussa on Egypt's Revolution, His Potential Presidential Candidacy and Middle East Uprisings," *Democracy Now*, Mar. 1, 2011, http://www.democracynow.org/2011/3/1/arab_league_secretary. Compare also the comments by Dina Mansour: "Sparked by the aspiration to end a 30-year rule that vigorously repressed freedom of expression and opposition . . . , January 25, 2011 came to mark the day in Egypt's modern history that opened the door for freedom and democracy in Egypt. None of the protesters that went down on the street held a single religious slogan. . . . Slogans mainly focused on calling for socioeconomic rights and most importantly political reform." See "The Aspirations of the Muslim Brotherhood," in *2011: Reset Dialogues on Civilizations*, http://www.resetdoc.org/story/00000021506 (accessed Feb. 12, 2012).

20. See Mohammed Khan, "The Prospect for a New Arab Century," in *Opinion: Al Jazeera English*, Feb. 22, 2011, http://english.aljaceera.net/indepth/opinion/2011/02/2011/21912.

21. Ramin Jahanbegloo, "Could Uprisings in Egypt and the Arab World Produce a 'Muslim Gandhi'?" *Christian Science Monitor*, Jan. 31, 2011, http://www.csmontior.com/Commentary/Global-Viewpoint/2011. As it happens, many insurgents in both Tunisia and Egypt were influenced by the political theorist and Gandhi scholar Gene Sharp, well known for his books *The Politics of Nonviolent Action* (Boston: Sargent, 1973), *Gandhi Wields the Weapon of Moral Power* (Canton, ME: Greenleaf Books, 1983), and *Waging Nonviolent Struggle* (Boston, MA: Extending Horizons Books, 2005), and for numerous other writings and pamphlets. Compare also Anthony J. Parel, ed., *Gandhi, Freedom, and Self-Rule* (Lanham, MD: Lexington Books, 2000); and my "Gandhi and Islam: A Heart-and-Mind Unity?" in *Peace Talks—Who Will Listen?* 132–51.

22. In the words of Amara Lakhous: "I believe that the reference model in today's Arab societies is not Khomeini's Iran, but the Iran of the young who joined the Green Wave two years ago. And I believe that the elites, especially the educated, are looking to Erdogan's Turkey with interest and admiration. The great challenges posed by the present consist in conciliating democracy and Islam, traditions and modernity, the past and the future." See "Today's Models: The Iranian Green Wave and the Turkish AKP," in *2011 Reset Dialogues on Civilizations*, http://restdoc.org/story/00000021479 (accessed Feb. 20, 2012). Compare also Nader Hashemi, "The Arab Revolution of 2011: Reflections on Religion and Politics," and Alper Y. Dede, "The Arab Uprisings: Debating the 'Turkish Model,'" both in *Insight Turkey* 13 (Apr.–June 2011): 15–21, 23–32. See also Alfred Stepan, "Contrasting Progress on Democracy in Tunisia and Egypt," *Immanent Frame* (Social Science Research Council, Apr. 21, 2011).

12. Opening the Doors of Interpretation

1. Ahmad Hissou and Stefan Weidner, "Interview mit Nasr Hamid Abu Zayd," http://www.NEFAIS.net/2010/07/06/interview.abu-Zayd/ (accessed Mar. 1, 2012). (I have translated the above and subsequent passages from the interview from German.)

2. Hissou and Weidner, "Interview mit Nasr Hamid Abu Zayd." For Abu Zayd's discovery of hermeneutics and his study of the works of Gadamer, Ricoeur, and others, see also his *Ein Leben mit dem Islam,* narr. Navid Kermani, translated from Arabic by Cherifa Magdi (Freiburg: Herder, 2001), 114–18; and his *Gottes Menschenwort: Für ein humanistisches Verständnis des Koran,* ed. and trans. Thomas Hildebrandt (Freiburg: Herder, 2008), esp. 159–228. Compare also Michaelle Browers, "Islam and Political *Sinn:* The Hermeneutics of Contemporary Islamic Reformists," in *An Islamic Reformation?* ed. Michaelle Browers and Charles Kurzmann (Landham, MD: Lexington Press, 2004), 54–78.

3. Hissou and Weidner, "Interview mit Nasr Hamid Abu Zayd."

4. Hissou and Weidner, "Interview mit Nasr Hamid Abu Zayd."

5. Hissou and Weidner, "Interview mit Nasr Hamid Abu Zayd."

6. See http://en.wikipedia.org/wiki/Nasr_Abu_Zayd, 4 (accessed Mar. 1, 2012).

7. Abu Zayd, *Rethinking the Qur'an: Towards a Humanistic Hermeneutics* (Utrecht: Humanistic University Press, 2004), 27–28.

8. Abu Zayd, with Ester R. Nelson, *Voice of an Exile: Reflections on Islam* (Westport, CT: Praeger Publishing, 2004), 3–4.

9. Zayd, with Nelson, *Voice of an Exile,* 57. At this point, Zayd offers a genealogy of his position (57–58): "I see my scholarship as a continuation of the rational school of thought started by the Mu'tazilites and further developed by Muslim philosophers such as al-Kindi, al-Farabi, Ibn Sina (Avicenna), and Ibn Rushd (Averroes)." At the same time, greatly attracted to Ibn Arabi's *The Meccan Revelation,* "I proposed to study the hermeneutics of the Qur'an from a mystical (Sufi) perspective."

10. Zayd, with Nelson, *Voice of an Exile* 169–70, 185, 199.

11. Abu Zayd, *Reformation of Islamic Thought: A Critical Historical Analysis* (Amsterdam: Amsterdam University Press, 2006), 98–99.

12. I do not wish to minimize the intellectual differences between the two thinkers. Al-Jabri was more a classical rationalist and seemed to be unfamiliar with hermeneutics. His comments on "Eastern" Islamic thought were sometimes harsh (and would hardly have been endorsed by Abu Zayd in this form). See, e.g., the statement in his *Arab-Islamic Philosophy:* "With his Eastern philosophy, Avicenna (Ibn Sina) consecrated a spiritualist and gnostic trend whose impact was instrumental in the regression of Arab thinking from an open rationalism, spearheaded by the Mu'tazilites, then by al-Kindi, and culminating with al-Farabi, to a pernicious irrationalism which

inaugurated the 'gloom thinking' that scholars like al-Ghazali, Suhrawardi of Aleppo and others simply spread and popularized in various circles. Such is my judgment against Avicenna." See *Arab-Islamic Philosophy: A Contemporary Critique*, trans. Aziz Abbassi (Austin: University of Texas Center of Middle Eastern Studies, 1999), 58. Broadly speaking, in the idiom of German philosophy, one might say that al-Jabri was closer to Kant, while Abu Zayd was closer to Heidegger and Gadamer. However, the distance is not absolute. With the notion of a "critique of *Arab* reason," al-Jabri introduced into critical reason an element of religion and culture that Kant would hardly have endorsed. Moreover, the political implications of their respective writings seem to be quite compatible.

13. See http://en.wikipedia.org/wiki/Mohammed_Abed_al-Jabri, 1 (accessed Mar. 5, 2012).

14. Al-Jabri, *Arab-Islamic Philosophy*, 1–3.

15. Al-Jabri, *Arab-Islamic Philosophy*, 6–7, 9, 57.

16. Muhammad Arkoun, *The Unthought in Contemporary Islamic Thought* (New York: St. Martin's Press, 2002), 125. Compare also his comment (20): "The *unthinkable* and the *unthought* are inherent in the linear structure of any discursive statement; and also in the fact that any proposition is an act of power whether followed by a result or not."

17. Abdolkarim Soroush, *The Expansion of Prophetic Experience: Essays on Historicity, Contingency and Plurality in Religion*, trans. Nilou Mobasser, ed. and intro. Forough Jahanbakhsh (Leiden and Boston: Brill, 2009), 61, 90–91. In his writings, Soroush occupies a position somewhere between Abu Zayd and al-Jabri. Like the latter, he places himself in the tradition of critical and scientific reason (Jahanbaksh calls his position "neo-rationalist"). However, like Abu Zayd, Soroush is able to invoke both the rationalist legacy and the legacy of Sufism (especially Rumi). Unlike Abu Zayd, however, he does not seem to be influenced by hermeneutics (as is evident in his sharp distinction between essence and accidentals). On the whole, by comparison with both Abu Zayd and al-Jabri, Soroush's work seems to exude more the aura of neoplatonic Shiism.

18. Gadamer, *Truth and Method*, 329.

Appendix A. Beyond Multiculturalism?

1. See Bhikhu Parekh, *Rethinking Multiculturalism: Cultural Diversity and Political Theory* (London: Macmillan, 2000); Fred Dallmayr, "Multiculturalism and the Good Life: Comments on Bhikhu Parekh," *Good Society* 12 (2003): 40–44. The latter review is reprinted in my *In Search of the Good Life*, 237–45.

2. Parekh, *Rethinking Multiculturalism*, 6, 15. Compare also my *Dialogue among Civilizations*.

3. Fay Weldon, *Sacred Cows* (London: Chatto and Windus, 1989).

Compare also P. Kelly, ed., *Multiculturalism Reconsidered* (Cambridge, UK: Polity, 2002); and Christian Joppke, "The Retreat of Multiculturalism in the Liberal State," *British Journal of Sociology* 55 (2004): 237–57.

4. Compare in this context Thilo Sarrazin, *Deutschland schafft sich ab: Wie wir unser Land aufs Spiel setzen* (Munich: Deutsche Verlagsanstalt, 2010); and Derek McGhee, *The End of Multiculturalism? Terror, Integration, and Human Rights* (Maidenhead, UK: Open University Press, 2008). In the United States, parallel sentiments can be found in Samuel P. Huntington, *Who Are We? The Challenges to American Identity* (New York: Simon and Schuster, 2004).

5. See Tariq Modood, "Multiculturalism and Integration: Struggling with Confusions," in *Defending Multiculturalism: A Guide for the Movement*, ed. Hassan Mahamdallie (London: Bookmarks, 2011), 5–18. The paper is also available as part of the "Accept Pluralism" project of the European University Institute (San Domenico di Fiesole, Italy).

6. Tariq Modood, "The Liberal Dilemma: Integration or Vilification?" *International Migration* 44 (1006): 6. See also his *Multicultural Politics* (Edinburgh: Edinburgh University Press, 2005).

7. Tariq Modood, "Multiculturalism's Civic Future: A Response," *Open Democracy* (June 2007): 10; see also Modood, *Multiculturalism: A Civic Idea* (London: Polity, 2007).

8. See Nick Pearce, ed., *An Ambiguous Rescue: Multiculturalism and Citizenship; Responses to Tariq Modood*, http://www.opendemocracy.net/conflict-europe_Islam/response_modood_4630 (accessed Feb. 10, 2012). See also Per Mouriben and Knud Erik Jørgensen, eds., *Constituting Communities: Political Solutions to Cultural Conflict* (London: Palgrave, 2008); and Anne Phillips, *Multiculturalism without Culture* (Princeton: Princeton University Press, 2007). The latter text resonates with German (and European) discussions of *Leitkultur*; see, e.g., Bassam Tibi, *Europa ohne Identität? Die Krise der multikulturellen Gesellschaft* (Munich: Bertelsmann, 1998).

9. See Nasar Meer and Tariq Modood, "How Does Interculturalism Contrast with Multiculturalism?" *Journal of International Studies* 32 (2011): 1–22; Leonard M. Hammer, "Foreword," in *Interculturalism: Exploring Central Issues*, ed. David Powell and F. Sze (Oxford: Interdisciplinary Press, 2004), 2; Pearce, *Ambiguous Rescue*, 8; and "It's All in the Mix," *New Start Magazine*, June 7, 2006. Compare also Jagdish S. Gundara, *Interculturalism, Education, and Inclusion* (London: Paul Chapman, 2000); Gundara and Sidney Jacobs, eds., *Intercultural Europe: Diversity and Social Policy* (Aldershot: Ashgate, 2000); Beatriz P. Ibañez and Carmen Lopez Saenz, eds., *Interculturalism: Between Identity and Diversity* (New York: Peter Lang, 2006); and Michael Emerson, ed., *Interculturalism: Europe and Its Muslims in Search of Sound Societal Models* (Brussels: Center for European Policy Studies, 2011).

10. Parekh, *Rethinking Multiculturalism*, 167.

11. Meer and Modood, "How Does Interculturalism Contrast with Multiculturalism?" 9, 18.

12. See Charles Taylor, "Modes of Secularism," in *Secularism and Its Critics*, ed. Rajeev Bhargava (Oxford: Oxford University Press, 1998), 50–51; Parekh, *Rethinking Multiculturalism*, 332. Compare also Roger Trigg, *Religion in Public Life: Must Faith Be Privatized?* (Oxford: Oxford University Press, 2007); Brendan Sweetman, *Why Politics Needs Religion: The Place of Religious Arguments in the Public Square* (Downers Grove, IL: InterVarsity Press, 2006); Nancy Rosenblum, ed., *Obligations of Citizenship and Demands of Faith: Religious Accommodation in Pluralist Democracies* (Princeton: Princeton University Press, 2000); Ronald Thieman, *Religion in Public Life: A Dilemma for Democracy* (Washington, DC: Georgetown University Press, 1998); and Paul J. Weithman, ed., *Religion and Contemporary Liberalism* (Notre Dame: University of Notre Dame Press, 1997).

13. Sonia Sikka, "Liberalism, Multiculturalism, and the Case for Public Religion," *Politics and Religion* 3 (2010): 580–609, at 582–83, 588, 593; Parekh, *Rethinking Multiculturalism*, 334. For the distinction between a shallow and a "deep" or ethically engaged multiculturalism see also Janice Stein, "Searching for Equality," in *Uneasy Partners: Multiculturalism and Rights in Canada*, ed. Janice Stein et al. (Waterloo, Ontario: Wilfrid Laurier University Press, 2007), 19.

14. Sikka, "Liberalism, Multiculturalism," 599. For a critique of the twin dangers of privatization and politicization see also my "Religion and the World."

15. Parekh, *Rethinking Multiculturalism*, 306–9, 341. See also Arendt, *Human Condition*. 45–53.

Appendix B: Cosmopolitan Confucianism?

1. This paper was presented at the Second Nishan Forum on Confucianism and World Civilization, held near the birthplace of Confucius, May 21–23, 2012.

2. For different forms of dissemination and cultural borrowing, short of outright domination, see my discussion in "Modes of Cross-Cultural Encounter," in *Beyond Orientalism*, 1–37.

3. For the persistence of "empire" and "imperialism" in our time, see Said, *Culture and Imperialism;* see also Hardt and Negri, *Empire*. Regarding "hegemony" see especially Ernesto Laclau and Chantal Mouffe, *Hegemony and Socialist Strategy: Towards a Radical Democratic Politics*, trans. Winston Moore and Paul Cammack (London: Verso, 1985).

4. Admittedly, this is a broad, metaphysical speculation that is challenged by a great array of conflicting evidence. For some thoughts on the topic see, e.g., W. Somerset Maugham, *East and West* (Garden City, NY:

Doubleday, 1934); C. Northcote Parkinson, *East and West* (Boston: Hough-ton Mifflin, 1963); and Charles A. Moore, ed., *Philosophy and Culture—East and West* (Honolulu: University of Hawaii Press, 1962).

5. See on this point Connolly, *World of Becoming;* see also my "Being in the World: A Moving Feast" (chap. 1 above).

6. Liu Shuxian, "Contemporary New Confucianism: Background, Va-rieties, and Significance," in Dallmayr and Zhao Tingyang, *Contemporary Chinese Political Thought*, 94.

7. Jiang Qing and Sheng Hong, *To Nurture Virtue with Virtue* (in Chi-nese) (Shanghai: Jointly Press, 2003), 56, 59, 184.

8. Jiang and Sheng, *To Nurture Virtue with Virtue*, 161. Compare also Jiang Qing, *Political Confucianism* (in Chinese) (Beijing: Jointly Press, 2003); and his *A Confucian Constitutional Order: How China's Ancient Past Can Shape Its Political Future*, ed. Daniel A. Bell and Ruiping Fan, trans. Edmund Ryd (Princeton: Princeton University Press, 2012).

9. Kang Xiaoguang, *Benevolent Government: The Third Road to Chi-na's Political Development* (in Chinese) (Singapore, 2005), vii–xlix.

10. For details of the Manifesto see Liu Shuxian, "Contemporary New Confucianism," 96, 104–5.

11. See, e.g., Anja Steinbauer, "A Philosophical Symphony: Tang Jun-yi's System," http://www.fed.cuhk.edu.hk (accessed Feb. 20, 2012); Mou Zongsan, *Intellectual Intuition and Chinese Philosophy* (in Chinese) (Tai-pei, 1971); Mou Zongsan, *Treatise on Summum Bonum* (in Chinese) (Taipei, 1985).

12. See Zhao Tingyang, "All-Under-Heaven and Methodological Re-lationism," in Dallmayr and Tingyang, *Contemporary Chinese Political Thought*, 60; see also Du Weiming, *Confucian Thought: Selfhood as Cre-ative Transformation* (Albany: State University of New York Press, 1985), 81, 88.

13. Wing-tsit Chan, "Chinese and Western Interpretations of *Jen* (Hu-manity)," *Journal of Chinese Philosophy* 2 (1975): 109.

14. Du Weiming, "*Jen* as a Living Metaphor," in *Confucian Thought*, 81. As he remarks in another context, *jen* also mediates between humanity and nature, as well as between humanity and "Heaven." Thus, a person striving for *jen* "must also be able to realize the nature of the 'myriad things' and assist Heaven and Earth in their transforming and nourishing functions." See *Humanity and Self-Cultivation: Essays in Confucian Thought* (Berkeley: Asian Humanities Press, 1979), 97.

15. See Du Weiming, "Neo-Confucian Religiosity and Human Related-ness," in *Confucian Thought*, 133, 137.

Appendix C: The Complexity of Difference

1. Zhang Longxi, "The Complexity of Difference: Individual, Cultural, and Cross-Cultural," *Interdisciplinary Science Reviews* 35 (2010): 341–52. Compare also Longxi, ed., *The Concept of Humanity in the Age of Globalization* (Taipei: National Taiwan University Press, 2012).

2. See Fred Dallmayr, "On the Natural Theology of the Chinese: A Tribute to Henry Rosemont, Jr.," *Ex/Change*, no. 13 (June 2005): 16–22.

3. See Hilary Putnam, *Realism with a Human Face*, ed. James Conant (Cambridge: Harvard University Press, 1990); Donald Davidson, *Inquiries into Truth and Interpretation*, 2nd ed. (Oxford: Clarendon Press, 2001); and Lindsay Waters, "The Age of Incommensurability," *Boundary 2* 28 (Summer 2001): 133–72.

4. Longxi, "Complexity of Difference," 347.

5. Benjamin Schwartz, *China and Other Matters* (Cambridge: Harvard University Press, 1996), 5, 7.

6. See Guo Qiyong, ed., *Debates on Confucian Ethics* (in Chinese) (Wuhan, China: Wuhan Jiaoyu Chubanshe, 2004); Liu Qingping, "Confucianism and Corruption: An Analysis of Shun's Two Actions Described by Mencius," *Dao: A Journal of Comparative Philosophy* 6 (2007): 1–19; Guo Qiyong, "Is Confucian Ethics a 'Consanguinism'?" *Dao: A Journal of Comparative Philosophy* 6 (2007): 21–37; and Huang Yong, ed., "Symposium: Filial Piety as the Root of Morality or the Source of Corruption," *Dao: A Journal of Comparative Philosophy* 7 (March 2008).

7. Fred Dallmayr, "On Love with Distinction: A Chinese Debate," in *Integral Pluralism*, 185–90. Compare also Du, *Confucian Thought*. and Du, *Humanity and Self-Cultivation*.

8. Longxi, "Complexity of Difference," 345.

Appendix D: Dialogue in Practice

1. This conversation was held during a meeting of the World Public Forum in Rhodes, Greece, in Oct. 2010.

Index